POCA 2005

Postgraduate Cypriot Archaeology

Proceedings of the Fifth Annual Meeting of Young Researchers on Cypriot Archaeology, Department of Classics, Trinity College, Dublin, 21-22 October 2005

Edited by

Giorgos Papantoniou

in collaboration with

Aoife Fitzgerald and Siobhán Hargis

BAR International Series 1803
2008

Published in 2016 by
BAR Publishing, Oxford

BAR International Series 1803

POCA 2005. Postgraduate Cypriot Archaeology

ISBN 978 1 4073 0290 4

BAR Publishing is the trading name of British Archaeological Reports (Oxford) Ltd.
British Archaeological Reports was first incorporated in 1974 to publish the BAR
Series, International and British. In 1992 Hadrian Books Ltd became part of the BAR
group. This volume was originally published by Archaeopress in conjunction with
British Archaeological Reports (Oxford) Ltd / Hadrian Books Ltd, the Series principal
publisher, in 2008. This present volume is published by BAR Publishing, 2016.

Printed in England

BAR
PUBLISHING

BAR titles are available from:

BAR Publishing
122 Banbury Rd, Oxford, OX2 7BP, UK
EMAIL   info@barpublishing.com
PHONE   +44 (0)1865 310431
FAX   +44 (0)1865 316916
www.barpublishing.com

CONTENTS

ACKNOWLEDGEMENTS

We would like to thank a number of individuals and groups for their support of POCA 2005:

This event could not have taken place without the generous support and assistance of the Centre for the Mediterranean and Near Eastern Studies (MNES) at Trinity College Dublin, the Irish Institute of Hellenic Studies at Athens and Cyprus Tourism at Dublin. Therefore, we would like to particularly express our sincere gratitude to Professor Sean Freyne and Professor Brian McGing (MNES), Mr Jason O'Brien (Odaios Foods; Irish Institute of Hellenic Studies at Athens), and Mr Shay Bollard (Cyprus Tourism at Dublin). We thank BAR for agreeing to publish the proceedings and being supportive and available throughout the process.

We would particularly like to thank the Embassy of the Republic of Cyprus in Dublin and, especially, the former Ambassador Mr Andreas Kakouris, the former consul of the Embassy, Mrs Maria Hadjitheodhosiou, and the secretary of the Ambassador, Mrs Anna Vernardou, for their valuable moral and financial support.

Many thanks are due also to Professor Maria Iacovou, of the University of Cyprus, who kindly accepted our invitation to give the plenary lecture for the workshop, and for participating actively in POCA through her generous advice to a new generation of scholars on Cypriot Studies.

We are very grateful to the Classics Department, and particularly to Dr Christine Morris, who teaches Cypriot Archaeology at Trinity, for her valuable encouragement, assistance with ideas, and for her solutions in every difficulty which we confronted in the process of organising this workshop and editing the volume. Our thanks are also due to Dr Hazel Dodge of Trinity College Dublin for her availability and support.

Our special thanks and gratitude are also due to all the anonymous reviewers who kindly agreed to carry out all the valuable and time-consuming process of peer-reviewing all the published articles.

The logo of the conference was kindly drawn by Anna Georgiadou.

In addition, we would like to thank all the participants and attendants of POCA, some of whom traveled from distant parts in order to attend the workshop: Greece, Cyprus, England, Scotland, Italy, Poland and the USA were all represented. Finally, we would like to thank all of those who attended the plenary lecture and the workshop for their participation and enthusiasm. It was indeed a great honour for Cyprus and Cypriot archaeology to be so wholeheartedly welcomed in another insular unit such as Ireland, lying at the other edge of Europe.

A BRIEF MESSAGE FROM THE INITIATOR AND ORGANISER OF THE FIRST POCA

Dear POCA 2005 organisers and participants,

I would like to take this opportunity to congratulate POCA on its 5th year.

Unfortunately, due to teaching and research commitments, I will not be able to participate in person on this occasion, but would nevertheless like to pass my congratulations and thanks for all the hard work of the people involved in organising POCA conferences during these past five years – POCA 2001 in Cambridge, POCA 2002 in Glasgow, POCA 2003 in Dublin, POCA 2004 in Reading, and now, POCA 2005 here in Dublin again. Thanks are also due to the sponsors, and the participants through the years.

I first conceived the idea of POCA while conducting doctoral research in Cyprus, meeting young researchers with a keen interest in Cyprus, with archaeological or other foci. The many interesting and stimulating, but necessarily brief discussions with fellow researchers on archaeological excavations, at museums, at CAARI, and on the road, made me think of setting up a forum catering for the perceived need for in-depth, critical, and constructive discussion of work in progress. The first POCA, POCA 2001, was realised at the McDonald Institute of Archaeology, at University of Cambridge, on 10th November 2001.

I am sure you agree with me that POCA provides a valuable forum for young researchers, both post-graduate and post-doctoral, to constructively discuss issues of Cypriot archaeology, as well as research relating to the neighbouring disciplines. One indication of this is that POCA in its 5th year continues to reach for new horizons. It has now grown into a truly international event, with participants arriving from far and wide, including the UK, Ireland, Greece, Poland, USA, and, I am glad to note, Cyprus itself. I look forward to hearing the result of the bids for organising POCA 2006.

It is the participant input and interaction that makes a conference a success – I wish you all a stimulating, enjoyable, and productive POCA 2005.

Kirsi Lorentz
Newcastle, Friday 14th October 2005

Dr Kirsi O. Lorentz
Lecturer in Archaeology
Director of the Wolfson Bioarchaeology Laboratory
School of Historical Studies
1st Floor Armstrong Building   UK
University of Newcastle   Office Tel.: (00-44)-(0)191-2225754
Newcastle-upon-Tyne   FAX: (00-44)-(0)191-2226484
NE1 7RU   Email: K.O.Lorentz@newcastle.ac.uk

PREFACE

The fifth Postgraduate Cypriot Archaeology (POCA) workshop took place from the 21st to 22nd October 2005, hosted by the Department of Classics, Trinity College Dublin. POCA is a workshop originally designed to provide postgraduate researchers in Cypriot archaeology with a forum in which to present their work, discuss some central themes of their research, meet people who work in the same area and exchange ideas and information in a friendly and collegial environment.

Cypriot Archaeology is well established at Trinity College Dublin, and the Department of Classics was happy to be hosting the workshop for the second time in the five years of POCA's existence. This year, one of the main aims of the organisers was to make the workshop inclusive of time periods not usually covered by the conference. This aim was satisfactorily achieved with presentations ranging chronologically from the Bronze Age to Byzantine and Medieval ages, but also including modern heritage management. Perceiving the need for the survival of such a forum for postgraduates and young researchers of Cypriot studies, and the usefulness of interdisciplinary and multidisciplinary studies, we were happy to welcome participants from disciplines other than pure archaeology.

In addition, as postgraduate students working on Cypriot archaeology, we felt that this year we had an additional mission: the International Conventions of UNESCO stipulate that it is illegal to conduct excavations or any other archaeological fieldwork in the occupied territory of the Republic of Cyprus. For the past thirty years this principle had been duly respected by all international institutes, universities and archaeologists who specialise in the archaeology of Cyprus. We were concerned, therefore, to learn that German archaeologists were currently actively engaged in the illegal excavation of the well-known archaeological site of Galinoporni in the occupied peninsula of Karpasia. By means of a petition signed by any participants who wished to protest against this, we took the opportunity of this workshop to request that this violation of international law should come to an end.

Professor Maria Iacovou of the University of Cyprus opened the workshop with a public lecture entitled *Let the 'ancient island' speak: A Cyprocentric Approach to the History of the Cypriote Kingdoms*. The forum was concluded by Professor Maria Iacovou and Dr Christine Morris, the A.G. Leventis Senior Lecturer in Greek Archaeology and History at the Department of Classics, Trinity College Dublin. Some suggestions and key questions for the new directions and the new, expanded form that POCA was starting to take were raised.

POCA 2005 was a great success, attracting thirteen presented papers, thus making this the largest POCA up to that date. In this context, it also has to be said, that this is the first time in POCA's existence that the proceedings have been published. All the papers that were finally submitted for publication were subject of peer review by the most appropriate academics and scholars. The sessions and participants were as follows:

People and Cultural Interaction

Daisy Knox (University of Cambridge): Script in Context: The Cypro-Minoan Script and its Place in Late Bronze Age Cypriot Society

Eleni Christou (University of Cyprus): The Demographic Minorities of Cyprus during the 12th century

Jimmy Schryver (University of Minnesota): Cyprus at the Crossroads: Intercultural Contact on Frankish Cyprus

Power and Ideology

Anna Satraki (University of Cyprus): Manifestations of Royalty in Cypriot Sculpture

Giorgos Papantoniou (Trinity College Dublin): Sacred Landscapes from *Basileis* to *Strategos*: Methodological and Interpretative Approaches

Celine Marquaille-Telliez (Kings College London): Female Representation in Hellenistic Cyprus: The Ptolemaic Court

Art and Religion

Katarzyna Zeman (University of Warsaw): Aegean Origin of Aniconic Cult of Aphrodite in Paphos

Lesley Bushnell (University College London): The Wild Goat-and-Tree Icon and its Special Significance for Ancient Cyprus

Doria Nicolaou and Evi Karyda (Pontificio Istituto di Archeologia Cristiana/Newcastle University): The Fish and its Symbolism in the Early Christian Mosaics of Cyprus

Savvas Neocleous (Trinity College Dublin): Music in Medieval Cypriot Iconography: Evidence from Nativity Representations

Landscape Studies and Heritage Management

Konstantinos Raptis and Olga-Maria Bakirtzis (Archaeological Expedition in Cyprus of the Directorate of Byzantine and Post-Byzantine Antiquities of the Hellenic Ministry of Culture/Aristotle University of Thessaloniki): Agios Georgios, Pegeia – Cape Drepanon: Integrating an Excavation Site into an Archaeological Landscape

Deirdre Stritch (Trinity College Dublin): A Comparative Study of Heritage Management in Israel and Cyprus

Technology

Maria Dikomitou (University College London): An Analytical Approach to the Study of Middle Bronze Age Pottery from Deneia, Cyprus

We hope that POCA will continue to grow and reach for new horizons.

POCA 2005 Committee

PART 1:

PEOPLE AND CULTURAL INTERACTION

SCRIPT IN CONTEXT: THE CYPRO-MINOAN SCRIPT AND ITS PLACE IN LATE BRONZE AGE CYPRIOT SOCIETY

DAISY-KATE KNOX

At the beginning of the Late Bronze Age (c. 1550 BC-1050 BC), a new script emerged on Cyprus. Thanks to its apparent linguistic similarity to Cretan Linear A, noted by Arthur Evans in 1909, this script came to be known as Cypro-Minoan. Its use is attested for about five hundred years, between the 16th and 11th centuries BC, and its influence can be felt through to the Classical period in the idiosyncratic Cypriot syllabic script used to write Greek.

The Late Bronze Age saw distinct changes in Cypriot society which are evident in virtually every sphere. Landscape survey evidence in particular, has shown that the population began to nucleate into large, coastal emporia sites, such as Enkomi or Hala Sultan Tekke, and sizeable inland settlements like Kalavasos. A wider range of settlement types started to appear, including specialist production sites for pottery, for example, and others, such as Politiko-*Phorades*, devoted to copper-mining. This move towards the coast, the increasing evidence of Cypriot material found outside the island, and the wide range and number of imported goods found within it, indicate an escalating interest in foreign trade (Catling 1962: 142-4; Knapp 1997: 56-63; Steel 2004: 156-171). Finally, burials began to take place within the settlements, showing a marked shift away from the large extramural cemeteries of the previous period (Keswani 2004: 84-88).

The introduction of the Cypro-Minoan script coincided with, and was perhaps symptomatic of, these complex changes in social practice and organisation. Unfortunately, despite a great deal of effort by various linguists (notably Daniel 1941, O. Masson 1956, E. Masson 1974, Faucounau 1977; see also Knapp & Marchant 1982; Palaima 1989), the script remains undeciphered. Most scholars agree that there is not yet sufficient evidence of it for this to be possible (Palaima 1989: 123-4). As a consequence, therefore, the Cypro-Minoan script might not seem a particularly useful tool in helping to understand the society in which it was used. Indeed, until very recently, attempts to utilise it in this way have been

extremely thin on the ground. In 2002, however, Smith introduced the possibility of an archaeological approach to the study of Cypro-Minoan (2002: 1-32) and the papers within her volume (notably Webb 2002, Hirschfeld 2002) represent the first strides in this new direction.[1] It is within this tradition that I believe the study of Cypro-Minoan currently holds the most potential.

This paper aims to show how a detailed analysis of all the non-linguistic elements of Cypro-Minoan can illuminate not only how the script was used, but also what it might mean for the nature of Late Bronze Age Cypriot society. Although the inscriptions themselves should not be ignored, the focus of this paper will be placed on the geographical and chronological spread of Cypro-Minoan, the types of object which were inscribed and the contexts in which those objects have been found.

This approach is not without its problems, which Smith explains in detail (2002: 3-32). As with any study of archaeological context, it is plagued by the biases of preservation, excavation and publication. The corpus of Cypro-Minoan inscribed objects which exists today necessarily comprises only those which have been able to survive the millennia and which happen to have been deposited in those sections of sites which archaeologists have chosen to excavate. Of these objects, many, particularly those found in the early years of archaeology, can no longer be linked to their specific findspot. Yet, providing these problems are acknowledged, they are not insurmountable. Although some perishable inscribed objects may not have survived, many different types of object have, and most of these can be linked at least to a site, a significant portion to a specific area of it. Conse-

---

[1] My thanks to an anonymous reviewer who has drawn my attention to a recently-completed PhD addressing the Cypro-Minoan script from an interdisciplinary perspective, without attempting decipherment (Ferrara 2005, unpublished). Unfortunately, the present article was written in 2004 and it has been impossible to take proper account of Ferrara's extensive and detailed study when revising it for publication. Reference will be made to the unpublished manuscript where possible.

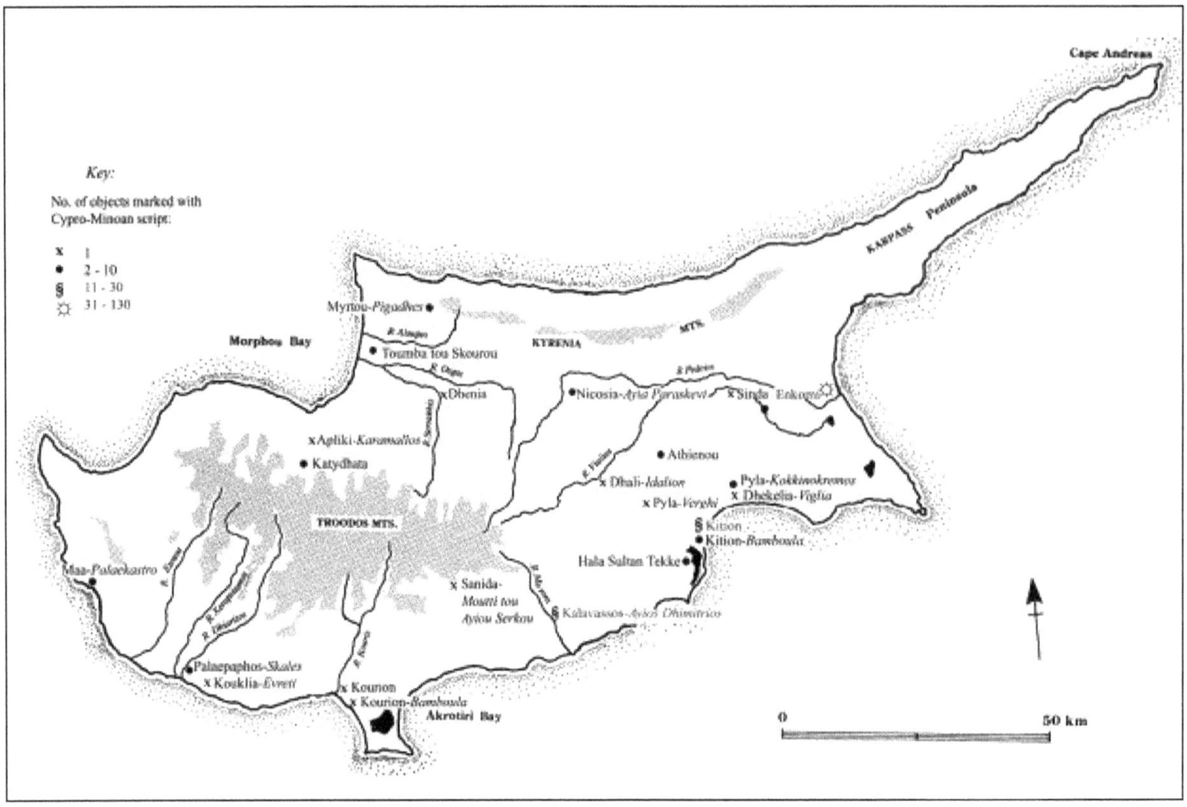

Fig 1 – Geographical Distribution of Objects Inscribed with Cypro-Minoan

quently, there remains enormous potential to study the nature and context of Cypro-Minoan inscribed objects.

CYPRO-MINOAN

There are 232 known objects inscribed with Cypro-Minoan,[2] of which 224 have been found in Cyprus.[3] The script occurs on a variety of media, including clay and metal vessels, seal stones, gold rings, lead sling 'bullets', clay balls, clay cylinders and tablets. It is likely that it was also written on perishable media, such as wood or wax, as appears to have been the case in contemporary Egypt and the Near East (Powell 2002: 239). Nothing of this kind has yet been discovered within a Late Bronze Age Cypriot context.[4]

Cypro-Minoan objects have been found over a broad geographical area (Fig. 1). The script occurs in both ceremonial and domestic contexts, in tombs and in settlements, on the coast and inland, although certainly not at every Late Bronze Age site. This pattern may have been influenced by inconsistent scales of excavation or publication at different sites. The inscribed cylinder seal from Pyla-*Verghi* (Cyprus Museum 1949/XI-30/1), for example, was discovered during a clandestine sondage in 1949 (Masson, O. 1957: 12-13); whereas the Cypro-Minoan objects from Hala Sultan Tekke were found during extensive excavations over several years (for a summary see Åström 1986: 1-17). Similarly, it is now apparent that examples of Cypro-Minoan have been found at Maroni, but since these are still awaiting publication, they could not be included in the present study.

Nevertheless, there are certain important trends within the data which cannot be completely explained away by excavation or preservation biases. The site of Enkomi is a case in point. Although examples of Cypro-Minoan generally occur in rather small numbers, this site has produced 123 inscribed objects, its closest competitor, Kition, only twenty-seven (Dikaios 1969: 882-90; Masson, E. 1971a: 479-504, 1985: 280-92). One may initially ascribe the reason for this discrepancy to the four extensive excavations which have been carried out at

[2] The corpus of Cypro-Minoan inscriptions used in this paper is largely based on material collected in the PASP database of Cypriot Scripts (Hirschfeld 1996). A small number of additional examples which were not included in this database, but which have been identified in excavation reports as Cypro-Minoan, have also been incorporated. All figures are consequently likely to be approximate.

[3] The remaining seven provenanced examples were found at Ugarit on the Levantine coast. This non-Cypriot context has been excluded from the present analysis as it can offer little relevant information on the significance of Cypro-Minoan within Cyprus itself. It has even been conjectured that these Levantine examples write a different language (E. Masson 1974; but see also Knapp & Marchant 1982; Palaima 1989:121-162 who argue against this). For a further examination of Ugarit examples, see Ferrara 2005:114-121.

[4] One wooden diptych was discovered amongst the cargo of the Ulu Burun shipwreck, much of which originated in Cyprus. Whilst this may

have been used to record Cypro-Minoan, the diptych can neither be categorically identified as Cypriot in origin, nor did it preserve any evidence of script.

Enkomi.[5] However, of these, only Dikaios' project has been systematically published to date and furthermore, the excavations at Kition were hardly small-scale. There is a difference also in the types of object found at each different site. More than half of the inscribed objects found at Enkomi, for example, were clay balls, whereas no such item was found at Kition. All of this suggests that Cypro-Minoan script, although widespread, was not used on the same scale or in the same way throughout Cyprus.

The script itself is syllabic and carries strong structural parallels with near-contemporary Cretan Linear A (Chadwick 1990: 183-5; Palaima 1989: 135-40). Linear A is also syllabic and undeciphered. It is attested slightly earlier than Cypro-Minoan, between the 18th and 14th centuries BC. The range of inscribed objects is broadly similar to that of the Cypriot script, including clay and metal vessels, sealings, tablets and apparently ceremonial objects such as double axe heads.[6] However, there are approximately 2500 examples of Linear A, found in at least thirteen major centres across Crete and the Cyclades, illustrating a significant difference in the scale of use of the two scripts. In her extensive study of Linear A, Schoep used the linguistic and non-linguistic characteristics of the script in order to reconstruct its economic and social significance and the administrative processes in which it was involved (Schoep 2002). The approach to Cypro-Minoan in this paper is partly inspired by Schoep's research into the archaeological contexts of Linear A. In addition, I have incorporated a comparison with the Linear A corpus in order to help understand the socio-economic implications of the Cypro-Minoan evidence.

CYPRO-MINOAN IN ADMINISTRATION

One of the most striking aspects of the Linear A corpus is that, like its successor Linear B, it was used predominantly for administration. The evidence of several types of inscribed object – in particular vessels, tablets and sealings – support this claim. These same types of object also occur inscribed with Cypro-Minoan, and might plausibly suggest that this script too was being used in an administrative context. The following demonstrates, however, that in the case of Cypro-Minoan, the evidence is a little more ambiguous.

There are seventy-three examples of clay storage vessels – primarily jugs, jars and pithoi – inscribed with Cypro-Minoan. These inscriptions all consist of two or three signs, usually positioned on the handle (e.g. Fig. 2) or, more occasionally, the rim or upper body. Since the positions of these inscriptions seem to indicate that they were meant to be readily visible, they could have

functioned as labels of contents. Evidence against this, however, may be found in studies of potmarks, which are clearly a phenomenon related to these Cypro-Minoan marks. These studies, in particular that by Hirschfeld (2002) on the Enkomi material, have shown that there is no correlation between a vessel's likely contents and the sign marked upon it.

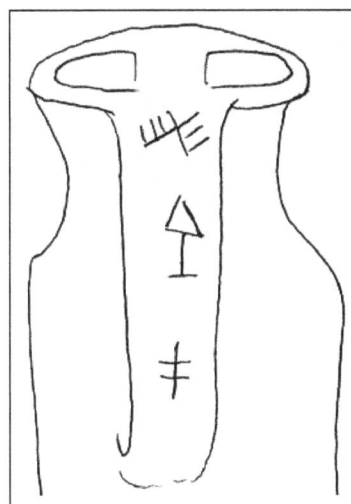

Fig 2 – Clay jug handle, Tomb 11.11, Katydhata (after Åström 1989: fig. 181, drawn by author)

Potmarks found in Minoan contexts, such as the inscribed vessels from Kommos, also do not seem to have functioned as labels (e.g. Bennet et al. 1996: 243-377). The majority of marks found on vessels in Crete were inscribed before firing, most likely by the potters themselves. In contrast, however, almost all of the vessels with Cypro-Minoan marks, along with the majority of single-sign potmarks, were inscribed after firing. Since it is far easier to inscribe soft, wet clay, the Cypro-Minoan inscriptions on these objects probably do not represent makers' marks or similar. Most of these vessels were found in storage rooms or domestic contexts, such as Area 3 at Maa-*Palaekastro* (Karageorghis & Demas 1988: 17-50, 399-403). These signs, therefore, could have been added later as part of a process of controlling or monitoring the movement of goods.

This kind of produce-management is familiar from Late Bronze Age Crete, from the tablets and sealings found in the archives and storerooms of the palaces. Evidence for it in Cyprus, however, is more elusive. Only a single example of an Aegean-style accounting document, inscribed with Cypro-Minoan and found from a Cypriot Bronze Age context, has been found to date. Figure 3 is an example of a Linear A inventory document – a type common in Late Bronze Age Crete (Schoep 2002: 67-87). Figure 4 shows the Cypro-Minoan document, a potsherd found down a well in Dikaios' Area I at Enkomi (#4025, Dikaios 1969: 778, 891). Although there is clearly a difference in media – a re-used potsherd as opposed to a

---

[5] Excavations at Enkomi were carried out by the British Museum (Murray, Smith et al. 1900), the Swedish Cyprus Expedition (Gjerstäd et al. 1937), a French project led by Schaeffer (Schaeffer 1952, 1971; Courtois 1981, 1984) and Dikaios' Greek excavations (Dikaios 1969).

[6] Two specifically Cypriot inscribed objects – clay balls and clay cylinders – which do not occur in Crete will be discussed below.

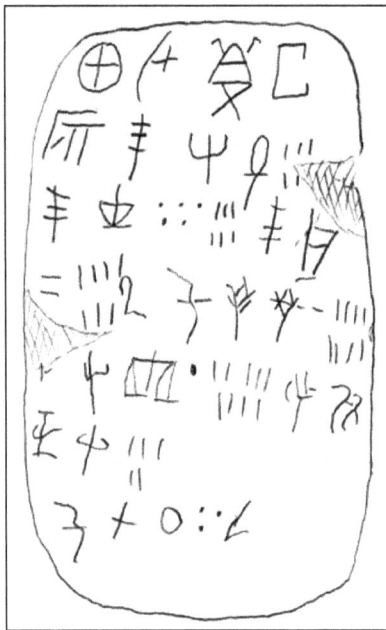

Fig 3 – Clay Linear A tablet, #13, Ayia Triada, Crete
(after Chadwick 1990: fig. 26, drawn by author)

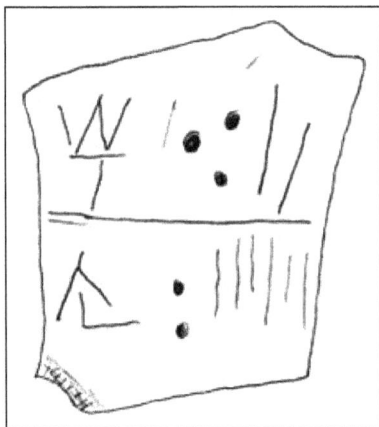

Fig 4 – Potsherd, #4025, Enkomi
(after Dikaios 1969: pl. 149.21, drawn by author)

specially made clay tablet – a definite similarity exists between the arrangements of symbols, which are possibly ideographic, alongside what appear to be numerals.[7] This unique fragment suggests that Cypro-Minoan may have been used in albeit limited stock-taking activities at Enkomi.

Tablets, such as that discussed above, containing lists of ideograms and numbers, provide some of the clearest evidence for the administrative use of Linear A. Made in unbaked clay and housed in archives, they were temporary documents, specifically designed and used for stock-taking and recording the movement of goods.

Tablets inscribed with Cypro-Minoan also exist (e.g. Fig. 5), but they are so different in form that it is difficult to support a similar administrative function for these objects. They were inscribed in continuous sequences on both sides with hardly any apparent numbers. When Ventris turned his famously successful linguistic hand to these Cypro-Minoan tablets, he believed that their structure suggested they were poems (Ventris 1956: 41-2).

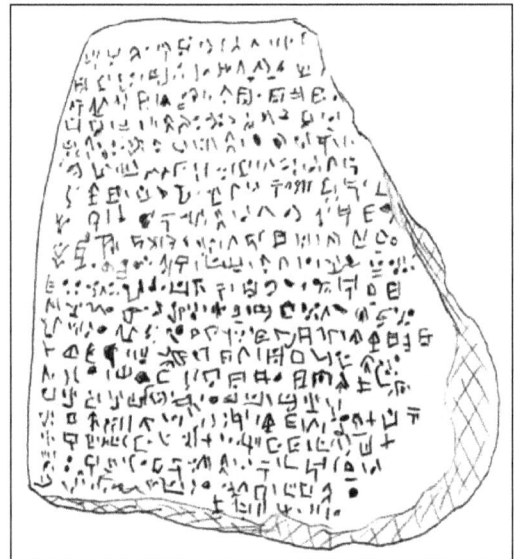

Fig 5 – Clay Cypro-Minoan tablet, #1687, Enkomi
(after Dikaios 1953: 234, drawn by author)

Only four Cypro-Minoan tablets have been found in Cyprus itself, and all of these from Enkomi (Dikaios' #1193, #1687, #1885 and Schaeffer's AM2336 (Louvre); Dikaios 1953, 1956, 1963; Masson, E. 1969, 1970). Their use was clearly extremely limited and their existence may reflect a particular local concern peculiar to this site. One possibility is that they record diplomatic letters in the Near Eastern manner (see Knapp 1996) and in that regard, it is perhaps significant that the only other four Cypro-Minoan tablets which exist were discovered at Ugarit, on the Levantine coast.

By far the most striking body of evidence for Linear A administration is provided by the 2105 clay sealings which survive from Crete. They were preserved in the fiery destruction horizons which were particularly widespread on the island at the end of the 15th century BC. Although similar destruction horizons are much rarer in a Late Bronze Age Cypriot context, they do exist – for example at several points during the Bronze Age history of Enkomi, (see Dikaios 1969). But despite these opportunities for preservation, only a single seal impression survives from Late Bronze Age Cyprus, apparently made by a cylinder seal of Eastern Mediterranean/Mesopotamian type. This impression was found in Rm 24 (Floor III), Area I at Enkomi (Fig. 6; #1905.9; Dikaios 1969: 178-9).

---

[7] There is also a single example of Linear A being inscribed on a potsherd in a similar way – the so-called 'ostrakon' from Thera (Michailidou 1993, 2000).

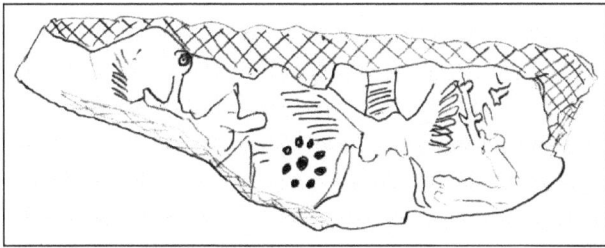

Fig 6 – Clay Cylinder Seal Impression, #1905.9, Enkomi (after Dikaios 1969: 179, drawn by author)

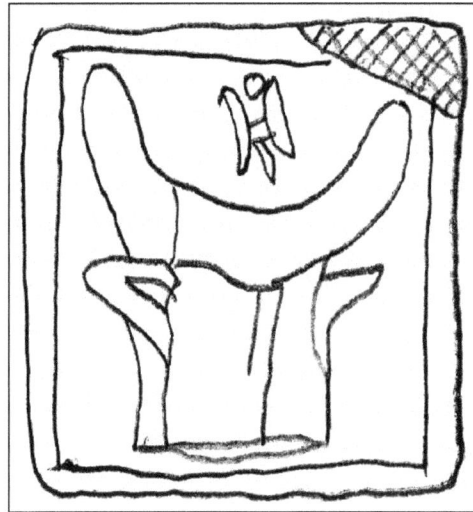

Fig 7 – Serpentine Stamp Seal, Rm3, House A, Apliki-Karamallos (after O. Masson 1957: 19, drawn by author)

There is some other evidence to support the practical use of seals in Late Bronze Age Cyprus, in particular the impressions found on some pithoi and large basins (Webb 2002: 126-8). Yet there are only twenty-seven published examples of this kind of impression and none of the seals used included Cypro-Minoan signs. Some have suggested that despite this meagre physical evidence, the practical use of inscribed seals in Cyprus can be proven by the orientation of the inscriptions on the seals themselves (Masson, O. 1957; Smith 2002: 10-12). Thus, if the Cypro-Minoan characters were written 'backwards' this would imply that they were supposed to be read in impression. Unfortunately, although significant strides have been made in refining the syllabary (Ferrara 2005), we do not have sufficient evidence of the script to be able to tell firstly, in which direction every sign should point, and secondly, that Cypro-Minoan signs were not reversible as, for example, Egyptian hieroglyphs. The sign on the Enkomi seal impression is, like the majority of those in the Cypro-Minoan syllabary, unfortunately symmetrical.

Although seal impressions are evidently rare, inscribed seals are slightly more common.[8] Those seals which were found in settlements, such as the serpentine stamp seal from Apliki-Karamallos (Fig. 7) or the haematite cylinder seal from Sinda (Masson, O. 1957: 14-15, 19-20), are all inscribed with one or two signs.[9] Those which can be linked to primary depositional contexts, such as the seal from Kalavasos, Building III (#455, South 1983: 103; Smith 2002: 13-4), which was found amongst a large cache of weights, do suggest administrative function. Although it is difficult to speculate, their short inscriptions may perhaps represent the mark of an individual or place.

Simply because there is scant evidence for Aegean-style administrative documents and practices on Cyprus, does not necessarily mean that Cypro-Minoan was not being used for administration on the island, albeit in a rather idiosyncratic way. The Cypro-Minoan corpus does include

two types of object which are distinctly Cypriot, without direct parallel in the Aegean, and which could support administrative activity on the island. Firstly, a small number of clay cylinders (e.g. Fig. 8) have been found at Enkomi and Kalavasos. They were inscribed with around twenty lines of text, including apparent numerals, and show evidence of erasures and overwriting. Smith has carried out a detailed study of the context of the Kalavasos cylinders (2002: 20-5). These were found in Building X, an ashlar-faced, monumental structure, used partly as a storage centre for olive oil and partly as an arena for élite feasting. They were preserved in the fire that destroyed the building in the 13th century BC. Smith concludes that they were probably used to record the goods stored in Building X, updated and corrected over time as the quantities changed. This is certainly plausible, yet the large quantity of non-numeric information included indicates a very different system of administration to that of the Aegean. Although these cylinders could indicate some sort of distinctly Cypriot administrative practice, since only six have been discovered (five from Kalavasos, one from Enkomi) they probably had very limited, localised use.

Secondly, some of the most curious objects inscribed with Cypro-Minoan could also provide evidence for the administrative use of the script. The small balls, around 4cm in diameter (e.g. Fig. 9) made of unbaked clay, which have been found predominantly, but not exclusively, at Enkomi, have been variously identified as weights, tokens, counters and even marbles (Masson, E. 1971b; Dikaios 1969: 884), but their actual use remains obscure. Those found within Dikaios' Enkomi sectors cluster in two adjacent rooms (Western sector, Area 3, Levels IIB-IIIB; Dikaios 1969: 884, 887). Dikaios found shallow pits in the floors of these rooms and, on this basis, concluded that they were spaces for playing marbles. However, the quantities of slag, tools and mortar-lined pits encrusted with metal also found within

---

[8] Twenty-six examples are listed in the PASP database.

[9] It is acknowledged that a single sign would not be considered an 'inscription' proper by those who study Aegean Linear scripts. However, given that the single signs inscribed on objects discussed in this paper have been identified in other, longer inscriptions and are therefore definitely part of the Cypro-Minoan syllabary, they will be included in this investigation.

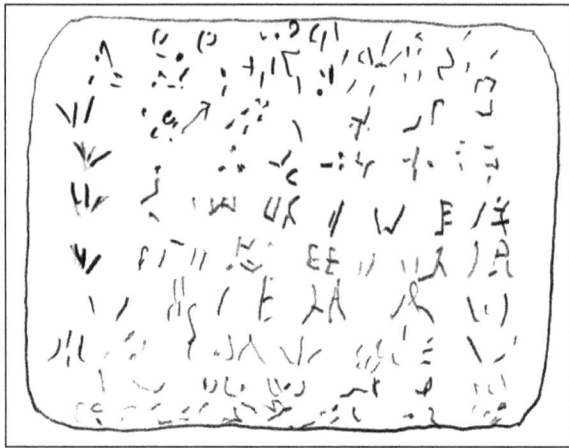

Fig 8 – Clay Cylinder, #19.10, Enkomi
(after Schaeffer 1971, drawn by author)

Fig 9 – Clay Ball, #1282, Enkomi
(after Dikaios 1969: pl.164.41, drawn by author)

and around these rooms, suggest instead that this part of the site was probably used for processing copper. The single provenanced clay ball from Hala Sultan Tekke, found in Rm 2, Area 22, Layer 2, was also associated with a crucible (Öbrink 1979: 3, 46-7). Some practical use, therefore, connected with the administration of this copper processing could be conjectured. Perhaps the inscriptions recorded the origin of the raw material or the destination of the finished product.[10]

It does seem that there is some evidence that Cypro-Minoan was used in administration. However, this evidence must be kept in perspective. Inscribed vessels constitute only a tiny proportion of the hundreds of thousands of vessels found from Late Bronze Age Cyprus. In House B at Toumba tou Skourou, for example, out of the thousands of pithos sherds it contained, only two are inscribed (Vermeule & Wolsky 1990: 109-16).

---

[10] See Ferrara 2005: 82-108 for some forward steps in the interpretation of clay balls.

Likewise, of the hundreds of surviving Late Bronze Age seals, only twenty-six are inscribed and of those, only five have clear administrative use. The clay cylinders and clay balls are very localised phenomena – the former predominantly from Kalavasos, the latter, Enkomi. So whatever administration these inscribed objects might suggest, it was certainly not common practice. Furthermore, objects with possible administrative uses simply cannot account for the whole Cypro-Minoan corpus. The script must have had another function.

CYPRO-MINOAN AND SYMBOLIC STATUS DISPLAY

In a society whose general population would not know even how to begin to read or write, where they might not even understand the concept of the written word, a script like Cypro-Minoan, and the ability to use it, could be a powerful tool. It is no coincidence that at least a third of the objects on which Cypro-Minoan is found are made of what could be considered 'precious material', such as bronze, gold or lapis lazuli, or can be connected with activities which might be seen as 'high status'.

Of all the inscribed vessels, it is bowls, made from both clay and metal (bronze or silver), which stand out as the only vessels to have long inscriptions of up to ten signs (e.g. Fig. 10). Unfortunately, only one of these bowls retains a secure provenance (Schaeffer's #16.63, Q4E, level 12, Enkomi; Courtois 1984: 52-3, 1986: 24-7) These bowls may plausibly have been used in activities such as group feasting. Their inscriptions could indicate the owner of the object perhaps, its heritage or worth, or record a dedication or message specifically relevant to this activity.

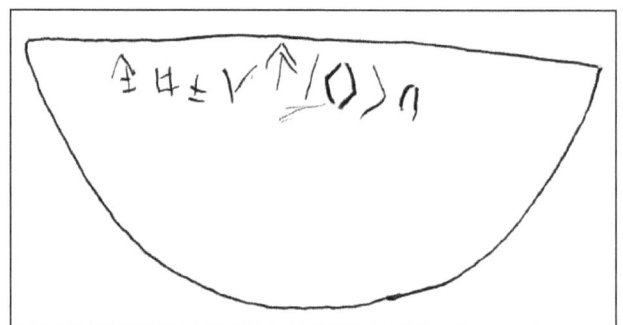

Fig 10 – Bronze Bowl, Cyprus Museum #25, Enkomi
(after O. Masson 1968: 73, drawn by author)

Uncharacteristically long inscriptions also appear on those seals which have been found in burial contexts, such as that from Tomb 2 at Hala Sultan Tekke (Fig. 11). There is some evidence that seal stones were used as jewellery, as illustrated by the cylinder seal set into a gold necklace found at Ayios Iakovos (Gjerstäd *et al.* 1937, pl. CXLVII, 9), and at least one of the inscribed examples was imported from Babylonia (British Museum 97.4-1.711, Enkomi; Masson, O. 1957: 8-9). The objects themselves, therefore, already have 'prestige value', by virtue of their material, age or provenance. It is thus not inconceivable that the inclusion of Cypro-Minoan inscriptions could have been used to enhance this still further, demonstrating some extraordinary knowledge. Objects like these were probably part of a mechanism of status legitimation, for which burial in particular was an appropriate arena.

Fig 11 – Haematite Cylinder Seal, Tomb 2.230, Hala Sultan Tekke (after Åström et al. 1976: 99, drawn by author)

A whole host of inscribed objects have also been found in ritual contexts, the storerooms of the sanctuaries at Myrtou-Pigadhes for example (du Plat Taylor 1957: 95-6), or the temple complex at Kition (Karageorghis 1985a, 1985b) in rooms full of precious objects such as bronze tripods, offering stands, stone rhyta, and even a fragmentary larnax. Many of these objects were probably deposited as votives. Those which were inscribed, including elaborate bronze stands or imported ivories, are exotic, prestige goods. They illustrate their owners' ability to import rare materials and access skilled craftsmanship, as well as wield this mysterious new technique of 'writing'. So, much in the same way as the seals found in burials, their deposition in these ritual contexts appears to be a form of conspicuous consumption.

Many of the inscriptions on these votives seem to have been added after their initial design. An ivory plaque of the Egyptian god Bes, for example, found in Rm 38C, Temple 4, Area 2 at Kition, is inscribed on the base, an area which would originally have been obscured by its mounting (Karageorghis 1985a: 151, 1985b: 116, 280, 330-1). At least two of the burial seal-stones, including a steatite cylinder seal found at Kourion Bamboula (#B1625; Benson 1972: 144) and the Babylonian example mentioned above, also seem to have been inscribed later. This may have been done just prior to their deposition as votives, specifically to add a kind of spiritual force to the object. Given how uncommon script was at this point, it is quite possible that it was viewed by some as possessing this sort of power. This would add yet more potential for

Cypro-Minoan inscribed objects to demonstrate high-status.

Objects inscribed with Linear A, such as the so-called 'offerings tables', have also been discovered in apparently ritual contexts on Crete. Like the Cypriot examples, such objects were plausibly dedicated as votives. As for their inscriptions, the majority consist of one of three recognised sign-groups which have been convincingly interpreted as dedications, possibly including the name of a deity (Olivier 1989: 240). There is almost no overlap between the groups of Linear A signs found on ritual objects and those found on administrative documents such as the clay tablets (Dickinson 1994: 194), illustrating a clear distinction in the types of statement being inscribed.

In the case of Cypro-Minoan, however, it is not possible to separate fully those objects apparently used in administration and those associated with symbolic or status display. The inscriptions on some metal bowls and votives are identical to those on some clay balls. Two clay balls from Enkomi, for example, (e.g. Schaeffer #1961.33; Masson, E. 1971a: 488) share their inscriptions with the reverse of the ivory Bes plaque found at Kition (Masson, E. 1985: 280). This overlap could be explained if these inscriptions referred to a place, person or perhaps group (c.f. Ferrara 2005: 104-8). Yet, it may also illustrate that Cypro-Minoan inscriptions had a multi-tiered signifycance, dependant on the context in which they were found. A name, for example, inscribed on any object may serve as a label, a marker of ownership. But whatever practical purpose that may have served in a copper-smelting environment, for example, this same inscription might take on a second, more abstract role when enlisted into activities of status display in the tombs and temples, enhancing the social profile and perceived power of the owner.

DISCUSSION

To assess what the corpus of Cypro-Minoan objects suggests about the nature of Late Bronze Age Cypriot society, it is necessary to return to where this paper began – administration and Linear A. It is clear that Cypro-Minoan, at least in part, was used in administration. Signs on the handles of clay vessels appear to have been used in controlling or monitoring the movement of goods, and even the peculiar clay balls may have had a role in the copper industry. Yet the number of surviving examples of Cypro-Minoan is small and those with discernable administrative function even smaller. We cannot possibly estimate what proportion of the original corpus either has not survived or has yet to be found. However, given what is extant, it seems likely that Late Bronze Age Cypriot written administration was neither comprehensive nor particularly complex.

There is some apparent regionalism in the types of inscribed objects. Most of the clay cylinders were found in Kalavasos and Kition's inscribed corpus consists almost entirely of votives. Enkomi's assemblage in particular stands out, both in the number and the range of inscribed objects. The earliest examples of the script also come from LCI Enkomi – a 'loomweight' (#19:13, Q5E; Schaeffer *et al.* 1968: 266-7), which may plausibly be interpreted as a label (Ferrara 2005: 56-7), and a tablet fragment (#1885, Area III; Dikaios 1969: 882), both of which have conceivable administrative use. Thus, one is left with the overriding impression of the small-scale adoption, during the early Late Bronze Age, of simple written administration at particular sites – with Enkomi at the forefront.

This is in stark contrast to the complex and widespread written administration implied by the large number of administrative inscriptions surviving from Bronze Age Crete.[11] In this context there existed an intricate system of sealings – noduli, roundels, clay bars – and tablets, in use on a huge scale. This elaborate administration implies a highly-organised, largely centralised political and economic system in each region. Yet on Cyprus, the evidence suggests not only that the use of writing in administration was limited, but that the administrative mechanisms themselves were rudimentary. Consequently, a comparable level of complexity and organisation for Cyprus simply cannot be assumed.

The different contexts in which Linear A and Cypro-Minoan developed had definite implications for the later significances of both scripts. Late Bronze Age Cretan society had a long history of using seals in administration, introduced in the Early Bronze Age. There is also some evidence that other scripts, such as the obscure Archanes script or the better-known Cretan Hieroglyphic, were already in use on the island.[12] LC I Cyprus, on the other hand, had no such traditions on which Cypro-Minoan could expand. At this time, Cypriot society was in a state of flux. Social complexity was increasing but it had probably not yet reached any kind of 'state' level (Keswani 1996: 238-9; see also Peltenburg 1996: 13-43 against this view). Even if Cypro-Minoan was initially invented for an administrative purpose, the socio-economic environment of Bronze Age Cyprus may simply not have been appropriate to sustain this as the script's primary use. Whereas on Crete, the background of literacy and the bureaucratic concerns of the palaces nurtured the administrative role of Linear A, on Cyprus, the ambiguous, less established social structure left Cypro-Minoan grappling for definition.

The arena of status display, already firmly established and increasingly important in the Late Bronze Age, was a natural sphere in which Cypro-Minoan could find a niche.

This would account for the existence of script on such a large number of objects with no perceivable administrative function – objects like the Bes plaque, which combine precious material with rare script, demonstrating the resources and knowledge of their owners.

Even the objects with plausibly administrative function could be seen in a similar light. On Crete, it is certainly possible to see the Linear A administrative documents, which make up more than 95% of the total corpus, as physical symbols of palace-centred control. These inscriptions, therefore, combine a practical and a symbolic function. On Cyprus, the cross-over between the inscriptions on votives, metal bowls and clay balls suggests that there could be a link between Cypro-Minoan administration, such as it was, and élite status display.

It may be implausible to suggest that the very adoption of written administration on Cyprus was a conscious attempt by certain élite groups to demonstrate their status by reference to the Aegean world. Nevertheless, no such administration existed before the Late Bronze Age and the invention of Cypro-Minoan. Similarly, early Late Bronze Age Cypriot society was not sufficiently centralised or complex to have required the sort of intricate administration which the use of a script made possible. Even in the latter stages of the Late Bronze Age, when this level of complexity appears to have been reached, Cypro-Minoan remained encumbered by the associations it had gained during the earlier period.

The surviving Cypro-Minoan evidence certainly implies that the script was never used to its full administrative potential. Far more appropriate for Late Bronze Age Cyprus was the utilisation of the script as a further tool of status negotiation. It is possible then, that the script and the administration were introduced as a package of élite self-definition, based on a model seen at work in Neo-Palatial Crete. Cypro-Minoan was yet another weapon in the struggle for superiority amongst the élite groups of Late Bronze Age Cyprus.

---

[11] It is true that the archive at Ayia Triada accounts for some 45% of these Linear A administrative documents (Schoëp 2002:16-7). However, even if it had never been discovered, the range and number of objects remaining would still imply a similarly extensive system, quite different in scale from that of contemporary Cyprus.

[12] For further information on the Archanes script, which was possibly in use as early as MMIA, see Sakellarakis & Sapouna-Sakellaraki 1997.

Bibliography

ÅSTRÖM, P. (1986) Hala Sultan Tekke – An International Harbour Town of the Late Cypriot Bronze Age. *Opuscula Atheniensia* 16, 1-17.

ÅSTRÖM, P. (1989) *Katydhata: A Bronze Age Site in Cyprus*. Göteborg, Paul Åströms Forlag.

ÅSTRÖM, P., D. BAILEY and V. KARAGEORGHIS (1976) *Hala Sultan Tekke I: Excavations 1897-1971*. Göteborg, Paul Åströms Forlag.

BENSON, J.L. (1972) *Bamboula at Kourion: the Necropolis and the Finds*. Philadelphia, University of Pennsylvania Press.

BENNET, J., M. DABNEY, O. KRYSZKOWSKA, D. REESE, K. SCHWAB, C. SEASE, M. SHAW and H.

WHITTAKER (1996) Catalogue of Miscellaneous Finds. IN: Shaw, J. and M. Shaw eds, *Kommos: an Excavation on the South Coast of Crete. Vol I: The Kommos Region and Houses of the Minoan Town. Part 2: The Minoan Hilltop and Hillside Houses.* Princeton, Princeton University Press, 243-377.

CATLING, H.W. (1962) Patterns of Settlement in Bronze Age Cyprus. *Opuscula Atheniensia* 4, 129-69.

CHADWICK, J. (1990) Linear B and Related Scripts. IN: Hooker, J. ed. *Ancient writing from cuneiform to the alphabet*, London, British Museum Press.

COURTOIS, J-C. (1981) *Alasia II: Les Tombes d'Enkomi. Fouilles Claude Schaeffer 1947-1965.* Paris, Mission archéologique d'Alasia.

COURTOIS, J-C. (1984) *Alasia III : Les Objets des Niveaux Stratifiés d'Enkomi. Fouilles CFA Schaeffer 1947-70.* Memorie 32, Paris.

COURTOIS, J-C. (1986) *Enkomi et la Bronze Récent à Chypre.* Nicosia, Chypre: Impr. Zavallis.

DANIEL, J.F. (1941) Prolegomena to the Cypro-Minoan Script. *American Journal of Archaeology* 45, 249-82.

DICKINSON, O. (1994) *The Aegean Bronze Age.* Cambridge, Cambridge University Press.

DIKAIOS, P. (1953) Inscribed Tablet from Enkomi, Cyprus. *Antiquity* 27, 103-5; 233-7.

DIKAIOS, P. (1956) A New Inscribed Clay Tablet from Enkomi. *Antiquity* 30, 40-1.

DIKAIOS, P. (1963) The Context of the Enkomi Tablets. *Kadmos* 2:1, 39-52.

DIKAIOS, P. (1967) More Cypro-Minoan Inscriptions from Enkomi. IN: Brice, W.C. ed. *Europa. Studien zur Geschichte und Epigraphik der Frühen Aegaeis. Festschrift für Ernst Grumach.* Berlin, Walter de Gruyter and Co., 80-7.

DIKAIOS, P. (1969) *Enkomi Excavations 1948-1958: Volumes I-IIIb.* Mainz am Rhein, Verlag Philipp von Zabern.

EVANS, A.J. (1909) *Scripta Minoa I*, Oxford, Clarendon Press.

FAUCOUNAU, J. (1977) Études chypro-minoennes I-III. *Syria* 54, 211-49.

FERRARA, S. (2005) *An Interdisciplinary Approach to the Cypro-Minoan Script*, unpublished PhD thesis, University College London.

GJERSTAD, E. *et al.* (1937) *The Swedish Cyprus Expedition: finds and results of the excavations in Cyprus 1927-1931.* Vol.1, Stockholm, The Swedish Cyprus Expedition.

HIRSCHFELD, N. (1996) *The PASP Data Base for the Use of Scripts on Cyprus.* Minos Supplement 13, Salamanca, Ediciones Universidad de Salamanca.

HIRSCHFELD, N. (2002) Marks on Pots: Patterns of Use in the Archaeological Record at Enkomi. IN: Smith, J. ed. *Script and Seal Use on Cyprus in the Bronze and*

Iron Ages. Boston, Archaeological Institute of America, 49-109.

KARAGEORGHIS, V. (1985a) *Excavations at Kition V, Volume I.* Nicosia, Department of Antiquities.

KARAGEORGHIS, V. (1985b) *Excavations at Kition V, Volume II.* Nicosia, Department of Antiquities.

KARAGEORGHIS, V. and M. DEMAS (1984) *Pyla-Kokkinokremos: A Late Thirteenth Century BC Fortified Settlement in Cyprus.* Nicosia, Department of Antiquities.

KARAGEORGHIS, V. and M. DEMAS (1988) *Excavations at Maa-Palaekastro 1976-1986.* Nicosia, Department of Antiquities.

KESWANI, P.S. (1996) Hierarchies, Heterarchies and Urbanization Processes: The View from Bronze Age Cyprus. *Journal of Mediterranean Archaeology* 9, 211-50.

KESWANI, P.S. (2004) *Mortuary Ritual and Society in Bronze Age Cyprus.* London, Equinox.

KNAPP, A.B. (1996) *Near Eastern and Aegean Texts from the Third to the First Millennia BC. Sources for the History of Cyprus Volume II.* New York, Altamont.

KNAPP, A.B. (1997) *The Archaeology of Late Bronze Age Cypriot Society: The Study of Settlement, Survey and Landscape.* Glasgow, University of Glasgow.

KNAPP, A.B. and A. MARCHANT (1982) Cyprus, Cypro-Minoan and Hurrians. *Report of the Department of Antiquities Cyprus*, 15-30.

MASSON, E. (1969) La Plus Ancienne Tablette Chyprominoenne. *Minos* 10.1, 54-77.

MASSON, E. (1970) Remarques sur les Fragments de Tablette Chyprominoenne. *Studi Micene ed Egeo-Anatolici* 11, 73-102.

MASSON, E. (1971a) Les boules d'argile inscrites d'Enkomi. IN: Schaeffer, C.F.A. ed. *Alasia I*, Paris, Mission archéologique d'Alasia. 479-504.

MASSON, E. (1971b) *Étude du vingt-six boules d'argile inscrites trouvés à Enkomi et Hala Sultan Tekke (Chypre).* Studies in Mediterranean Archaeology, 31.1, Göteborg, Paul Åströms Förlag.

MASSON, E. (1974) *Cyprominoica. Répertoires, Documents de Ras Shamra, Essais d'interprétation.* Studies in Mediterranean Archaeology 31:2. Göteborg, Paul Åströms Förlag.

MASSON, E. (1985) Inscriptions et marques Chypro-Minoennes a Kition. IN: Karageorghis, V. *Excavations at Kition V, volume II.* Nicosia, Department of Antiquities, 280-92

MASSON, O. (1956) Les écritures chyro-minoennes et les possibilités de déchiffrement. IN: *Études mycéniennes: Actes du colloque international sur les textes mycéniens*, Paris, C.N.R.S., 199-206.

MASSON, O. (1957) Cylindres et cachets chypriotes portant les characteres chypro-minoens. *Bulletin de Correspondance Hellénique* 81, 6-37.

MASSON, O. (1968) Three Bronze Bowls in Nicosia Museum. *Minos* 9, 66-72.

MICHAILIDOU, A. (1993) 'Ostrakon' with Linear A Script from Akrotiri (Thera). A Non-Bureaucratic Activity? *Minos* 27-8, 7-24.

MICHAILIDOU, A. (2000) Indications of Literacy in Bronze Age Thera. *Minos* 35-6, 7-30.

MURRAY, A.S., A.H. SMITH and H.B. WALTERS (1900) *Excavations in Cyprus*. London, Printed by order of the Trustees of the British Museum.

ÖBRINK, U. (1979) *Hala Sultan Tekke V: Excavations in Area 22, 1971-1973 and 1978*. Göteborg, Paul Åströms Forlag.

OLIVIER, J-P. (1989) Les Écritures Crétoises. IN: Treuil, R., P. Darque, J-C. Poursat and G Touchais, *Les Civilisations égéennes du Néolithique et de l'Age du Bronze*. Book 2, Chapter 2. Paris, Presses Universitaires de France.

OVERBECK, J.C. and S. SWINY (1972) *Two Cypriot Bronze Age Sites at Kafkallia (Dhali)*. Göteborg, Paul Åströms Forlag.

PALAIMA, T. (1989) Cypro-Minoan Scripts: Problems of Historical Context. IN: Duhoux, Y., T. Palaima and J. Bennet eds, *Problems in Decipherment*. Louvain-la-Neuve, Peeters, 121-87.

PELTENBURG, E. (1996) From Isolation to State Formation in Cyprus, *c.* 3500-1500 B.C. IN: Karageorghis, V. and D. Michaelides eds, *The Development of the Cypriot Economy: From the Prehistoric Period to the Present Day*. Nicosia, University of Cyprus, 17-44.

du PLAT-TAYLOR, J. (1957) *Myrtou-Pigadhes: A Late Bronze Age Sanctuary in Cyprus*, Oxford, Dept. of Antiquities, Ashmolean Museum.

POWELL, B.P. (2002) Seals and Writing in the Ancient Near East and Cyprus: Observations from Context. IN: Smith, J. ed. *Script and Seal Use on Cyprus in the Bronze and Iron Ages*. Boston, Archaeological Institute of America, 227-48.

REYES, A.T. (2002) The Stamp Seals of Cyprus in the Late Bronze Age and the Iron Age: An Introduction. IN: Smith, J. ed. *Script and Seal Use on Cyprus in the Bronze and Iron Ages*. Boston, Archaeological Institute of America, 213-26.

SAKELLARAKIS, Y and E SAPOUNA-SAKELLARAKI (1997) *Archanes: Minoan Crete in a New Light*. Athens, Ammos.

SCHAEFFER, C.F.A. (1952) *Enkomi-Alasia I*. Paris, Mission archéologique d'Alasia.

SCHAEFFER, C.F.A. (1971) *Alasia I*. Paris, Mission archéologique d'Alasia.

SCHAEFFER, C.F.A., J-C. COURTOIS and J. LAGARCE (1968) Fouilles d' Enkomi-Alasia dans l'île de Chypre, campange de 1967. *Syria* 45, 263-74.

SCHOEP, I. (2002) *The Administration of Neopalatial Crete: A Critical Assessment of the Linear B Tablets and their Role in the Administrative Process*. Minos supplement 17, Salamanca, Ediciones Universidad de Salamanca.

SMITH, J.S. (2002) Problems and Prospects in the Study of Script and Seal Use on Cyprus in the Bronze and Iron Ages. IN: Smith, J. ed. *Script and Seal Use on Cyprus in the Bronze and Iron Ages*. Boston, Archaeological Institute of America, 1-47.

SOUTH, A.K. (1983) Kalavasos-Ayios Dhimitrios 1982. *Report of the Department of Antiquities Cyprus*. 92-116.

STEEL, L. (2004) *Cyprus Before History: From the Earliest Settlers to the End of the Bronze Age*. London, Duckworth.

VENTRIS, M. (1956) Notes on the Enkomi 1955 Tablet. *Antiquity* 30, 41-2.

VERMEULE, E.T. and F.Z. WOLSKY (1990) *Toumba tou Skourou*. Harvard, Harvard University Press.

WEBB, J.M. (2002) Device, Image and Coercion: The Role of Glyptic in the Political Economy of Late Bronze Age Cyprus. IN: Smith, J. ed. *Script and Seal Use on Cyprus in the Bronze and Iron Ages*. Boston, Archaeological Institute of America, 111-54.

CYPRUS AT THE CROSSROADS: UNDERSTANDING THE PATHS TAKEN IN THE ART AND ARCHITECTURE OF FRANKISH CYPRUS
JAMES G. SCHRYVER

INTRODUCTION

The idea of Cyprus as a crossroads of the eastern and larger Mediterranean has long been a popular one, as can be seen in its use in the titles of articles and books written by scholars in various fields (Government of Cyprus 1952; Edbury 1998; Karageorghis 2002). From what we are able to observe concerning Cyprus during the Lusignan period, the image is also an appropriate and useful one. However, one danger exists that we must acknowledge if we are to continue to use this notion to aid our understanding of the types of interactions between various cultures that occurred on the island during this time. That danger results from the fact that the neat image of Cyprus being located at the crossroads of various Mediterranean cultures that this brings up in our minds belies the complexities that underlie it (Fig. 1). It is exactly these complexities that we must seek to understand if we are to attempt to sort out the various and intricate traffic patterns that these cultures move within once they reach the island.

Although one could argue that the relevant events reach back as far as the Crusader defeat at the Battle of Hattin in July 1187, the story of the Lusignan kingdom of Frankish Cyprus begins locally in May 1191 with the conquest of the island by Richard the Lionheart on his way to the Third Crusade (Edbury 1991: 1-12; Nicolaou-Konnari 2000). Richard soon sold the island to the Templars for 100,000 Saracen bezants. Before paying the full amount, however, the Templars returned the island to him, most likely as a result of the popular revolt they had suffered on April 4-5 of 1192. Richard then turned around and sold the island to Guy de Lusignan, again for the sum of 100,000 bezants. It is not known whether Guy ever paid the full amount (Edbury 1991: 9 and 28; Nicolaou-Konnari 2000: 67-8). What is known, however, is that by selling the island to Guy, Richard not only freed himself once again of the responsibility of administrating it, but also solved the problem that had been caused by Guy's

loss of Jerusalem to the Moslems (Edbury 1991: 24-9; Nicolaou-Konnari 2000: 65-7). Although some scholars claim that it was Guy's brother Aimery who really founded the Lusignan dynasty on the island, it is with the settlement policies of Guy, starting in 1192, that the prolonged cultural contact and thus the period of interest for this article begins (Edbury 1989: 17; 1991: 16-17).

During the nearly 300 years that the island remained in Lusignan hands (*de jure*), a rich variety of artistic cultures came to and crossed paths on Cyprus: among others, Armenian, Byzantine, Crusader, French, Islamic, Italian and Levantine (Fig. 1). The numerous material culture traditions that travelled down these pathways individually, together with the various combinations of these traditions that formed on the island, produced a diverse array of artistic expressions. The range of these expressions extends from the continuation of certain individual styles and elements, such as fourteenth-century French cathedral architecture (one-way traffic), to more complete syntheses of various artistic elements (complex traffic patterns). As a result, if one approaches these artistic works as a homogeneous group, as products of one coherent society, subject to a rigid set of behavioral rules that remained static throughout the long period of Lusignan rule, there are always some pieces of evidence and/or works of art that do not fit. This problem remains regardless of whether or not these rules involve integration of all the various communities living on the island, segregation, or instances of both (Schryver 2005: 20-47).

CHALLENGES

A number of challenges make finding the definitive conclusion concerning just how these cultures intersected on the island very difficult. These are important to understand because they are in part the products of our own approach to the topic. Moreover, they hinder our

Fig. 1 – Map of Cyprus with arrows representing the numerous cultural paths
that came to the island (image by author)

understanding of the cultural interactions that are the current focus of study. They are the reason that certain pieces of evidence, artifacts and works of art do not fit within the proposed models of Cypriot society at that time.

One of the most significant problems is present in the basic statement of the issues under investigation. For example, when I say that I am studying the interaction between the Franks and Greeks in Frankish Cyprus, I have already come to three important conclusions without necessarily having looked at any of the supporting evidence. First, I have concluded that the Franks and Greeks were and remained two distinct groups throughout the period of Lusignan rule. Second, I have concluded a number of things about the nature of their opposition. Third, I have concluded that they did indeed interact. What is more, even if I have only done it subconsciously, I have also made two problematic assumptions: first, I have assumed that these are the only two groups upon which I must focus. Second, I have assumed that their interaction with one another was the same in every context.

The idea that Cyprus is a cultural crossroads makes the notion of a simple and all-encompassing model of interaction quite attractive. In terms of methodology, when looking superficially at the evidence with the assumption of interaction in mind, it is easy to imagine that we should be able to examine the artistic traditions that arrive on the island as paths that remain isolated for the most part, but nevertheless do cross once in a while at various intersections. It might even prove quite satisfying

to state that understanding the intersections of these various paths that cross on Cyprus is as easy as locating their point of origin and tracing them through to their various junctions.

In this regard, we might imagine that if Figure 2 represents a model for the interaction of the Frankish and Greek paths, the results of these intersections would also be easy to understand or to quantify. Interactions between the Franks (Group A) and the Greeks (Group B) would in time result in a mixed cultural group of Franco-Greeks or Franco-Cypriotes (Group AB). The period of time needed for this to occur would be short, perhaps one or two generations. As time continues on, more interactions between different members of this group would simple increase the mixed nature of this group, perhaps creating what we might symbolize as group AB^2. The point is that once the initial interactions caused the creation of a new hybrid culture, this new culture would determine the nature and the outcome of any future interactions.

Unfortunately, the situation is not so simple. Certainly, from the outside, it is tempting to view Frankish Cyprus after a few generations as one whole, coherent, cultural unit, especially since the single name, the period's clear chronological boundaries (1191-1489), and the island's geographical limits invite such a conception. But, as in so many other cases, the devil is in the details. For example, the efforts of a number of scholars have revealed that a larger variety of societies and cultures or communities were present on the island during the Lusignan period than previously assumed (Prawer 1977a; 1977b; Richard 1979; 1987; 1991; Schryver 2005: 190-6). Other scholars,

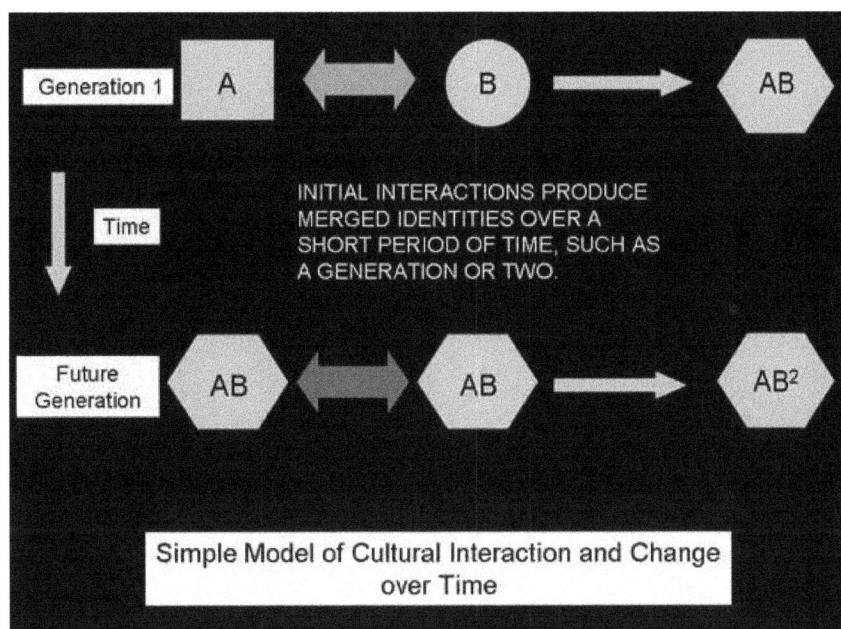

Fig. 2 – Simple Diagram/Model of Cultural Interaction and Change (image by author)

such as Tassos Papacostas, have reminded us that in trying to understand the intersections occurring on the island, we perhaps also need to consider the presence of western merchants there before 1191 (Papacostas 1999). Taking a step back, it becomes clear that this demographic complexity is something that is recognisable and perhaps even inherent in the notion that there are many paths that intersect on the island during this time (Fig. 1). Nonetheless, these minor communities of Armenians, Jacobites, Melkites and Nestorians are often benignly neglected by scholars who focus instead on the Franks and the Greeks. Although these studies are extremely useful in their own right, they can lead to the assumption that the latter are the only two cultures and paths that require our attention as we seek to understand the culture of the island during this period. Once again, although this is a seductive idea, its simplicity is belied by the complexity of the road map of Frankish Cyprus. Each of the other (minor) groups had their own traditions that they brought with them to the island along their paths. In the very least, we must acknowledge the possibility of the influence of these communities on the Franks and the Greeks.

For the sake of clarity, let us return to the discussion of Frankish and Greek interaction. Now, if these groups and the nature of the context between them were all static (another pothole awaiting scholars along this path of inquiry) and if the local social and political context at the point of origin of each of these various paths was the same, then the solution would be simple: the evidence would either prove or disprove the assumption that their interaction was always the same/was the same in every context. There would be evidence for interaction or there would not, and the conclusions concerning one area would apply for the entire 300-year period. I will dispense

with a discussion of the problems of absence of evidence vs. evidence of absence for now.

An additional factor should also be discussed at this point. Just as a simplistic understanding of the interaction of these two groups is problematic, even more problematic is any understanding based on the belief that they remained segregated. These communities did not simply co-exist next to one another as independent or singular entities, moving along in the same general direction like cars in a multi-lane highway, yet never crossing over into each other's lanes. Examining the evidence we can see that they did indeed 'cross over'. In fact, this idea is inherent in the notion of Cyprus as a crossroads of intersecting cultures. What is perhaps more difficult to grasp is the idea/notion that singular instances of interaction did not necessarily set the tone for future interactions. Nor should we take it for granted that any given interactions would result in cultural exchange. To return to the argument and simple model put forward above, the interactions of Group A and B as shown in Figure 2 does not necessarily lead to the creation of a Group AB. If these groups were static entities, then perhaps that would have been the case. But these groups were actual fluid bodies, changing as a result of interactions with one another, but also as a result of internal developments and conditions. Not to mention the fact that what we are really seeking to understand involves the actions and interactions of individual members of these groups. In other words, given any two groups who might interact during two different time periods 1 and 2, which we might out of convenience limit to a generation, these groups would never be the same at any given point during time 2 as they had been prior to the interaction during time 1. At the least, even if there were not any internal development, the actual interaction that occurred at any specific point during time 1 would

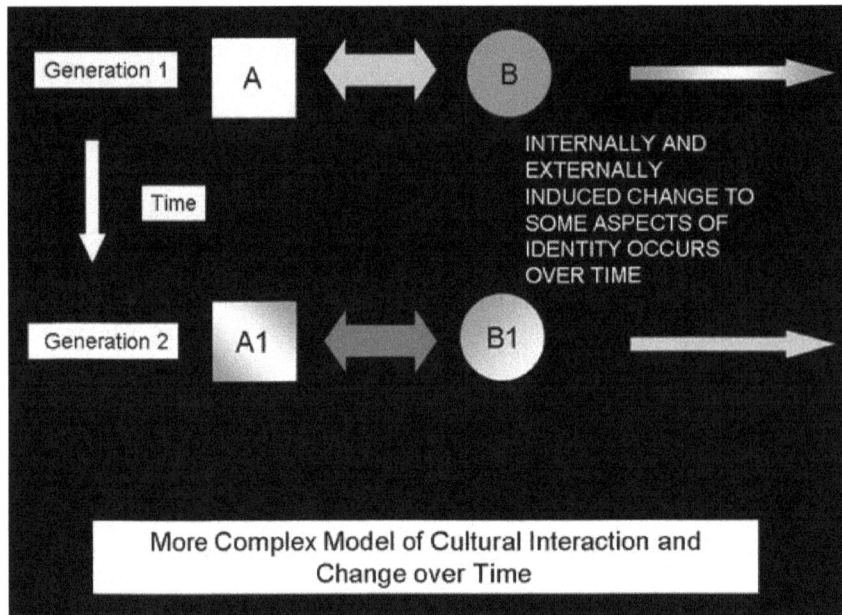

Fig. 3 – Modified Diagram/Model of Cultural Interaction and Change (image by author)

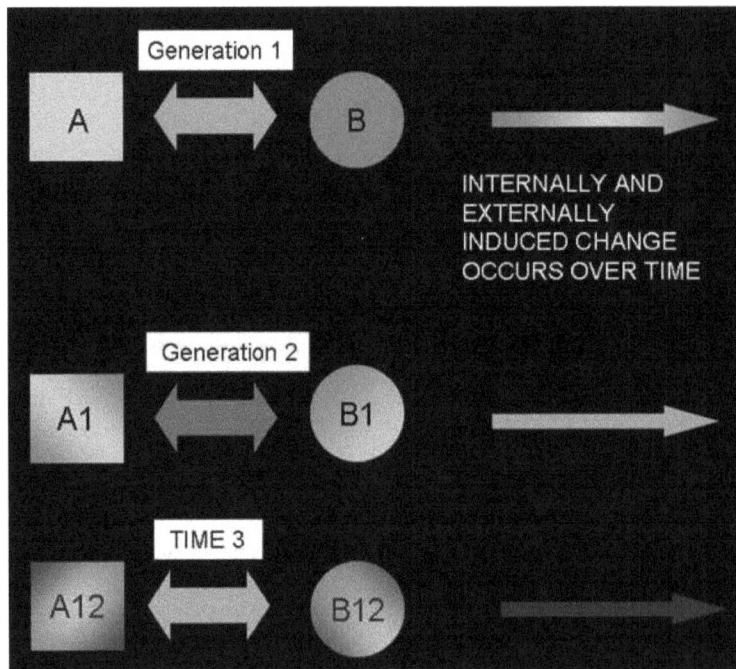

Fig. 4 – Complex Diagram/Model of Cultural Interaction and Change (image by author)

produce some difference in the groups that would prevent the interaction occurring during time 2 from being the same. Figure 3 is an attempt to diagram this idea. If we were talking about group A and group B interacting during a period we might call time 1, after that we would be talking about group A1 and group B1. What is more, I would argue that in many respects these interactions are cumulative, so that after the interaction occurring during time 2, we should not speak of group A2 and group B2, but instead of group A12 and group B12. After all, it would be wrong to assume that all of the changes that

might have occurred as a result of the interaction during time 1 would be wiped out or erased as a result of the interaction during time 2. These changes would, of course, then also affect the types of interactions that would occur at any point in the future (Fig. 4).

Once we recognise the complexity of the situation, the importance of issues such as the intended function and audience for different monuments and works of art and architecture and the changing nature of the different communities present on Frankish Cyprus that produced them to any examination of the material culture become ever more apparent. These factors make an in-depth study of the various contexts of these works essential in order to understand them. This issue is one that is ignored within a conception of Frankish Cyprus as a whole, singular entity as seen from outside.

These issues may seem somewhat obvious to many of us who are actively wrestling with trying to understand just what kind of intersections occurred on the island, but this has not always been the case. In fact, the previous models of the society that formed in the Latin East assumed a situation in which there was either total interaction or total segregation (Ellenblum 1998: 3-11). And they found both historical and art historical evidence (often even the same evidence) to support and illustrate their claims. Thus, until very recently, the student of society in any portion of the Latin East, including Cyprus, was faced with a choice between two societal models, both of which were quite convincing on the surface (Schryver 2005: 20-47 with further references). Again, the reason for this is that there are a range of artistic expressions that are possible.

Although acknowledging these challenges is only half the journey, to use the metaphor of choice for this article, I believe that such an acknowledgement puts us on the right track towards overcoming them. It does so by allowing us to consider four important factors from the beginning. 1) Many of these works provide examples of the complex ways in which both artists and patrons on Frankish Cyprus combined contextual considerations (local, regional and Mediterranean-wide) in the expressions of their identity through art. 2) The identities of these artists and patrons were multi-layered in themselves, motivating them to privilege certain aspects over others in any given situation. 3) Just as these individuals had to be able to convey different messages about themselves to different audiences in different contexts, many of these works of art (especially those commissioned by the Lusignan family) had to be able to perform in the same way. 4) When these groups did interact, whether personally or artistically, and even when they began to merge with one another in certain aspects of their identity, this did not erase other aspects of these same identities (in this case Frankish and Greek) that continued to remain distinct. By taking these 'new' factors into account when examining the works of art and architecture previously used to support one cultural model or another, it will become clear that we must be more careful in how we interpret many of these works and the various cultural paths and intersections that they represent.

Therefore, in addition to pointing out the potholes along the road ahead, I wish to suggest that by looking at all of the issues addressed above, we can better understand the paths that enter the crossroads of Cyprus and how they act when they get there. At the least, I hope to demonstrate that the intersections that are formed are not simply one-way. I will do this by discussing two works of art that are

at first glance at odds with one another: the cathedral of St. Nicholas in Famagusta and a donor portrait from Asinou (Fig. 5 and Fig. 7). Regardless of their different functions and media, as cultural products of one coherent society they do not seem to belong together because the Frankish identities they express would seem to be in contrast. Through this discussion, I hope to demonstrate why a deep understanding of the interplay of the different contexts or road systems and the range of possible resulting 'traffic' patterns that I have highlighted is so important for the correct interpretation of these works of art. I believe that both works do actually 'fit' into the same chronological period, the same political kingdom, and the same broad culture and society. The challenge for us is to understand how this is so.

Fig. 5 – Cathedral of St. Nicholas, Famagusta, façade (photo by author)

Like many of its cousins along the European pilgrimage route, the cathedral of St. Nicholas in Famagusta dominates the cityscape of the walled portion of the town (Fig. 8). It has a flat concrete roof and was built in bright yellow limestone. The building consists of a nave and two aisles, each of seven bays and each ending in an apse. Documents imply that work was underway at least by August of 1300. The Western façade (Fig. 5) was originally framed between two identical towers, which were later altered when the building was converted into a mosque after 1571 (Jeffery 1918: 116-27 and 150-4; Enlart 1987: 222 and 227-45).

Fig. 6 – Reims Cathedral, façade (photo by bodoklecksel)

Whereas the local elements seem limited to the palm trees and the flat roof, the fourteenth-century French elements in the architecture of St. Nicholas are immediately apparent to the viewer in both the details and general appearance of the building: for example, the use of sharply gabled doorways to create a tri-partite division of the façade and the elaborate tracery. By weaving in the threads of evidence provided by an examination of the history of the cathedral, we can identify trends that help to narrow down the sources of this influence. In his study of the cathedral, Camille Enlart identified parallels with 'the style of Champagne' (Enlart 1987: 223). And along with others, he noted that St. Nicholas also 'imitates Rheims Cathedral' (Enlart 1987: 224; Andrews 1999; Weyl Carr 2005: 314-15). The connections with the Champagne region involved the physical movement of individuals from one area to the other. During the initial period of building, the archbishop of Famagusta was one Gerard of Langres, who was from that region. It is reasonable to assume that the local urban bishop of the cathedral, Baldwin Lambert, not only requested permission to erect the cathedral, but asked the archbishop that an architect and masons be sent as well (Enlart 1987: 223).

The masons and artisans who arrived brought with them knowledge of styles and techniques from the West. As Robert Ousterhout has recently cautioned regarding the Crusader mainland, the patron's identity and experience was not necessarily always the same as that of the majority of the builders (Ousterhout 2004: 92). However, in this case it does seem that the patrons brought their people with them.

There may have been an added level of incentives for Western artisans to come to Cyprus, such as that offered by the Papal Bull of 1347 granting a 100-day indulgence for those contributing to the completion of St. Sophia (Enlart 1987: 56; Coureas and Schabel 1997: no. CXXIV). Other personal connections are just as important in regards to the influence of the art of southern France on certain elements of these and other churches on the island (Enlart 1987: 55-67). For example, trade connections existed between Marseilles, Montpellier and Narbonne on one side and Famagusta on the other (Enlart 1987: 55 with further references). In addition, a number of men from the south of France were sent by the Church to serve on the island and when these had to hire artists to carry out work on Cyprus, they brought them from the same region (Enlart 1987: 56 with further references).

The physical parallels with Reims (Fig. 6) such as those found in the decorative program of the façade are also worth exploring on a different level (Andrews 1999). Reims had been the royal coronation site for five centuries by the 1300s and as a result had become an important symbol of the power of these 'French' kings (Sadler-Davis 1984: 16; 1995: 49-68). In this connection, it is important to mention that in the fourteenth century, Famagusta Cathedral became the coronation spot for certain of the Lusignan kings as King of Jerusalem (Enlart 1987: 224; Edbury 1991: 141, 150, and 199). The new monarch would travel to Famagusta for the second coronation after he had been crowned at the cathedral of St. Sophia in Nicosia as King of Cyprus. By recalling Reims, the decorative program thus focuses the viewer's attention on Cyprus as the last Western outpost in the eastern Mediterranean and the only link to Jerusalem. It also emphasises the Western aspects of the island's identity, reminding those who might be planning future Crusades which side Cyprus was on, and perhaps also enforcing the idea that they should not be considered another Constantinople; both messages that were extremely appropriate as a backdrop for the coronation ceremony.

In addition, by co-opting traditional iconography and well-established rituals as their own, the Lusignans could establish themselves within the tradition of European kingship. As Peter Edbury has rightly observed, they were thus able to gain access to equal treatment by other kings crowned in the same way, namely, those of Latin Christendom (Edbury 1991: 184). The Western façade and the use made of St. Nicholas are the physical expressions of this strategy.

Examples of French Gothic architecture imported to Cyprus, such as at St. Nicholas, have been used by scholars to support both a model of cultural integration and a model of cultural segregation (Schryver 2005: 20-

Fig. 7 – Donor Portraits from Our Lady of Asinou (with the kind permission of Dumbarton Oaks)

47). Such cases are seen as examples of acculturation or symbolic stamps of authority, respectively. Enlart discussed architectural works, such as St. Nicholas, as proof of the cultural melange that had developed on Frankish Cyprus (Enlart 1987: 15). Other scholars working in the Latin East might be more inclined to view

Fig. 8 – Cathedral of St. Nicholas, Famagusta (photo by author)

these works as a stamp of authority and control over the local population (Georgopoulou 1996: 467-96). This point of view would explain that the Latin cathedrals dominated other buildings in the city just as the Latin Church (i.e. Rome) and the Franks held dominion over the other peoples living on the island. Neither explanation is completely satisfactory because both are belied by the complexity of the situation, by the intricacy of the road system.

Monuments such as the Cathedral of St. Nicholas were used as physical representations of a specific strategy and show elements of French-Gothic style brought over from the West for Western patrons who wanted Western cathedrals. Often, the patron arranged for Western masons and sculptors to come and do the work (De Vaivre 2001). Interestingly, unlike media such as icons and manuscript illumination, which were filtered through the Holy Land on their way to Cyprus, many of the architectural elements show little stylistic assimilation (Coldstream 1987: 5). There are of course a few exceptions to this notion (Andrews 1999: 42-5). However, in my view, the French architecture of the Cathedral of St. Nicholas and the apparent attempts at association with Reims Cathedral indicate a conscious assertion of a separate Western identity by a certain portion of the Frankish population on the island. In addition, it asserts this separation through a link with the French royalty and the traditions associated with it.

What can the cathedral tell us about the interaction between the Frankish and Greek communities or the types of intersections formed when their paths crossed? Not much, but this was not the purpose of the monument. It was never intended as a place where Frankish and Greek cultural paths would intersect. Therefore, to look at these French details and declare on that basis that the cathedral is a symbol of segregation on the island, not only ignores

many of the other monuments of this period, but also the function of the building. In addition, this is only one of the many possible physical manifestations of religious art or cultural 'traffic patterns' on the island.

Balancing the paths coming to the island from the West are those that originate in the local context. The composition of the Frankish society of Cyprus was not limited to elements imported directly from France. On the contrary, the community also comprised generations of Franks or *poulains* born into the culturally mixed environment of the island (Prawer 1977a; Richard 1987: 158-9). In addition, many of the refugees who came to Cyprus from the Crusader mainland had themselves been born in the Latin East (Richard 1979). These refugees brought with them their devotion to various local saints, their participation in local forms of worship and their patronage of local artists (Hunt 1991). One example of this patronage is the antependium of Othon de Grandson (Fig. 9), someone whom the Templar of Tyre describes as a 'Western knight of great renown' (Crawford 2003: 134, §542). This altar hanging is thought to have been commissioned on the island as an offering of thanks for de Grandson's safe arrival there after escaping from the mainland and the advancing Muslim armies (Stettler 1959: 34-7 and 49; Weyl Carr 1995: 243; 2005: 307-8).

Two other more well-known examples of such offerings are the icon of St. Nicholas from the Church of Agios Nikolaos tis Stegis and the icon of the Virgin Cassianos (Schryver 2005: 125-33). Scholars have typically seen these three works as representative of the mixed culture that formed on Cyprus in the thirteenth-century, although Annemarie Weyl Carr has, rightly I think, and for quite a while, been pressing us to re-evaluate this stance (Weyl Carr 1995; 2005). More specifically, these icons actually represent the mixed culture of the Franks who were coming or fleeing to Cyprus from the mainland in this

Fig. 9 – Antependium of Othon de Grandson (Weyl Carr, 1995, fig.8,
with the kind permission of the Bernese Historical Museum)

same period. More importantly for our discussion here, they are essentially non-Western works of art commissioned by Franks who are also depicted within the works as the patrons. In the latter two cases, the 'Western' identity of these Franks is made obvious.

ASINOU

The further development of this mixed culture on Cyprus and the interaction between Latins and Greeks in the sphere of religion can be seen in two fourteenth-century murals (Fig. 7) in the Church of Our Lady Phorviotissa, better known as Our Lady of Asinou (Weyl Carr 1995: 242-3; 1998/1999). The mural is painted on the semi-dome of the southern apse of the narthex. It depicts a Latin lady kneeling in petition for protection from the Virgin Mary who appears above and to her right. On the other side of the Virgin kneel two male figures who we can assume are members of the lady's family. Mary extends her cloak over her female devotee and looks benignly towards the males on her left, while the Christ-child reaches out to bless the Latin lady. Annemarie Weyl Carr has pointed out the similarity of this protective gesture (known as the Schutzmantel motif) to that found in the Armenian Gospel Book of Prince Vasak and attributed the mural to a local, presumably Orthodox painter (Weyl Carr 1995: 243).

Once again, most significant from the point of view of cultural interaction within the sphere of religion, and as a contrast to the Cathedral of St. Nicholas, is the Latin identity of the donor. This identity is clear for two reasons: her clothing and her posture. The lady's décolletage and the other pieces of Frankish clothing are the standard dress of Western donors (Rice 1937: 100-39). Here, there is perhaps a relationship with historian's observations concerning the desire of the Frankish nobility to keep up with the latest fashions from the West (Prawer 1972: 396). Another insight into the importance of clothing as an identity marker in Frankish society is

provided by some of the earliest laws of the Kingdom of Jerusalem. Canon sixteen of the Council of Nablus held in 1120 threatens that any Saracen dressing in the Frankish manner with seizure (Prawer 1972: 519; Kedar 1999: 334). The position of prayer of all the figures, kneeling with their hands together (as opposed to standing, which is the position associated with the Greeks), is also traditionally associated with the Latins (Weyl Carr 1998/1999: 66). Thus, as with the donors of the two large icons, the donor here is conspicuous in her identity. But this is not a Western patron in the same sense as those involved in the building of St. Nicholas and I think that this distinction is extremely important. Instead, she is from the Frankish world of Cyprus. Is she Cypriot? I am not sure. Most likely the answer would depend on whom we asked. As noted, her clothing and her posture mark her as Latin. She has openly patronised this local Greek Orthodox church, but apparently that has not changed her affiliations, or her expressed identity as a Frankish woman. And although it is extremely difficult for us to know, I would also venture that this act did not change her own view of her identity as a Latin-rite Christian.

IN CONCLUSION

The two monuments just discussed demonstrate two different examples of the various possibilities open to the artistic paths (Frankish and Greek) that cross on Cyprus. They can remain dominated by one-way traffic (i.e. rigidly French or Byzantine) or they can intersect with other paths to create a series of two-way streets. Yet even in the process of intersecting, both cultures maintain certain aspects central to their different identities even while emerging on the other side of the intersection transformed. By examining the different monuments just discussed in their various contexts, we are able to understand how they could possibly be the product of the same general society of Frankish Cyprus, how they do belong. Their contribution to the crossroads of Cyprus is in the different goods they bring along their respective paths. In this way, we can also understand how other works of art might fit into the picture of Frankish Cyprus we are creating. For example, a discussion of the damascened basin of Hugh IV would take us down yet another series of paths and through new intersections, ones leading away from the realm of religion and into the realm of politics (Rice 1956). But that is a journey for another time.

Bibliography

ANDREWS, J.M. (1999) Santa Sophia in Nicosia: The Sculpture of the Western Portals and its Reception. *Comitatus* 30, 63-80.

bodoklecksel. *Cathedral of Reims.* 28 October 2007 <http://commons.wikimedia.org/wiki/ Image:Reims_Kathedrale.jpg>.

COLDSTREAM, N. (1987) Introduction: Camille Enlart and the Gothic Architecture of Cyprus. IN: Enlart, C. *Gothic Art and the Renaissance in Cyprus.* Edited and translated from the French by D. Hunt. London, Trigraph, 1-10.

COUREAS, N. and C. SCHABEL (1997) *The Cartulary of the Cathedral of Holy Wisdom of Nicosia*, Nicosia, Cyprus Research Centre.

CRAWFORD, P. trans. (2003) *The 'Templar of Tyre': Part III of the 'Deeds of the Cypriots',* Crusade Texts in Translation 6, Aldershot, Hampshire, Ashgate.

De VAIVRE, J.B. (2001) Sculpteurs parisiens en Chypre autour de 1300. IN: Balard, M., B.Z. Kedar, and J. Riley-Smith eds, *Dei gesta per Francos.* Aldershot, Hampshire, Ashgate, 373-88.

EDBURY, P.W. (1989) Cypriot Society under Lusignan Rule. IN: Hunt, D. and I. Hunt eds, *Caterina Cornaro, Queen of Cyprus.* London, Trigraph, 17-34.

EDBURY, P.W. (1991) *The Kingdom of Cyprus and the Crusades, 1191-1374.* Cambridge, Cambridge University Press.

EDBURY, P.W. (1998) Cyprus at the Crossroads: Crusaders and Pilgrims. IN: Papanikola-Bakirtzis, D. and M. Iacovou eds, *Byzantine Medieval Cyprus.* Nicosia, Bank of Cyprus, 27-33.

ELLENBLUM, R. (1998) *Frankish Rural Settlement in the Latin Kingdom of Jerusalem.* Cambridge: Cambridge University Press.

ENLART, C. (1987) *Gothic Art and the Renaissance in Cyprus.* Edited and translated from the French by D. Hunt. London, Trigraph.

GEORGOPOULOU, M. (1996) Mapping Religious and Ethnic Identities in the Venetian Colonial Empire. *Journal of Medieval and Early Modern Studies* 26, no. 3, 467-96.

Government of Cyprus (1952) *Cyprus, Cross-roads of the Middle East.* Nicosia, Government Printer.

HUNT, L.-A. (1991) A Woman's Prayer to St. Sergios in Latin Syria: Interpreting a Thirteenth-Century Icon at Mount Sinai. *Byzantine and Modern Greek Studies* 15, 96-124.

JEFFERY, G. (1918) *A Description of the Monuments of Cyprus.* Nicosia, Government Printing Office.

KARAGEORGHIS, V. (2002) *Early Cyprus: Crossroads of the Mediterranean.* Los Angeles, J. Paul Getty Museum.

KEDAR, B.Z. (1999) On the Origins of the Earliest Laws of Frankish Jerusalem: The Canons of the Council of Nablus, 1120. *Speculum* 74, no. 2, 310-35.

OUSTERHOUT, R. (2004) The French Connection? Construction of Vaults and Cultural Identity in Crusader Architecture. IN: Weiss, D.H. and L. Mahoney eds, *France and the Holy Land: Frankish Culture at the End of the Crusades.* Baltimore, John Hopkins University Press, 77-94.

NICOLAOU-KONNARI, A. (2000) The Conquest of Cyprus by Richard the Lionheart and its Aftermath. *Επετηρίδα* 26, 25-123.

PAPACOSTAS, T. (1999) Secular Landholdings and Venetians in 12th-Century Cyprus. *Byzantinische Zeitschrift* 92, no.2, 479-501.

PRAWER, J. (1972) *The Latin Kingdom of Jerusalem: European Colonialism in the Middle Ages.* New York, Praeger.

PRAWER, J. (1977a) Social Classes in the Latin Kingdom: The 'Minorities'. IN: Hazard, H.W. and N.P. Zacour eds, *The Impact of the Crusades on the Near East.* Setton, K.M. ed., *A History of the Crusades*, V, Madison, University of Wisconsin Press, 59-115.

PRAWER, J. (1977b) Social Classes in the Latin Kingdom: The Franks. IN: Hazard, H.W. and N.P. Zacour, eds, *The Impact of the Crusades on the Near East.* Setton, K.M. ed., *A History of the Crusades*, V, Madison, University of Wisconsin Press, 117-92.

RICE, D.S. (1956) Arabic Inscriptions on a Brass Basin made for Hugh IV de Lusignan. IN: *Studi Orientalistici in Onore di Giorgio Levi della Vida,* vol. 2. Pubblicazioni dell'Istituto per l'Oriente, 52, Roma, Istituto per l'Oriente, 390-403.

RICE, D.T. (1937) *Icons of Cyprus.* London, George Allen & Unwin, Ltd.

RICHARD, J. (1979) Le peuplement latin et syrien en Chypre au XIIIe siècle. *Byzantinische Forschungen* VII, 157-73.

RICHARD, J. (1987) Culture franque et culture grecque: le royaume de Chypre au XVème siècle. *Byzantinische Forschungen* XI, 399-415.

RICHARD, J. (1991) Culture franque, culture grecque, culture arabe, dans le royaume de Chypre au XIIIème et au début du XIVème siècle. *Hawliyat Far' al-Adab al-'Arabiyah (Annales du Départment del Lettres Arabes)* 6, no. B, 235-45.

SADLER-DAVIS, D. (1984) *The Sculptural Program of the Verso of the West Façade of Reims Cathedral.* Ph.D. dissertation, Indiana University.

SADLER-DAVIS, D. (1995) Lessons fit for a King: The Sculptural Program of the Verso of the West Façade of Reims Cathedral. *Arte Medievale* 9, no.1, 49-68.

SCHRYVER, J. (2005) *Spheres of Contact and Instances of Interaction in the Art and Archaeology of Frankish Cyprus, 1191-1359.* Ph.D. dissertation, Cornell University.

STETTLER, M. (1959) *Bildteppiche und Antependium im Historischen Museen, Berne.* Bern.

WEYL CARR, A. (1995) Art in the Court of the Lusignan Kings. IN: Coureas, N. and J. Riley-Smith eds, *Cyprus and the Crusades: Papers Given at the International Conference 'Cyprus and the Crusades', Nicosia, 6-9 September, 1994.* Nicosia, Society for the Study of the Crusades and the Latin East and the Cyprus Research Center, 239-74 (with plates).

WEYL CARR, A. (1998/1999) Correlative Spaces: Art, Identity, and Appropriation in Lusignan Cyprus. *Modern Greek Studies Yearbook* 14/15, 59-80.

WEYL CARR, A. (2005) Art. IN: Nicolaou-Konnari, A. and C. Schabel eds, *Cyprus, Society and Culture 1191-1374.* The Medieval Mediterranean: Peoples, Economies and Cultures, 400-1500, 58, Leiden, Brill, 285-328.

PART 2:

POWER AND IDEOLOGY

MANIFESTATIONS OF ROYALTY IN CYPRIOT SCULPTURE
ANNA SATRAKI

INTRODUCTION

The first large scale representations of the human body appear in the archaeological record of Cyprus, around the middle of the 7th century BC (Karageorghis 1993: 6). The sanctuary of Agia Irini, at the west coast of the island, has yielded the earliest group of medium and large-size terracotta statues, which Einar Gjerstad dates from the mid-7th to the mid-6th century BC (Gjerstad *et al*. 1935: 777-83). By the end of the 7th century BC the local limestone (due to the lack of local sources of marble) is widely used throughout the island, its limitations becoming one of the major factors for the formation of the distinct stylistic and typological tradition of local sculpture. Although limestone becomes the preferred medium in areas with abundant sources of the local stone, the production of small and large-scale terracotta statuary never ceases during the Archaic and Classical periods.

The creation of a strict typological framework for the study of Cypriot sculpture usually proves to be an unproductive exercise, and efforts to understand its function in contemporary contexts seem even less promising. However, it should be said that the parallel analysis of the corpus of sculpture together with the other surviving archaeological evidence might result in a higher degree of appreciation of this kind of artistic expression. In the present paper it will be argued that sculpture served as one of the means of manifestation of royal power during the Archaic and Classical periods.

It should be stressed that the identification of particular statue figures with textually known Cypriot kings or *anaktes* is hard to achieve. However, this is not the objective of this paper. The main argument presented in this paper is that a number of large male statues may represent royal or aristocratic figures (based on grounds that will be explained), and therefore, their distribution at the sanctuaries of the archaic and classical period is connected to the political configuration of Cyprus during this time. It is widely accepted that both media, terracotta and stone, serve the same function so they will be analysed together.

STATE OF RESEARCH

It is to be regretted that the corpus of Cypriot sculpture was created by illicit digging at the ancient sites or by expeditions that did not employ scientific methods in the field. As a result, our knowledge of the material is limited in some cases to the mere fact of the provenance of certain types from a specific sanctuary of the island, while in other instances statues even seem to have been detached from their bases, depriving us from important information about the conditions of the dedication.

Despite the lacunae in the documentation of the circumstances of discovery, certain facts seem to be unquestionable. First, that sanctuaries are par excellence places of finding stone and terracotta statues and statuettes from the Archaic and Classical period (Hermary 2001a) (Fig. 1). It should also be noted that the distribution of stone sculpture is not confined to the areas in close proximity to the quarries, that is eastern Cyprus (the Athienou formation), but instead limestone statues of monumental size are to be found as far west as Kourion and Palaepaphos. Moreover, the great majority of the material is dated to the Archaic period; this should not be attributed to chance. On the contrary, it should be related to the long chain of events that constitute the historical framework of the age of the kingdoms.

CYPRIOT KINGSHIP AND THE MANIFESTATION OF ROYAL POWER

Life-size sculpture appears for the first time in Cyprus shortly after the first written reference to Cypriote kings in an official Assyrian document: an inscribed basalt stele erected at Kition at the end of the 8th century, during the reign of the Assyrian king Sargon II (722-705 BC) is to

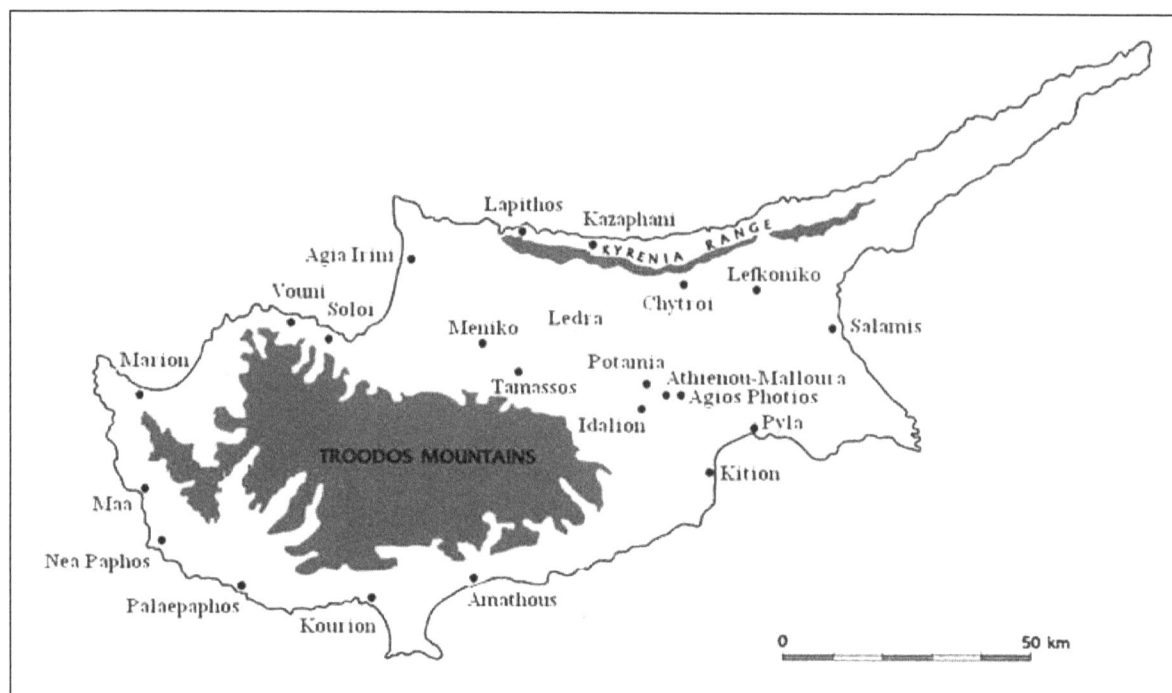

Fig. 1 – Map with sites mentioned in the text

date the earliest reference to the political landscape of Iron Age Cyprus (Stylianou 1989: 8-21; Iacovou 2002: 83-4). Malbran-Labat, who has thoroughly studied the document, asserts that, although the Assyrian king seemingly boasts the subjugation of the Cypriot polities, it is in fact safer to see it as an alliance on economic terms that serves both the interests of the Assyrian empire and Cyprus itself (Yon and Malbran-Labat 1994: 173-4).

It should be stressed that the local rulers of the small territorial polities (admittedly their number – seven – may be used as a sacred formula) are actually called (and evidently recognised as) kings: down to the end of the 4th century BC, when the Cypriot kingdoms were abolished by Ptolemy I, no other term will ever be used in any epigraphic source to address these men but the Greek term *basileus* (king), with the exception of the Phoenician dynasty of Kition, which consistently uses the word *mlk*, the Phoenician equivalent of the Greek *basileus* (Iacovou 2006). Respectively, the members of the royal families will diachronically be called *anaktes* (Phoenician *adon*). *Basileis* and *anaktes* become visible in the archaeological record through royal inscriptions that make use of the syllabic script (the successor of the indigenous prehistoric system of writing) the earliest of which date back to the beginning of the 7th century BC. These texts are rightfully regarded as the first eloquent declarations of the authority of the Cypriot kings and invariably prove to be a reliable evidence for the identification of the independent Archaic and Classical Cypriot states (Iacovou 2002: 76).

The first so-called 'royal' built tombs predate the earliest royal inscriptions only by about half a century. The deceased in these monuments have never proved to be of royal descent, although the discovery of an inscription that mentions two kings of Palaepaphos in a half-carved, half-built tomb at the site (Maier and Karageorghis 1984: 217) could provide satisfactory evidence to this. Otherwise, their size and wealth in offerings and the sophisticated burial customs, best illustrated at the 'Royal Necropolis' of Salamis (Karageorghis 1969: 23-130) leave little doubt to the validity of the hypothesis that they were designed to house the kings and their families.

The elegant weaponry, including remnants of chariots, along with the equipment for rich symposia found in these tombs, especially those of Salamis, display the prominent and leading position of the dead in the Archaic societies of the Cypriot polities (Buchholz *et al.* 2002: 229-30). In political terms, they may have been employed by the local dynasties as symbols – drawn from the Homeric epos – to express a fundamental aspect of their claims to authority: their power to protect the state.

The same applies to sculpture: the first 'generation' of figures that can justifiably be called statues (and not statuettes) demonstrate features that could qualify as royalty or signify persons from the upper strata of society. Life-size figures from the sanctuary at Agia Irini reveal a strong military character as they are most often accompanied by swords and armor (Karageorghis 1993: 8-18) (Figs 2-3). This seems to be a recurring feature in the repertoire of male iconography and could be based on the desire of the ruling class to visually transfer a message with strong ideological implications: its will and power to protect the state and its political and economic functions against any internal or external enemy.

Fig. 2 – Terracotta figures from the sanctuary
at Agia Irini, Cyprus Museum
(provided by the Department of Antiquities)

Fig. 4 – Kazaphani no. 74A, Cyprus Museum
(provided by the Department of Antiquities)

Fig. 3 – Agia Irini no. 2102, Cyprus Museum
(provided by the Department of Antiquities)

Fig. 5 – Lefkoniko, Inv. No. 1940/XI-4/1, Cyprus
Museum (provided by the Department of Antiquities)

Additionally, other characteristics such as size (some of the earliest statues reach the colossal), long hieratic beards and richly adorned garments (e.g. mantles with fringed borders) indicate the existence of a hierarchy among the sculptures with (most probably) social and (perhaps) political implications (Figs 4-5). The combined use of these traits on one statue could hypothetically be taken as a conscious effort on behalf of the sculptor to ascribe social connotations to a piece that otherwise conforms to the basic outlines of a widely used type.

To sum up, the emergence of monumental large-size sculpture at about the same time that royal inscriptions and built tombs began to appear as a means of confirming and promoting the high political status of the rulers of Iron Age polities, cannot be coincidental. This is apparently a time of consolidation for the institution of kingship, a process begun with the inception of the first millennium BC and enhanced when the island entered the economic sphere of the Assyrian empire (Iacovou 2002: 83). Sculpture could only have served the same purpose as the royal inscriptions and built tombs did, an argument strengthened by the observation of the pattern of spatial and temporal distribution of stone and terracotta statuary.

Epigraphic documents that testify to the existence of portraits of kings and *anaktes* are eventually key evidence for this argument. The minute corpus of this category consists of three late 4th century BC inscribed statue bases that record the erection on the first of a statue of the last king of Palaepaphos, in Greek alphabetic script (Mitford 1961: 136-8) and on the other of the images (most probably statues) of the sons of the last king of Amathous, in Greek alphabetic and Eteocypriot syllabic script (Masson and Hermary 1982: 240-1; Hermary 1983: 298-9). Unfortunately, none of these bases has been discovered together with the figures they once supported. Nonetheless, the fact remains that royal images are most likely included in the surviving material even if we fail to identify them beyond any doubt.

TYPOLOGY OF MALE ICONOGRAPHY

One generic type, a standing draped figure carrying a gift to be presented to the god is, from the 7th century BC down to the end of the 4th BC (and through the Hellenistic period), the most common statue offering to the sanctuaries of the island (Mylonas 1998: 123). Modern scholarship shows general agreement regarding the decipherment of the identity of these figures: they most probably represent worshipers whose act of dedication is thus being kept alive (Counts 2001: 160-1). The secular character of these representations cannot be verified by any external evidence, except for the fact that divine images can be securely identified by the consistent use of certain symbols and attributes that follow the demands of a strong religious conservatism.

Variation to the type of the standing votary is achieved with the use of different headgear and garment. The most common type of male representation during the 7th and 6th centuries wears a conical cap with upturned cheek-pieces and is dressed in a long unpleated chiton and a mantle that covers one or both shoulders. One leg is usually advanced and one arm is bent across the chest (Mylonas 1998: 124-30). By the end of the 6th century BC it is being replaced by the more 'Hellenised' version of the male with a wreath (Mylonas 1998: 135-44). These figures wear the archaising pleated Greek chiton with a mantle and as a rule carry a wide variety of gifts, such as birds and incense burners. This large group of sculptures is believed to have been widely used by different social classes. They could portray from royalty to peasantry (Mylonas 1998, 128). Size, garments, the rendering of the hair and beard and the existence of certain symbols (e.g. winged solar disc) are the only indications that could help identify the social status of these figures.

Other categories appear occasionally in sculptural groups and these are also classified on the basis of their headgear. The males with rosette-decorated diadems, which never seem to reach life-size, are attested in relatively large numbers from the end of the 7th century. The type falls out of use by the beginning of the 5th century BC

(Mylonas 1998: 132-5). The characteristic dress-type for these figures is the 'Cypriot shorts', with rosette decoration in bas-relief. A. Hermary (1989: 44) has suggested that they represent young *anaktes*, whose involvement in ceremonial activities is highly possible. The enigmatic garment and diadem along with the terracotta representation of two such figurines escorting a large bull from a sanctuary site at Meniko, near Tamassos, support this theory (Fig. 6).

Fig. 6 – Menoiko no. 16, Cyprus Museum
(provided by the Department of Antiquities)

Egyptianising elements in hairstyle and costume are frequently attested throughout the 6th century BC. These are mainly the hair that is rendered as a plastically uniform mass resembling the Egyptian wig *klaft*, the Egyptian kilt *shenti*, occasionally with a devanteau and the short-sleeved bodice with a collar (*oushek*). G. Markoe (1990) suggested that these types were actually used to express ethnicity, although the mixture of such traits does not in any way alter the strong Cypriot character of the result. The difficulties in interpreting these figures cannot at the present be overcome.

However, the royal connotations of a small group within this category seem to be indisputable. The almost exclusively limestone male representations with double crowns (of which we usually have only the heads) are unanimously recognized as royal portraits (Fig. 7). Their large (often colossal) size, the long plastically rendered hieratic beards along with the Egyptian royal crown, often decorated with pharaonic symbols such as Uraei and winged solar discs, could only be signs of royal iconography. In its new Cypriot context the double crown of Egypt, adopted by the Cypriot Kings at least in their sculptural representations, retained its status as 'a traditional and powerful symbol of royalty' (Maier 1989: 383). Small-sized, beardless variants of this type do occur

Fig. 7 – Aloa, Inv. No. 1940/XI-19/1,
Famagusta Museum – until 1974
(provided by the Department of Antiquities)

but they are as a rule late 6th- early 5th century BC pro-ducts, that is, they belong to a time when probably the type has already lost its original significance. In cases where the body is preserved, this kind of headgear is associated with Egyptianising garments (Brönner 1994; Mylonas 1998: 146-9).

One more type seems to be exclusively used to portray royalty. If the identification is correct (of which we have no definite indication), then a kind of turban that crowns a small number of bearded limestone heads is the sculptural version of the *mitra*, the headgear worn by the Cypriot kings during the time of the Ionian Revolt, according to the descriptions of Herodotus (VII.90) (Hermary 1989b: 180-1). Over life-size and colossal limestone and terracotta examples of this type, whose number does not exceed ten, are dated from the second half of the 7th century BC to the middle of the 5th century BC; where the body is preserved, they wear the long chiton and mantle (Mylonas 1998: 144-5).

PLACING THE MATERIAL ON THE POLITICAL MAP OF ARCHAIC AND CLASSICAL CYPRUS

All of the above mentioned types have a wide geographic distribution. Typically, find groups of male representa-tions comprise mainly of figures with conical caps and wreaths and also, in smaller numbers, of figures with rosette-decorated diadems. Males with turbans and double crowns and other less usual representations, created by intermingling elements from the standard repertoire

(Mylonas 1998), appear sporadically, but still never exclusively in any area of the island.

Such groups come mainly from sanctuaries usually referred to as rural; they are, to be exact, located in some distance from the known capitals of the kingdoms. As a rule the earliest pieces are dated to the end of the 7th to the beginning of the 6th century BC; it is far from common to witness the beginning of such tradition in the Classical period. On the contrary, sometime during the 5th century BC the act of dedicating sculpted votives is suddenly terminated in a number of such sites, pointing, along with the testimony of other aspects of material culture, to the end of the life of the sanctuary. This undeniable fact clearly illustrates the political history of the island during these eventful years.

This is the case with Idalion. The sanctuary, just north of the Western Acropolis, excavated by Sir Robert Hamilton Lang in the 1860s, has yielded a large number of limestone and terracotta male representations that date from the end of the 7th century BC to the end of the Hellenistic period (Pryce 1931; Senff 1993). Colossal figures with conical caps or wreaths and three over life-size heads with turbans are included in the surviving material that is kept at the British Museum. However, none of these figures belongs to the 4th century BC; in fact, the latest pre-Hellenistic large-size figure is dated to the third quarter of the 5th century BC (Senff 1993: 41).

A combination of Greek and Phoenician documents informs us that sometime in the 5th century BC the Greek kingdom of Idalion was abolished and absorbed by the Phoenician kingdom of Kition. According to the numismatic evidence, the reign of king Azbaal, who is the first to bear the double title of 'king of Kition and Idalion' begins after the year 457 or 446 BC (Destrooper 1996: 108). Consequently, the abolition of the Greek kingdom of Idalion should be assigned to the second half of the 5th century BC, even at the very beginning of this period.

Therefore, it seems reasonable to assume that the dedication of large-size statues with probable royal connotations, attested in the sanctuary of Apollo from the end of the 7th century BC to the third quarter of the 5th century BC, but never again before the Hellenistic period, coincides with the time of the life of the independent kingdom of Idalion and that the Phoenician rulers of Kition did not maintain this tradition.

A comparable situation occurs at Kourion. The dedication of large size statues at the sanctuary of Hylates suddenly comes to an end around the middle of the 5th century BC (Hermary 1996: 148). At about the same time coin issues from the royal mint are interrupted; the autonomy of the kingdom of Kourion from this time on is put to question (Iacovou 2002: 78).

The tumultuous years of the beginning of the 5th century BC, marked by the Cypriot revolt of 498 BC and the efforts of the Phoenicians of Kition to obtain access to the copper ores of the inland, may have affected the life of the sanctuaries of eastern Cyprus. These are believed to have served as markers for the territorial limits of the archaic kingdoms (Fourrier 2002). The unstable situation of these years may have rendered some of them useless and led them to abandonment: the sanctuary at Athienou-*Malloura* could fall into this category (Counts 1998: 2). On the other hand, the production and dedication of large scale richly adorned male figures continues uninterrupted at the sites of Pyla (Hermary 1989; Pryce 1931), Athienou-*Agios Photios* (ancient Golgoi?) (Cesnola 1885; Myres 1914; Karageorghis 2000: cat. nos. 170-177, 180-182, 335-336) and Potamia (Karageorghis 1979).

Tamassos, at the centre of the island, close to the rich copper ores of the foothills of Troodos, appears to be of singular importance. While a king of Tamassos is mentioned on a number of Assyrian texts of the early 7th century BC, the lack of any royal inscriptions or coin issues points to the fact that it may have lost its autonomy sometime after 673 BC (the date of the last reference to a king of the city on epigraphic documents) (Iacovou 2002: 78). However, symbols of royal ideology do appear at the site: three archaic built tombs were excavated in the 19th century (Buchholz *et al.* 2002); they must have been once associated with three pairs of limestone lions and sphinxes of excellent craftsmanship, unearthed at some distance from the monuments (Solomidou-Ieronymidou 2001). Furthermore, a large group of terracotta and limestone male statues of monumental size was discovered at a sanctuary site at *Phrangissa* (Buchholz and Untiedt 1996: 47-51). Worthy of note is the colossal terracotta statue of a bearded male wearing a *shenti*, decorated with a winged solar disc and greaves. It is dated to the end of the 7th century BC (Karageorghis 1993: cat. no. 67) (Fig. 8).

No group of large male statues comes from the *polis* of Amathous (Hermary 1994) or its environs, a situation that I believe should not be attributed to the considerable distance of the stone quarries of the island: this hardly had any effect on the case of Kourion and Paphos. Besides, limestone was widely used for the production of male and female statuettes and other offerings as well as architectural members. Furthermore, this is the site that has by far produced the greatest number of large Hathoric capitals in limestone, coming mainly from the sanctuary and the administrative centre on the Acropolis (Hermary 1985). Even so, 'royal' iconography as is known from the rest of the island is attested here but not in sculpture in the round: a male figure wearing a turban is depicted in the centre of one long side of the early 5th century relief decorated sarcophagus that Luigi Palma di Cesnola had discovered at the cemeteries of the city, perhaps in one of its built tombs. He is most likely to be identified with the king at the time (Hermary 1981: 74-83).

Lastly, Palaepaphos and Marion have each yielded one group of large male statues. The group from Palaepaphos,

Fig. 8 – Tamassos statue no. B246, Cyprus Museum (provided by the Department of Antiquities)

that consists of limestone figures dressed in chiton and mantle with fringed borders as well as with figures that exhibit strong Egyptianising elements (e.g. double crowns) comes from the site of the so-called North-East Gate of the city (site KA) along with a number of syllabic inscriptions, some of which refer to royal activities (Fig. 9). The whole find group is dated from the end of the 7th century BC to the very end of the 6th century BC (Masson and Mitford 1986; Tatton-Brown 1994). Marion, on the other hand has mainly produced terracotta figures, Archaic and Classical, that still in cases reach the colossal (Childs 1994). The site, along with the sanctuary at nearby Pomos (Megaw 1954: 173), demonstrates clearly that the availability of stone could not directly affect (and in no way detain) the production of large-size male figures, as these, or at least some of them, were entrusted with a role much more meaningful than that of simple votives to the god: quoting Wriedt Sørensen, 'they were primarily used to convey a social message, although they functioned as dedications to the gods' (Wriedt Sørensen 1994: 79).

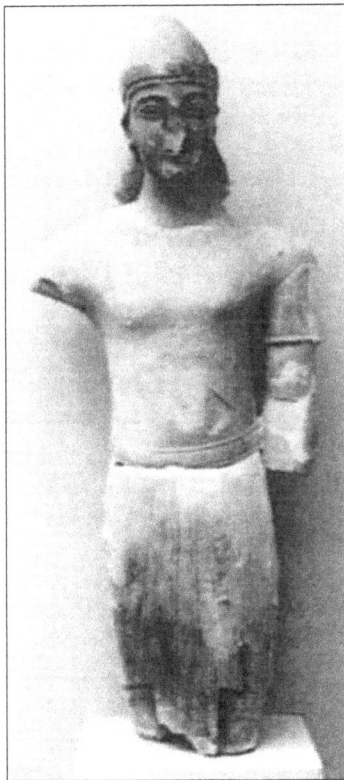

Fig. 9 – KA248, Paphos District Museum
(provided by the Department of Antiquities)

A SOLITARY EXAMPLE

A combination of factors needs to be considered in order to propose a conclusion, where a single inscription could beyond any doubt point to the identification of a royal portrait. However, a late 4th century BC statue from Golgoi (Hermary 2001b) perhaps stands a little closer to a secure recognition: the name Pnytagoras, used almost exclusively at pre-Hellenistic Salamis and twice by the royal family, can be read in incised alphabetic characters on the chiton of the standing male figure. The inscription dates to the Hellenistic period and it therefore postdates the act of dedication. In any case, it most probably points to the identity of the portrayed man, whose date coincides chronologically with the reign of the last but one king of Salamis, Pnytagoras. In this case, size at least is confirmed to be an essential element of royal iconography, supported by the bull mask, a possible reference to the involvement of the Cypriot Priest Kings in cult activities.

CONCLUSIONS

The study of the material evidently points to one conclusion: large-size stone and terracotta sculpture was used as a means of royal and princely manifestation, during the era of the ancient Cypriot kingdoms. If we accept this notion, then certain facts can be deduced. First, the spatial distribution of the supposedly royal types indicates that royal dynasties throughout the island used the same iconographic motifs for their sculptural representations, namely large size, long beards, rich garments and headgear and above all, symbols inspired by Egyptian and Achaemenid royal art. Second, the number of the so-called royal representations is gradually diminishing during the Classical period. This is evidently related to the fact that life is interrupted (either permanently or temporarily) at a number of sanctuary sites, sometime between the end of the 6th and the end of the 4th century (Papantoniou, this volume); the dedication of royal and princely figures is thus primarily a late 7th and 6th century BC phenomenon.

Case studies such as Idalion and Kourion, where the sculptural material can be put side-by-side with the testimony of the primary sources, reveal that the examination of the so-called royal types echoes the internal history of the Cypriot polities. Even if it is still impossible to read in detail these local histories through sculpture, it is nevertheless possible to outline implicit dynastic rivalries and inter-regional conflicts motivated by territorial claims. It does not come as a surprise that 'royal figures' are highly concentrated in eastern Cyprus, the field of military and ideological conflicts between the kingdoms of Idalion and Kition in the 5th century BC, and Salamis and Kition in the 5th and 4th centuries BC. Consequently, continuities and discontinuities in the practice of offering this class of votives to the sanctuaries of the island are a significant indicator of political stability or instability in each region.

In the end, what is evident from a brief review of the question is that sculpture was *chosen* as a vehicle of communication, with ideological significance, in the political environment of the Cypriot kingdoms, and as such is open to many readings with historical value.

Acknowledgements

My traveling expenses to Ireland were generously funded by the Department of History and Archaeology of the University of Cyprus. I gratefully acknowledge the work of the Organising Committee who have hosted a seminal Conference in the friendly environment of the Trinity College, Dublin. I am most grateful to Giorgos Papantoniou for his friendly support throughout the last years and for our long discussions on Cypriot archaeology, which have been proved to be of great value for my research. My warmest thanks are due to my supervisor Maria Iacovou for continuously, patiently and wholeheartedly providing me guidance and inspiration.

Bibliography

BRÖNNER, M. (1994) Heads with Double Crowns. IN: Vandenabeele, F. and R. Laffineur eds (1994), *Cypriote Stone Sculpture. Proceedings of the Second Inter-*

national Conference of Cypriote Studies, Brussels-Liège, 17-19 May 1993, Brussels-Liège, Buteneers s.p.r.l., 47-53.

BUCHHOLZ, H.-G. and K. UNTIEDT (1996) Tamassos. Ein antikes Königreich auf Zypern, Jonsered, Paul Åströms Förlag.

BUCHHOLZ, H.-G., H. MATTHÄUS and K. WALCHER (2002) The Royal Tombs of Tamassos. State of research and perspectives. Cahier du Centre d' Études Chypriotes 32, 219-42.

CESNOLA, L.P. di (1885) A Descriptive Atlas of the Cesnola Collection of Cypriote Antiquities in the Metropolitan Museum of Art, New York, vol. 1, New York, Metropolitan Museum.

CHILDS, W.A.P. (1994) The stone sculpture of Marion: a preliminary assessment. IN: Vandenabeele, F. and R. Laffineur eds (1994) Cypriote Stone Sculpture. Proceedings of the Second International Conference of Cypriote Studies, Brussels-Liège, 17-19 May 1993, Brussels-Liège, Buteneers s.p.r.l., 107-16.

COUNTS, D. (1998) Contributions to the Study of Cypriote Sculpture: Limestone Votives from Athienou Malloura. Unpublished Ph.D. Dissertation, Brown University.

COUNTS, D. (2001) Prolegomena to the study of Cypriote sculpture. Cahier du Centre d' Études Chypriotes 31, 129-81.

DESTROOPER-GEORGIADES, A. (1996) Les tortues d'Égine à Chypre. IN: Κυπραίου, Ε. ed., «Χαρακτήρ» Αφιέρωμα στη Μαντώ Οικονομίδου, Δημοσιεύματα του Αρχαιολογικού Δελτίου 57, Athens, Έκδοση του Ταμείου Αρχαιολογικών Πόρων και Απαλλοτριώσεων, 103-12.

FOURRIER, S. (2002) Les territoires des royaumes chypriotes archaiques: une esquisse de géographie historique. Cahier du Centre d' Études Chypriotes 32, 135-46.

GJERSTAD, E., J. LINDROS, E. SJÖQVIST and A. WESTHOLM (1935) The Swedish Cyprus Expedition. Finds and Results of the excavations in Cyprus 1927-1931, vol. II, text and plates, Stockholm.

HERMARY, A. (1981), Amathonte II, Testimonia 2: Les sculptures découvertes avant 1975, Paris, École Française d'Athenes: Editions Recherche sur les civilisations.

HERMARY, A. (1983) Deux têtes en marbre trouvées à Amathonte. Bulletin de Correspondance Hellénique 107, 289-99.

HERMARY, A. (1985) Un nouveau chapiteau hathorique trouvé à Amathonte. Bulletin de Correspondance Hellénique 109, 657-99.

HERMARY, A. (1989) Catalogue des antiquités de Chypre: Sculptures. Musée du Louvre, Département des antiquités orientales, Paris, Ministere de la culture, de la communication, des grands travaux et du

Bicentenaire. Editions de la Reunion des Musees Nationaux.

HERMARY, A. (1989b) Témoignage des documents figurés sur la société chypriote d'époque classique. IN: Peltenburg, E. ed., 1989 Early Society in Cyprus, Edinburgh, Edinburgh University Press, 180-96.

HERMARY, A. (1994) Sculptures d'Amathonte: Les découvertes de la mission française. IN: Vandenabeele, F. and R. Laffineur eds (1994) Cypriote Stone Sculpture. Proceedings of the Second International Conference of Cypriote Studies, Brussels-Liège, 17-19 May 1993, Brussels-Liège, Buteneers s.p.r.l., 117-25.

HERMARY, A. (1996) Les sculptures en pierre. IN: D. Buitron-Oliver ed., The Sanctuary of Apollo Hylates at Kourion: Excavations in the Archaic Precinct, Studies in Mediterranean Archaeology 109, Jonsered, Paul Åströms, 139-49.

HERMARY, A. (2001a) Lieux et formes du culte à Chypre sous la domination achéménide. Transeuphratène 22, 9-20.

HERMARY, A. (2001b) Sculptures de la collection Cesnola: le cas du 'prêtre' à la tête de taureau. IN: Tatton-Brown, V. ed., Cyprus in the 19th Century A.D. Fact, Fancy and Fiction, Papers of the 22nd British Museum Classical Colloquium, December 1998, Oxford, Oxbow, 153-9.

IACOVOU, M. (2002) From ten to naught. Formation, consolidation and abolition of Cyprus' Iron Age polities. Cahier du Centre d' Études Chypriotes 32, 73-87.

IACOVOU, M. (2006) From the Mycenaean qa-si-re-u to the Cypriote pa-si-le-wo-se: the basileus in the kingdoms of Cyprus. IN: S. Deger-Jalkotzy and I. S. Lemos eds, Ancient Greece: From the Mycenaean Palaces to the Age of Homer, Edinburgh Leventis Studies 3, Edinburgh, Edinburgh University Press, 315-35.

KARAGEORGHIS, V. (1969) Salamis in Cyprus. Homeric, Hellenistic and Roman, London, Thames and Hudson.

KARAGEORGHIS, V. (1979) Material from a sanctuary at Potamia. Report of the Department of Antiquities Cyprus, 289-315.

KARAGEORGHIS, V. (1993) The Coroplastic Art of Ancient Cyprus III. The Cypro-Archaic Period. Large and Medium Size Sculpture, Nicosia, Leventis Foundation.

KARAGEORGHIS, V. (2000) Ancient Art from Cyprus, The Cesnola Collection in the Metropolitan Museum of Art, New York, Metropolitan Museum.

MAIER, F.G. (1989) Priest Kings in Cyprus. IN: Peltenburg ed., Early Society in Cyprus, Edinburgh, Edinburgh University Press, 376-91.

MAIER, F.G. and V. KARAGEORGHIS (1984) Paphos. History and Archaeology, Nicosia, A.G. Leventis Foundation.

MARKOE, G. (1990) Egyptianizing Male Votive Statuary from Cyprus: A Reexamination. *Levant* 22, 111-22.

MASSON, O. and A. HERMARY (1982) Inscriptions d'Amathonte IV. *Bulletin de Correspondance Hellénique* 106, 235-42.

MASSON, O. and T.B. MITFORD (1986) *Les inscriptions syllabiques de Kouklia-Paphos*, Konstanz, Universitätsverlag Konstanz.

MEGAW, A.H.S. (1954) Archaeology in Cyprus, 1953. *Journal of Hellenic Studies* 74, 172-6.

MITFORD, T.B. (1961) Further contributions to the epigraphy of Cyprus. *American Journal of Archaeology* 65, 93-151.

MYLONAS, D.G. (1998) *Archaische Kalksteinplastik Zyperns. Untersuchungen zur Ikonographie, Typologie und formgeschichtlichen Entwicklung der kyprischen Rundplastik der archaischen Zeit*, Unpublished Ph.D. Dissertation, Universität Mannheim.

MYRES, J.L. (1914) *Handbook of the Cesnola Collection of Antiquities from Cyprus*, Oxford, Clarendon Press.

PAPANTONIOU, G. (this volume) Cypriot Sacred Landscapes from Basileis to Strategos: Methodological and Interpretative Approaches.

PRYCE, F.N. (1931) *Catalogue of Sculpture in the Department of Greek and Roman Antiquities of the British Museum, vol. 1, part II, Cypriote and Etruscan*, London, The British Museum.

SENFF, R. (1993) *Das Apollonheiligtum von Idalion. Architektur und Statuenausstattung eines zyprischen Heiligtums*, Studies in Mediterranean Archaeology 94, Jonsered, Paul Åströms Förlag.

SOLOMIDOU-IERONYMIDOU, M. (2001) The discovery of six unique Cypro-Archaic statues at Tamassos, *Report of the Department of Antiquities Cyprus*, 166-86.

STYLIANOU, P.J. (1989) The Age of the Kingdoms. A Political History of Cyprus in the Archaic and Classical Periods. IN: Ίδρυμα Αρχ. Μακαρίου Γ', Μελέται και Υπομνήματα, Nicosia, 375-530.

TATTON-BROWN, V. (1994) Phoenicians at Kouklia? IN: Vandenabeele, F. and R. Laffineur eds (1994) *Cypriote Stone Sculpture. Proceedings of the Second International Conference of Cypriote Studies, Brussels-Liège, 17-19 May 1993*, Brussels-Liège, Buteneers s.p.r.l., 71-7.

WRIEDT SØRENSEN, L. (1994) The Divine Image? IN: Vandenabeele, F. and R. Laffineur eds (1994) *Cypriote Stone Sculpture. Proceedings of the Second International Conference of Cypriote Studies, Brussels-Liège, 17-19 May 1993*, Brussels-Liège, Buteneers s.p.r.l., 79-89.

YON, M. and F. MALBRAN-LABAT (1994) La stèle de Sargon II à Chypre. IN: A. Caubet ed., *Khorsabad, le palais de Sargon II, roi d'Assyrie, Actes du Colloque du Louvre*, Paris, La Documentation française, 161-79.

CYPRIOT SACRED LANDSCAPES FROM *BASILEIS* TO *STRATEGOS*: METHODOLOGICAL AND INTERPRETATIVE APPROACHES
GIORGOS PAPANTONIOU

I will state as an introduction that landscape is polysemic and highly context dependent. However, I will not expand on the variable meanings attached to the term 'landscape' by scholars of various backgrounds.[1] The last few years have seen a surge of interest in the importance of 'bringing together geographical and sociological imaginations' (Agnew and Duncan 1989). 'Landscape is the arena in which and through which memory, identity, social order and transformation are constructed, played out, re-invented, and changed.' (Knapp and Ashmore 1999: 10). The term 'sacred landscapes' has been chosen in acknowledgment of the inspiration provided by the work of Alcock. By using this term in her examination of the Hellenistic and Roman sacred landscapes of Greek world, Alcock shows that the relationship between religion, politics and memory was in general more intimate and more involved that had often been assumed (Alcock and Obsorne 1994; Alcock 1993; 1994a; 1994b; 2002; Van Dyke and Alcock 2003).

My research on sacred landscapes is at a preliminary stage, and, therefore, this paper does not aim to reach final conclusions.[2] At this stage the most beneficial course of action might be: 1. to put forward, and thus open for discussion, some first thoughts about changes in the use and concept of sacred landscapes that had been originally constructed in the era of the Cypriot *Basileis* (Kings) but were now functioning under a new political environment, that of the rule of the Ptolemaic *Strategos* (General). 2. to suggest a contextualised methodology for approaching the study of sacred landscapes in ancient Cyprus, stressing at the same time the research restrictions and dangers we confront when undertaking this task. Emphasis will be given to the era of the transition from the rule of several

Basileis, who were the heads of independent polities, to the island-wide rule of the *Strategos*. This era should not be restricted within technical absolute chronologies, since our intention is to understand the transition not only in terms of political but also of socio-cultural and ideological conceptions. The discussion on the continuity or discontinuity of sacred landscapes is based partly on my personal research on published excavated sanctuaries and survey projects, and also on a catalogue of almost 210 sanctuary sites put together by Ulbrich.[3]

Let us begin by introducing the methodology with which we can approach the horizon of the transition. I will start from the Cypro-Classical sacred landscapes, namely those landscapes that were directly affected by the political change from *Basileis* to *Strategos*. In the context of the struggle of the *Diadochoi* (Successors) of Alexander the Great, Cyprus was annexed by Ptolemy I in 294 BC and stayed in Ptolemaic hands until it became a Roman province in 58 BC. The Iron Age city-kingdoms ceased to exist; for the first time, Cyprus turned from a segmented to a unitary government and administration, under the control of a *Strategos*, who was accountable to the king of Ptolemaic Egypt who ruled from Alexandria.

---

[1] On searching for definitions for 'landscape' see Bender 1993: 1-17; Knapp and Ashmore 1999: 5-8; Finlayson and Dennis 2002: 219-22.

[2] A finalised version of this paper will appear in my PhD dissertation 'Cyprus, from *Basileis* to *Strategos*: Social Power and the Archaeology of Religion', Trinity College Dublin.

[3] This catalogue is the product of doctoral research by A. Ulbrich and will be published in Ulbrich, A. (forthcoming), *Heiligtuemer weiblicher Gottheiten auf Zypern in der Kyproarchaischen und Klassischen Epoche (Koenigszeit). Alter Orient und Altes Testament 44, Muenster: Ugarit Verlag.* Ulbrich has included in her catalogue the excavated sites, sites derived from published survey projects, sites from the Cyprus Survey Inventory of the Department of Antiquities and sites from the announcements of the Director in Bulletin de Correspondance Hellénique. She includes in her catalogue only sites from the Archaic-Classical period, some of which continue to function until the Hellenistic or Roman period. When she was able to examine the material personally or when published photographs were available, she checked the proposed chronology, and the interpretation of the site as a sanctuary. If not, she had to adopt the proposals of published excavators and surveyors, and the Cyprus Survey Inventory (personal communication with Ulbrich). The purely Hellenistic sites have been located by myself, either through bibliography, or through examination of the Cyprus Survey Inventory and its finds.

Continuity of cult activity is confirmed by a great number of 'sanctuary sites' that survive into the Hellenistic period and, particularly, sites which survive well into the Roman period. However, a substantial number of Cypriot sanctuary sites which do not survive into the Hellenistic period disqualifies the assumption for generic continuity of religious activity. It needs to be said that many of these sites have been located by field survey alone, and thus, if it is already difficult to recognise sacred space even in excavated sites – which usually reveal some archaeological indicators of ritual (Renfrew 1985: 259-60) – then it will be even more difficult and ambiguous to try to assign sacred character when one works from surface finds alone. The criteria or the indicators for ritual activity that can be set in a survey program are significantly limited. Conclusions about the regional patterning of the Cypriot cult remain tentative, therefore, and the chronological range of such activities is equally problematic.

The discussion and improvement of survey systems is not our scope here.[4] We will only be concerned with those factors that could illuminate the restrictions and dangers we confront in our effort to interpret the Cypriot sacred landscapes working with off-site data. In earlier years, regional fieldwork on Cyprus, as everywhere in the Mediterranean (Alcock and Cherry 2004: 3), has been regarded primarily as a means of producing a sites and monuments record, or as a preliminary step in the process of locating a site suitable for excavation. More sophisticated notions of landscape archaeology and its relationship with social structures were completely missing from the process. Todd outlines clearly the problems faced by archaeological field survey in Cyprus: lack of tell or mound formations, erosion, agricultural terracing, alluviation and aggradation, and construction of major highways or minor roads because of the rapid agricultural and economic development (Todd 2004, 1-2). Regarding the chronological range of the sites, I would be very cautious when using the chronologies suggested by the various survey projects. The recent conference on the 'Archaeological field survey in Cyprus' has shown that 'a surface scatter can differ from excavation assemblages and that sub-surface features can occur in locations where no artifacts appear on the surface' (Iacovou 2004a: 14). In addition to that, I would say that the problem is above all ceramological, i.e. linked to the methods and approaches hitherto employed in the study of ceramics. Cypriot Iron Age pottery is far from being well studied and 'suffers' greatly from the Swedish Cyprus Expedition typological classification.

The practice of Cypriot fieldwork in the early days of archaeology raises the issue of the validity of the suggested spatial interpretation of the sites and the chronologies. Is there indeed a noticeable discontinuity in

the sacred landscapes from *Basileis* to *Strategos*, or is the aforementioned discontinuity in cult activity simply illusory? If the former is the case, should we connect the abandonment of these sacred places with the political and social environment of the Cypriot city-kingdom *Basileis* or with that of the Ptolemies? Furthermore, how can the continuation of other sites into the Hellenistic period be explained, and what is the relation between ancient Cypriot politics and religion?

To approach these enquiries, we need to turn our attention to excavated sanctuary sites. The majority of the sanctuary sites have been excavated in the previous centuries with antiquarian approaches and methods, usually with no topographical plans and are never systematically published (Ulbrich 2001). The change of cult activity or of religious adherence is not an overnight phenomenon! In addition, as Alcock well demonstrates when discussing the sacred landscapes of Greece (Alcock 1994b: 258), worship could have continued in some places in a less archaeologically visible way, leaving minimal material traces that the antiquarian approach of early excavations would hardly grasp. All this information should be kept in mind as we approach the problem. In what follows, I will argue that the only way to reach some conclusions is to view Cypriot sacred landscapes from a diachronic, intra-insular perspective. A historically contextual approach which seeks to relate the land with social power, considering elites and non-elites, as well as locals and settlers is necessary.

The direct relationship between political administration, economic activity and religion for the era of Cypriot city-kingdoms has been underlined by the Swedish expedition in the so-called palace of Vouni (Westholm 1937: 111-292), and more recently it has been reassessed and proven beyond question by the ongoing excavation of the French expedition in the so-called palace of Amathous, where storage jars, votive gifts (some of which might be directly associated with royalty), and evidence of archival work (including clay sealings and bronze styluses) have been found (Petit 1989; 1991; 1995; 1996a; 1996b; 2002). The excavator identifies at least three sanctuaries directly associated with the administrative building (Petit 2002). The palace with its sanctuaries was abandoned at the end of the Cypro-Classical period. The abandonment could have been an episode connected with the closure of the city-kingdoms, and consequently, with the military and political acts of the Hellenistic *Diadochoi*.

The only other destructions of sanctuaries which, according to literary and excavated evidence could have been attributed to the Ptolemies are those of the Kition shrines (Gjerstad 1937: 74-5; Nicolaou 1976: 105, 108; Karageorghis 1976: 116, 172; Collombier 1993: 133-4; Mehl 2000: 738-9);[5] archaeological evidence perhaps

---

[4] This has been done elsewhere, e.g. Alcock and Cherry 2004, even if the aim of the authors was to consider solutions, but not to develop agreed guidelines or standards for how surveys could or should be conducted. More specifically, for current issues and future trends in Cypriot survey, see Cherry 2004.

[5] More recently, the French expedition of Kition has challenged that the sanctuary was destroyed by Ptolemaic troops: Salles 1993, 106-10, 349, note 10. However, the temples at Kition-*Kathari* were in use from the beginning of the 9th until the end of the 4th century BC. The

indicates the same for the Tamassos precinct of Aphrodite (Karageorghis 1981: 997; Tatton-Brown 1985: 70). In each case, however, this should be perceived as a political rather than religious war (Mehl 2000: 738). This is further justified by anthropological and sociological theory which has shown that the political elites, usually, reinforce their dominant position by demonstrating their ability to manipulate the conquered land through agency and ideology, which reproduces rather than transforms the social order (Shanks and Tilley 1987: 130). Moreover, epigraphic and archaeological evidence, the transfer of the capital to Nea Paphos, constructions of temples with cella etc., strongly suggests that the active presence of Ptolemaic power on the island is late rather than the early 3rd century BC. Let us not forget that during the first decades they had to fight with the rest of the successors for political stability in their possessions, something which even later rarely existed of course. Furthermore, let us not forget that the main sanctuaries located within the immediate environs of the urban centers, such as the sanctuaries of Aphrodite in Palaipaphos and Amathous, and the sanctuary of Apollo Hylates at Kourion, continue to flourish during the Hellenistic period. While the Cypro-Classical and Hellenistic strata of the Palaipaphos sanctuary are less familiar to us, the massive amount of votive inscriptions highlights the importance of the sanctuary in the Hellenistic period (Mitford 1961). Architectural activity in the Kourion (Soren 1986: 39) and Amathous (Hermary and Schmid 1996: 120-2) sanctuaries is another element of continuity. Furthermore, the numerous votive terracottas from the Amathous sanctuary, which lies on the summit but close to the palace, are a major indicator of its enhancement in the Hellenistic period (Queyrel 1988). Besides, we have to remember that an equally considerable amount of sanctuary sites located beyond the urban horizon were not interrupted, but survived well into the Hellenistic period. We will be concerned with these sites later in this paper.

Bearing in mind the weakness and conjectural character in the use of terms such as 'rural' or 'territorial' sanctuaries in the case of Cyprus, I would prefer the term 'extra-urban'. With the exception of the palatial sanctuaries at Amathous and possibly the shrines of Kition and Tamassos, it is obvious that the majority of the abandoned Cypro-Classical sanctuaries belong to this category. Most of these sanctuaries were situated in the agriculturally rich inland plain of the Mesaoria, a place where the boundaries of significant Cypro-Classical city-kingdoms we will examine later would have been located. 'No honest scholar can claim precise knowledge of the number, let alone the names and the boundaries, of the Cypriote city-kingdoms at any one time during their existence' (Iacovou 2004b: 263).

Indication of the probable use of extra-urban sanctuaries as 'landmarks', has recently been observed by various

scholars (Hermary 1996a: 42; Fourrier 1999; 2002; Counts 2004: 175; Nys and Recke 2004: 213). The important contribution of Fourrier, influenced by de Polignac's model (Polignac 1984), to the discussion of boundaries in the Cypro-Archaic period should be acknowledged here (Fourrier 2002). One very interesting point that has been raised is that, according to epigraphic and votive evidence, many of those sanctuaries share a common preference for male divine types such as Apollo and Reshef (Hermary 1996a, 42), or Hercules, Zeus Ammon and Pan (Counts 2004), which might personify an ideological construction in regional cult activity possibly directly associable with political, cultural and social boundaries. By using a variety of literary and archaeological evidence, Fourrier explores religious and cultural spheres of influence. The Cypro-Archaic period is decisive for the consolidation of power of the city-kingdoms and the construction of their territories. It is in this period that the multiplication of the extra-urban sanctuaries, especially in the plain of Mesaoria, takes place. According to Fourrier this phenomenon cannot be explained by the demographic expansion alone (Fourrier 2002: 137). 'Les sanctuaires, en regroupant les communautés autour de cultes communs, jouent un rôle dans l' organization politique et culturelle du territoire, ou ils servent de relais et de marqueurs.' (Fourrier 2002: 137).

The absence of treatises in textual or epigraphic evidence and the absence of fortresses in the archaeological landscape of the era of city-kingdoms make it difficult to define the territories. Natural landscape phenomena, such as lakes, springs, rivers, mountains, paths, gardens, mines etc. should be accorded cosmic meanings (Crumley 1999: 271), and might work as frontiers, but in the case of Cyprus they do not necessarily define the political space; they only create regional units which might have helped the political organisation of the island (Collombier 1991: 25). This is definitely more apparent in the plain of Mesaoria, where the natural features, with the exception of Gialias and Pediaios rivers, are limited, and, where the boundaries of several city-kingdoms would have periodically been placed (Counts 2004: 174-175, note 3).

It is probably not accidental, or only because of access to limestone quarries, that the best corpus of monumental sculpture of probable 'royal types' (Satraki, this volume) comes from extra-urban sanctuaries, especially of the plain of the Mesaoria (Fourrier 2002: 141). Excavation of sanctuaries such as Achna, Idalion-Aphrodite and Agia Irini, just to mention a few, has produced evidence which is confirmed by contemporary excavation activity as well (Smith 1997), and which highlights the role of the Cypriot Iron Age sanctuary as a focus of wealth disposal and economic control in the community: evidence for the segmentation of space, display and disposal of votives, consumption of food and drink, industrial activities, and large-scale storage.

Fourrier, discussing terracotta figurines, highlights the importance of the diffusion of regional styles which we

abandonment level dates on pottery grounds at the very end of the 4th century BC. The cultic use of the place was abandoned and the strata of later periods include only some modest domestic building.

meet in the sanctuaries, which becomes more apparent in the Cypro-Archaic period, in an effort to define zones of cultural influence (Fourrier 1999; 2002: 139). However, she rightly stresses the difficulties and dangers inherent if we suppose that these zones coincide with the geographical or political ones (Fourrier 2002, 139-40). Regional styles have created a serious misunderstanding in the case of Iron Age Cyprus, to the point that because the majority of the sculpture from Tamassos can be placed within the 'Idalion Style', 'we might infer that Tamassos was in fact a subordinate polity, governed by local elites, but economically secondary to Idalion' (Nys and Recke 2004: 216). Furthermore, because of the existence of regional styles, *a priori* dictated or not by governing elites we might even address the issue of the political status of Cypriot craftsmen (Nys and Recke 2004: 213, 217-19). More paradoxically, again, the starting point for comparison and interpretation are Near Eastern and Aegean models. Of course, art has always been an agent of political power and ideology. However, we should be extremely cautious in our interpretations, remaining context oriented. Our decision regarding the subordination, or not, of Tamassos to Idalion or any other polity, is definitely not dependent on the 'Idalion style'! In other words, cultural influence is not always synonymous with political domination.

Art-historical approaches, based on the trilingual tradition of Iron Age Cyprus, and with the intention of relating material culture with ethnicities, cultural and political identities, have contributed greatly on the misunder-standing created by regional styles. Iacovou has been instrumental in advocating that the striking homogeneity of the material culture of the Iron Age Cyprus disqualifies this line of thought (Iacovou 1999; 2006). If sculptures and 'vases are unable to tell of "Greek", "Phoenician" or "Eteocypriot" ethnics in Cyprus' (Iacovou 2006: 41), they are equally unable to define political boundaries. Regional variation in the mechanics and elaboration of constructing tombs, sculptures, ceramics etc., of course exists, but this does not extend to any significant point which should be connected with political boundaries. We should rather associate the regional styles with technological considerations and workshops' spheres of influence (Counts 2004: 178) rather than with political entities.[6]

Let us return to the Cypro-Classical sacred landscapes. According to Ulbrich's catalogue, discontinuity of cult is evident at a significant number of sites (about 45) before the end of that period. Obviously, in most of the cases, we can only gain a very general relative chronology, for all the reasons that have been mentioned above. At this point, I am going to argue that, more likely, the abandonment of the majority of these sites should be primarily attributed to the political environment of the city-kingdom *Basileis*.

The plain of Mesaoria, where at least the boundaries of Salamis, Kition, Idalion and Tamassos would have been lying in the early Cypro-Classical period, could be used as our starting point again. Salamis and Kition, the two most powerful harbour city-kingdoms of East Cyprus, would have vied constantly for control of the agricultural production of the Mesaoria plain, and the metalliferous foothills and forestry activities of Troodos. The attempt of Iacovou to reconstruct the political map of the island at the age of the city-kingdoms has made it most clear that their number, and consequently their territorial formation, would have fluctuated – but always diminishing in number (Iacovou 2002). Epigraphic evidence confirms that by the 4th century BC, Idalion and Tamassos had already lost their autonomy to Kition.[7] According to Iacovou, Tamassos might have been the *chorion* lost to Salamis after the defeat of Evagoras and the triumph of Milkyaton, and thus, the place that Pnytagoras could have wanted back, because of his appeal to Alexander (Iacovou 2002: 79). Hence, the discontinuity of those sanctuaries that might have acted as 'landmarks' could have been connected with the political acts of the *Basileis* of Salamis and Kition and the change of political boundaries. This interpretation is further amplified by the fact that about 40 sanctuary sites were abandoned even earlier, during the course of the Cypro-Archaic period, as well, when inland polities such as Chytroi and Ledra, mentioned only once on Assyrian royal inscriptions, may have lost their status as city-kingdoms and consolidated into stronger territorial units (Iacovou 2002: 81). Moreover, after the second half of the 5th century BC, a time of important changes on the political map of Cyprus, the dedications of monumental male statues of the probable 'royal types' (Satraki, this volume) stop, at least at Idalion (Senff 1993, 41) and Kourion (Hermary 1996b, 140). I suggest that this could be directly associated with territorial claims. Further systematic study of sculpture in combination with land-scape studies and geographical patterning of the sanctuary sites could prove a very important area of research.

Up to this stage we have been concerned with the first two enquiries we posed. The proposed 'gap' in ritual activity from *Basileis* to *Strategos*, seemingly, is not illusory, and we should primarily connect it with the political environment of the former. Therefore, extra-

---

[6] Even Nys and Recke propose the same explanation as a negative reply to the thesis: 'Regional styles are the result of a deliberate monitoring by the upper strata of the Cypriote Iron Age society that are wishing to convey a cultural and political identity.' See Nys and Recke 2004: 216, 217-19.

[7] Iacovou 2002: 77-8. While inscriptions identify the last *Basileus* of Kition, Pummayyaton, as *Basileus* of Kition, Idalion and Tamassos, his father and predecessor, Milkyaton, was *Basileus* of Kition and Idalion alone. What is not often acknowledged is that only one *Basileus* of Kition has ever bore the title '*Basileus* of Kition, Idalion and Tamassos'. The epigraphic evidence could state that he did not bear this triple title to the end of his kingship. In fact, Pummayyaton is named '*Basileus* of Kition, Idalion and Tamassos' in a single non-royal inscription on a marble altar, securely dated in 341 BC. However, at least three inscripti-ons from Kition, which date from 332-320/19 BC describe Pummayyaton as *Basileus* of only Kition and Idalion. This might allow us to reach the conclusion that Tamassos was lost to the city-kingdom of Kition before the abolition of all the Cypriot city-kingdoms by Ptolemy Soter: see Sa-traki, this volume. This information further enhances Iacovou's argument that Tamassos might have been the *chorion* lost to Salamis after the defeat of Evagoras and the triumph of Milkyaton, and thus, the place that Pnytagoras would have wanted back, because of his appeal to Alexander.

urban sanctuaries should be directly connected with political power, sovereignty and domination of the *Basileis*. However, before we continue, we should clearly state that definitive evidence which informs us that a sanctuary was founded to stake territorial claims is absolutely missing from the island. The influential theory of de Polignac is extremely important, but we should be very cautious when applying it to Cyprus, where, unlike Greece, there is no evidence describing the circumstances of the foundation of sanctuaries. Nonetheless, the placement of the foundation legends of the Cypriot city-kingdoms within recent trends of theory and interpretation of myth and comparative mythology, under an approach which exceeds mere descriptive narration, could provide new insights into the association of ritual and state. Even de Polignac himself seems to have modified his idea of the *a priori* territorial significance of the sanctuaries in favour of a model of social mediation among various localities (Malkin 1996: 78; Polignac 1994: 3-18). Our assessment of what was centre and what was periphery or territory, especially in the case of Cyprus is too relative, and may hide anachronistic 'matter-of-fact' and 'heavy-symbolism' approaches (Malkin 1996). We have to consider the possibility that, if sanctuaries existed as 'landmarks', this might be the result of social developments and human feelings which follow their foundation. This would be a good starting point to move from ancient landscapes to ancient 'mindscapes'.

It is time now to turn our attention to the Hellenistic sacred landscapes. Apart from the proposed 'gap', the continuity of cult in a significant number of sites (about 60) into the Hellenistic period is another fact which supports the connection of the abandonment of the Cypro-Classical sites primarily with the political environment of the pre-Hellenistic city-kingdoms. With the exception of the palatial sanctuaries of Amathous and the case of Kition and Tamassos, we have already discussed the continuity of cult activity in the main sanctuaries located within the immediate environs of the urban centers. The majority of these sites, however, are extra-urban sanctuaries. How can this continuity be explained? The answer may be found, again, in connecting Hellenistic sanctuaries with social power.

Studying the sacred landscapes, we cannot overstate the importance of memory (Van Dyke and Alcock 2003). Ptolemaic annexation of the island brought significant changes in its wake and redefinition of relationships among the island's dominant elite families. However, is this change visible and readable in the archaeological record of sacred landscapes? Following Alcock's methodology again, it is important to examine what was remembered, where and how. The transformation of Hellenistic political topographies, as elsewhere (Alcock 1993; 1994a; 1994b; 2002), brought a marked urban and extra-urban change. The association of settlement patterns with demographic elements and the growth of urbanisation of the Hellenistic period should be acknowledged. Again, we can benefit strongly from the advantages of

survey, which informs us about demographic trends, settlement preferences and economic decision making, across the full spectrum of a society: elites and non-elites, locals and foreigners (Alcock 1994a: 175). Then, issues of continuities and ruptures can be re-examined.

The continuity or discontinuity of extra-urban cult activity could be attributed to a multi-polar memory trend: our above discussion has raised the issue of the nature of cult patronage. Political uses of archaeology in the past should be acknowledged (Van Dyke and Alcock 2003: Preface, 1-9). Local and non-local elites, in their effort to define or redefine their relationship with land for political and economical reasons, or in order to naturalise or legitimate authority, could have used sanctuaries as a place to demonstrate their status. Votive portrait-like sculpture of the period (Connelly 1988), found in these extra-urban sanctuaries, supports this idea.[8] If the sanctuaries existed as 'landmarks' in any stage of the pre-Hellenistic period, now, under a new unified political organisation, many of them were not directly necessary.

Of course, it should be kept in mind that sanctuaries, everywhere and in all periods, go in and out of use for numerous reasons, not all of which can be connected with major political or institutional changes (Alcock 1993: 200). Put differently, the formation of the Cypriot sacred landscapes cannot be reduced to a passive reflection of political and economic events. Minor extra-urban sanctuaries, would have been dependent on local people, or individual proprietors, or perhaps on small extra-urban communities. On the other hand, ritual supports a sense of community identity. Although in archaeological contexts it is easiest to see the use of memory in relation to elite groups, memory is also employed in the service of resistance for common people, or simply functions as the motive power for continuity of life. Following the work of Terrenato for the case of Italy (Terrenato 2005), it can be inferred that the response of local non-elite population to periods of transition might vary from those of local elites. The continuity or abandonment of sanctuaries in the agricultural areas could also be related to the actions of non-elite groups, who might or might not have felt compelled to adjust their religious habits in the face of political change. It is possible that life went on in some places for many years, with little or no thought of the new structures of authority. This perfectly explains the continuity of so many sanctuaries during the Hellenistic period.

Ex novo foundation of Hellenistic sanctuaries is rather rare on the island. Although the distribution of settlements is quite intensive in the various published survey projects and in the Cyprus Survey Inventory, I have managed to locate only about 25 sites that might have functioned as a sanctuary *ex novo* in the Hellenistic period. We should

---

[8] A detailed study of Cypriot portrait-like sculpture will appear in my PhD thesis addressing issues of social power and legitimacy and relating this evidence to the sacred landscapes.

probably connect the decrease of sacred building activity with the lack of a need to define territorial boundaries. Furthermore, we should examine how the unification of the political system might have resulted in a more unified cultic system as well. Instructive in this regard is the study of Counts on the merging of the cult and iconography of Hercules and Zeus Ammon with that of Pan in the Mesaoria plain from the Cypro-Archaic to the Hellenistic period (Counts 2004). Moreover, specialised studies on Cypriot epigraphy should address this issue. The new philosophical perceptions and scientific developments, as well as new attitudes about the divine and the changing religious fashions, accumulated under the term 'henotheism', that prevailed in the Hellenistic world, should have had at least a tentative influence in Cyprus, and they are obviously connected both with the decrease of building activity and with the foundation of sanctuaries *ex novo*. The foundation of new sanctuaries is also connected with the foundation of new cities of Hellenistic Cyprus (Collombier 1993) where necessity for sacred space would have existed.

Re-connecting the phenomenon with social power and the political ideology of the Ptolemies, however, archaeological and epigraphic evidence could shed more light on the foundation of sanctuaries *ex-novo* and a more unified politico-religious ideology. Epigraphic evidence informs us about the foundation of a *Ptolemaion* probably at Nea Paphos, namely a sanctuary or temple dedicated to the Ptolemies (Anastassiades 2003: 44). Moreover, inscriptions refer to Ptolemies as temple-sharing gods (Anastassiades 2003: 51). The only *ex-novo* sanctuaries that have been excavated – namely the sanctuary sites of Soloi-*Cholades*, Geronisos island and Kafizin – reveal evidence, direct or indirect, about Ptolemaic cult. The important site at Soloi-*Cholades* (Westholm 1936), for instance, has revealed marble portrait sculptures of probable Ptolemaic queens. Moreover, excavations at the Geronisos island, just off the western shores of Cyprus, where passage rites seem to have taken place, might supply strong evidence about the Ptolemaic ideology (Connelly 2007). Finally, at the Kafizin sanctuary inscriptions provide evidence related to the cult of Arsinoe Philadelphus (Mitford 1980: 262). Inscriptions also record the construction of temples, but their remains seldom survive. Exceptions are found at the temple of Zeus at Salamis, built on a podium in the 2nd century (Argoud *et al.* 1975: 138-9), and on the Phanari Hill at Nea Paphos (Młynarczyk 1990: 202-3), constructed on a stepped platform at about the same time. Finally, the podium of a small temple at Nea Paphos, may also date from the Hellenistic period (Maier and Karageorghis 1984: 231). We note that Greek-style temple architecture is added onto the Cypriot sacred landscapes, not in the extra-urban environment of Cyprus, but in the direct environs of the major urban centers where Ptolemaic power and cult would have been practiced more markedly. Furthermore, the aforementioned continuation in the pre-existing urban and peri-urban cult centers where evidence for the Ptolemaic cult has been discovered goes along with it.

It seems that in order better to appreciate the transition from *Basileis* to *Strategos*, we have to penetrate as late as the Roman sacred landscapes! While excavation and survey activity confirms that *ex-novo* foundation of sanctuaries is rare to non-existent in the Roman period (Given and Knapp 2003: 313), the use of pre-existing sanctuary sites is visibly reduced. Only about 25 possible sanctuary sites seem to provide probable evidence of cult in the Roman period, and these sites include the important time-honored sanctuaries in the direct environ of urban centers, such as the sanctuaries of Apollo Hylates at Kourion, of Aphrodite at Palaipaphos and Amathous and of Zeus at Salamis. It seems that the Romans invested in re-building and temple constructions, on those sites that their Ptolemaic attendant predecessors did.

As we have seen, after the end of Cypriot city-kingdoms, extra-urban sanctuaries might be greatly appealed to and depended upon the local extra-urban population. As far as can be determined, in the Roman period, the great majority of Hellenistic extra-urban sanctuaries are 'dead'. When social memory, elite or non-elite, that kept them alive 'dies', they 'die' with it. As Alcock observes in the case of the Hellenistic and Roman sacred landscapes of Greece (Alcock 1994b: 259), the Cypriot evidence reconfirms that what usually distinguishes the surviving sites is what the defunct sites lacked: scale and significance. The urbanisation of the Hellenistic and Roman periods might have acted as a catalyst for the decline of these extra-urban sanctuaries. However, a first glance at the survey fieldwork reports of the Cyprus Survey Inventory and the various survey reports reveals a 'full' Hellenistic extra-urban settlement landscape. At least in the case of the Paphos area, the survey projects have shown that the number of settlements used in the Hellenistic period was considerably higher than that of the Cypro-Classical period (Lund and Sørensen 1996: 145, fig. 4). Of course, more research on settlement patterns needs to be done, but seemingly, urbanisation is not the only reason for the abandonment of extra-urban sanctuary sites. On the other hand, time-honored sanctuaries, such as that of Palaipaphos, were associated with mythic or legendary events and, therefore, to civic memory and identity. Hence, attention to larger, mainly urban or peri-urban, more renowned 'higher status' sanctuaries was particularly manifested by Ptolemaic attendants, and later by the Romans in order to construct and transmit their power.

In conclusion, I hope that I have shown that the transition from *Basileis* to *Strategos* is also marked by the transition from 'full sacred landscapes' to 'half-full' and later, 'half-empty' ones (Fig. 1)! I have tried to show that the only way to interpret the transition of these landscapes is not by staying fixed on the 'froth on the crest of the waves' of the end of 4th/beginning of 3rd century BC, but by setting them into their individual macro-history which takes into consideration the full length of the first millennium BC, or even the late second millennium BC when it comes to time-honored 'high-status' sanctuaries as that of Palaipa-

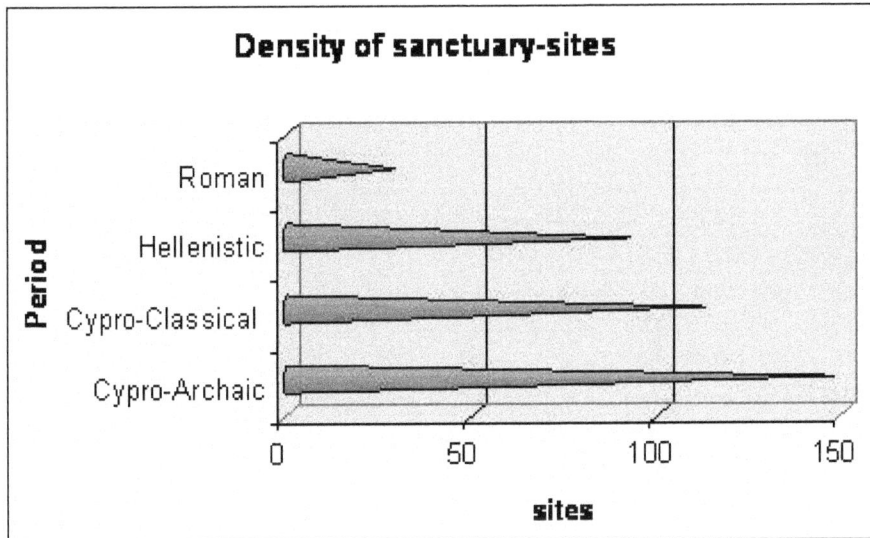

Fig. 1 – Density of sanctuary-sites (produced by author)

phos. Even when trying to examine the possible role of sanctuaries as 'landmarks' during the era of kingdoms, we are forced to search for the diachronic values and even penetrate into the Roman landscapes. Although we have to be aware of the work that has been done in areas of the Mediterranean with which Cyprus interacts it seems that it is time to turn 'to the long-term sustainable traditions of the geopolitical entity of Cyprus itself' (Iacovou 2002: 85), and then try to apply core-periphery models from the Levant or the Aegean to the island. In this paper, I have tried to treat archaeological landscapes as something dynamic and not static, as 'palimpsests of past activity' (Bender 1993: 9) which incorporate political and social action. It seems that a multidisciplinary and interdisciplinary approach, which seeks to read social power from landscapes, acknowledging at the same time its complexities, is our only investigative way. Recognition of the multiplicity of experience through time and space implies the recognition of the relativism of 'our' own modern experiences when we talk about ancient 'sacred landscapes'.

Acknowledgements

I wish to thank Prof. Maria Iacovou (University of Cyprus) and Dr. Christine Morris (Trinity College Dublin) for reading early drafts of this paper and providing valuable comments and discussion. My thanks are also due to my anonymous reviewer who kindly provided some valuable suggestions. Any mistakes and inconsistencies are of course mine. In addition, I would like to thank Dr. Anja Ulbrich for her kind help throughout my research on Cypriot sacred landscapes and for granting me permission to use a version of her unpublished sanctuary catalogue. Finally, I am most grateful to the Centre for Mediterranean and Near Eastern Studies, Trinity College Dublin for its academic and financial support during my post-graduate studies.

Bibliography

AGNEW, J.A. and J.S. DUNCAN eds (1989) The Power of Place. Bringing together Geographical and Sociological Imaginations. London, Unwin Hyman.

ALCOCK, S.E. (1993) Graecia Capta: The Landscapes of Roman Greece. Cambridge, Cambridge University Press.

ALCOCK, S.E. (1994a) Breaking up the Hellenistic World: Survey and Society. IN: Morris, I. ed., Classical Greece: Ancient Histories and Modern Archaeologies. Cambridge, Cambridge University Press, 171-90.

ALCOCK, S.E. (1994b) Minding the Gap in Hellenistic and Roman Greece. IN: Alcock S.E. and R. Osborne eds, Placing the Gods: Sanctuaries and Sacred Space in Ancient Greece. Oxford, Clarendon Press, 247-61.

ALCOCK, S.E. (2002) Archaeologies of the Greek Past: Landscapes, Monuments, and Memories. Cambridge, Cambridge University Press.

ALCOCK, S.E. and J.F. CHERRY eds (2004) Side-by-side Survey. Comparative Regional Studies in the Mediterranean World. Oxford, Oxbow Books.

ALCOCK, S.E and R. OSBORNE eds (1994) Placing the Gods: Sanctuaries and Sacred Space in Ancient Greece. Oxford, Clarendon Press.

ANASTASSIADES, A. (2003) Egypt in Cyprus: The Ptolemaic Royal Cult. Κυπριακαί Σπουδαί 64-65, 41-52.

ARGOUT, G., CALLOT, O., HELLY, B. and A.M. LARRIBEAU (1975) Le temple de Zeus à Salamine. Report of the Department of Antiquities Cyprus, 111-21.

BENDER, B. ed. (1993) Landscape: Politics and Perspectives. Oxford, Berg.

CHERRY, J.F. (2004) Cyprus, the Mediterranean, and Survey: Current Issues and Future Trends. IN: Iacovou M. ed., Archaeological Field Survey in Cyprus. Past History, Future Potentials. London, The British School at Athens, 23-35.

COLLOMBIER, A.M. (1991) Organization du territoire et pouvoirs locaux dans l'île de Chypre a l'époque perse. Transeuphratène 4, 21-43.

COLLOMBIER, A.M. (1993) La fin des royaumes chypriotes: ruptures et continuités. Transeuphratène 6, 119-147.

CONNELLY, J.B. (1988) Votive Sculpture of Hellenistic Cyprus. Nicosia, Department of Antiquities of Cyprus.

CONNELLY, J.B. (2007) Ptolemaic Sunset: Boys' Rites of Passage on Late Hellenistic Geronisos. IN: Flourentzos, P. ed., From Evagoras I to the Ptolemies. The Transition from the Classical to the Hellenistic Period in Cyprus. Nicosia, Department of Antiquities, Cyprus, 35-51.

COUNTS, D.B. (2004) Art and Religion in the Cypriote Mesaoria: The View from Athienou-Malloura. Cahier du Centre d' Études Chypriotes 34, 173-190.

CRUMLEY, C.L. (1999) Sacred Landscapes: Constructed and Conceptualized. IN: Ashmore, W. and B. Knapp eds, Archaeologies of Landscape: Contemporary Perspectives. Oxford, Blackwell, 269-76.

FINLAYSON B. and S. DENNIS (2002) Landscape, Archaeology and Heritage. Levant 34, 219-27.

FOURRIER, S. (1999) Chypre et la Grèce de l'Est à l'époque archaique (VIIe-Vie s.av. J-C). La petite plastique chypriote et les échanges en Méditerrané orientale. University of Lyon (unpublished Ph.D dissertation).

FOURRIER, S. (2002) Les territoires des royaumes Chypriotes archaiques: une esquisse de geographie historique. Cahier du Centre d' Études Chypriotes 32, 135-46.

GIVEN, M. and B. KNAPP eds (2003) The Sydney Cyprus Survey Project. Social Approaches to Regional Archaeological Survey. Monumenta Archaeologica Series 21, Los Angeles, Cotsen Institute of Archaeology, University of California.

GJERSTAD, E. (1937) Kition. IN: Gjerstad, E., Lindros, J., Sjöqvist, E. and A. Westholm, eds, The Swedish Cyprus Expedition. Finds and Results of the Excavations in Cyprus, 1927-1931, Vol. III, Stockholm, The Swedish Cyprus Expedition, 1-75.

HERMARY, A. (1996a) Les sanctuaires Chypriotes. L'Archéoloque, Archéologie Nouvelle 25, 38-43.

HERMARY, A. (1996b) Les sculptures en pierre, IN: Buitron-Oliver, D. ed., The Sanctuary of Apollo Hylates at Kourion: Excavations in the Archaic Precinct, Studies in Mediterranean Archaeology 109, Jonsered, Paul Åströms Förlag, 139-49.

HERMARY, A. and M. SCHMID (1996) Le Sanctuaire d'Aphrodite. IN: Aupert, P. ed., Guide d' Amathonte. Paris, De Boccard, 110-32.

IACOVOU, M. ed. (1999) Excepta Cypria Geometrica. Materials for a History of Geometric Cyprus. IN: Iacovou M. and D. Michaelides eds, Cyprus. The Historicity of the Geometric Horizon, Nicosia, Archaeological Research Unit, University of Cyprus, 141-66.

IACOVOU, M. (2002) From ten to naught. Formation, consolidation and abolition of Cyprus' Iron Age polities. Cahier du Centre d' Études Chypriotes 32, 73-87.

IACOVOU, M. (2004a) Editor's Preface, IN: Iacovou, M. ed., Archaeological Field Survey in Cyprus. Past history, Future Potentials, London, The British School at Athens, 11-15.

IACOVOU, M. (2004b) Mapping the Ancient Kingdoms of Cyprus. Cartography and Classical Scholarship during the Enlightenment, IN: Tolias, G. and D. Loupis eds, Eastern Mediterranean Cartographies, Τετράδια Εργασίας 25/26, Athens, Institute for Neohellenic Research, National Hellenic Research Foundation, 263-85.

IACOVOU, M. (2006) 'Greeks', 'Phoenicians' and 'Eteocypriots'. Ethnic identities in the Cypriot Kingdoms, IN: Chrysostomides, J. and C. Dendrinos eds, "Sweet Land...". Lectures on the History and Culture of Cyprus. Camberley, Porphyrogenitus, 27-59.

KARAGEORGHIS, V. (1976) Kition: Mycenaean and Phoenician Discoveries in Cyprus. London, Thames and Hudson.

KARAGEORGHIS, V. (1981) Chronique des fouilles et découvetes archéologiques à Chypre en 1980. Bulletin de Correspondance Hellénique 105.2, 967-1024.

KNAPP, A.B. and W. ASHMORE (1999) Archaeological Landscapes: Constructed, Conceptualized, Ideational, IN: Ashmore, W. and B. Knapp eds, Archaeologies of Landscape: Contemporary Perspectives. Oxford, Blackwell, 1-30.

LUND, J. and L.W. SØRENSEN (1996) The Hinterland of the Kingdom of Paphos in the Persian Period. Internal Developments and External Relations. Transeuphratène 12, 139-49.

MALKIN, I. (1996) Territorial Domination and the Greek Sanctuary. IN: Hellström, P. and B. Alroth eds, Religion and Power in the Ancient Greek World. Boreas 24, Upsala, Acta Universitatis Upsaliensis, 75-81.

MAIER F.G and V. KARAGEORGHIS, V (1984) Paphos. History and Archaeology. Nicosia, The A.G. Leventis Foundation.

MEHL, A. (2000) Ελληνιστική Κύπρος. IN: Papadopoulos T. ed., Ιστορία της Κύπρου. Αρχαία Κύπρος 2, 2, Nicosia, Archbishop Makarios III Foundation, 619-761.

MITFORD, T.B. (1961) The Hellenistic Inscriptions of Old Paphos. Annual of the British School at Athens 56, 1-41.

MITFORD, T.B. (1980) The Nymphaeum of Kafizin: The Inscribed Pottery. Kadmos, suppl. 2, New York, W. de Gruyter.

MŁYNARCZYK, Y. (1990) Nea Paphos in the Hellenistic Period, Nea Paphos III, Varsovie, Éditions Géologiques.

NICOLAOU, K. (1976) The Historical Topography of Kition. Göteborg, Paul Åströms Förlag.

NYS, K., and M. RECKE (2004) Craftsmanship and the Cultural/Political Identity of the Cypriote Kingdoms. The case of Idalion and Tamassos, Cahier du Centre d' Études Chypriotes 34, 211-22.

PETIT, T. (1989) Un depot de fondation au "palais" d'Amathontes, Bulletin de Correspondance Hellénique 113, 135-48.

PETIT, T. (1991) Syllabaire et alphabet au "palais" d'Amathonte, Phoinikeia Grammata. Actes du colloque de Liege, 15-18 nov. 1989, 481-490.

PETIT, T. (1995) Objects egyptiants et ideologie royale a Amathonte. Transeuphratène 9, 131-46.

PETIT, T. (1996a) Religion et royauté à Amathonte de Chypre. Transeuphratène 12, 97- 120.

PETIT, T. (1996b) Magasins Palatiaux de Chypre (En particulier Amathonte). Topoi 6, 113-30.

PETIT, T. (2002) Sanctuaires palatiaux d'Amathonte. Cahier du Centre d' Études Chypriotes 32, 289-326.

POLIGNAC, F. de (1984) La naissance de la cité grecque. Paris, Éditions La Découverte.

POLIGNAC, F. de (1994) Mediation, Competition, and Sovereignty: The Evolution of Rural Sanctuaries in Geometric Greece, IN: Alcock, S.E and R. Osborne eds (1994) Placing the Gods: Sanctuaries and Sacred Space in Ancient Greece. Oxford, Clarendon Press, 3-18.

QUEYREL, A. (1988) Amathonte IV: Les figurines Hellénistique de terre cuite. Paris, De Boccard.

RENFREW, C. (1985) The Archaeology of Cult: The Sanctuary at Phylakopi. London, Thames and Hudson.

SALLES, J.P. (1993) Conclusion, IN: Salles, J.F. ed., Les niveaux hellénistiques. Kition- Bamboula IV, Paris: Editions Recherche sur les Civilisations, 347-50.

SATRAKI, A. (this volume) Manifestations of Royalty in Cypriot Sculpture.

SATRAKI, A. (2006) Cypriot Kingship through Epigraphy and Numismatics. Paper read at the 2006 Postgraduate Cypriot Archaeology workshop, 27-8 October, Edinburgh.

SENFF, R. (1993) Das Apollonheiligtum von Idalion. Architektur und Statuenausstattung eines zyprischen Heiligtums, Studies in Mediterranean Archaeology 94, Jonsered, Paul Åströms Förlag.

SHANKS, M. and C. TILLEY eds (1987) Reconstructing Archaeology. Theory and Practice. Cambridge, Cambridge University Press.

SMITH, J.S (1997) Preliminary Comments on a Rural Cypro-Archaic Sanctuary in Polis-Peristeries, Bulletin of the American Schools of Oriental Research 308, 77-98.

SOREN, D. (1986) The Apollo Sanctuary at Kourion: Introductory Summary of the Excavation and its Significance. IN: Karageorghis, V. ed., Acts of the Archaeological Symposium: Cyprus, between the Orient and the Occident, Nicosia, Department of Antiquities of Cyprus, 393-404.

TATTON-BROWN, V. (1985) Archaeology in Cyprus 1960- 1985: Classical to Roman periods. IN: Karageorghis, V. ed., Archaeology in Cyprus: 1960-1985. Nicosia, The A.G. Leventis Foundation, 60-72.

TERRENATO, N. (2005) The Deceptive Archetype: Roman Colonialism in Italy and Postcolonial Thought. IN: Hurst, H. and S. Owen, eds, Ancient Colonizations: Analogy, Similarity and Difference, London, Duckworth, 59-72.

TODD, I. (2004) Vasilikos Valley Project 9: The Field Survey of the Vasilikos Valley, Vol. 1, Studies in Mediterranean Archaeology 71: 9, Sävedalen, Paul Åströms Forlag.

ULBRICH, A. (2001) An Archaeology of Cult? Cypriot Sanctuaries in 19th Century Archaeology. IN: Tatton-Brown, V. ed., Cyprus in the 19th Century A.D. Fact, Fancy and Fiction. Papers on the 22nd British Museum Classical Colloquium, December 1998, Oxford, Oxbow Books, 93-106.

Van DYKE, R. and S.E. ALCOCK eds (2003) Archaeologies of memory. Oxford, Blackwell.

WESTHOLM, A. (1936) The Temples of Soli. Studies on Cypriote Art during Hellenistic and Roman Periods, The Swedish Cyprus Expedition. Stockholm, The Swedish Cyprus Expedition.

WESTHOLM, A. (1937) Vouni. IN: Gjerstad, E., Lindros, J., Sjöqvist, E. and A. Westholm, eds, The Swedish Cyprus Expedition. Finds and Results of the Excavations in Cyprus, 1927-1931, Vol. III, Stockholm, The Swedish Cyprus Expedition, 76-292.

PTOLEMAIC POWER AND FEMALE REPRESENTATION IN HELLENISTIC CYPRUS
CÉLINE MARQUAILLE-TELLIEZ

With the support of an ever increasing body of epigraphical evidence combined with a renewed interest for Hellenistic urbanism, the Hellenistic period has shown how the Greeks, when forced to cohabit with royal power, reinvented the city and its institutions, extending the city's sacred landscape to give room to new religious practices, finding ways to remain active and sovereign without offending the king.[1] Royal houses may have imposed their domination through political and military power, they never spared efforts in order to gain prestige and legitimacy among citizens of the *koinē*, the community of Greeks that stretched from the Greek mainland to Asia Minor and North Africa, whose Greek culture the Hellenistic kings admired and wished to emulate. In this context of political compromise, the role of local elites illuminates the necessity of building new networks of power in a world subject to royal favour and benefaction. More specifically, the loyal followers and 'friends' of the Hellenistic dynasties form a fundamental part of the study of the projection and ideology of power in the history of empires (Mooren 1998; Savalli-Lestrade 2001; Cébeillac-Gervasoni and Lamoine 2003).

Evidence for the presence of Ptolemaic elites in Hellenistic Cyprus has often been discarded not only by specialists in the history of Cyprus but also by those in Ptolemaic Egypt, and in the Hellenistic period in general. This is partly due to the relative lack of interest in the Hellenistic period in Cyprus, a situation that found an appropriate adjustment in the last 20 years. The Hellenistic levels in Cyprus have produced disappointing results, mostly because of the disastrous earthquakes that shook the island in the 1st century BC and 1st century AD; they have nevertheless uncovered remarkable examples of ceramic and glass specimens, statues, as well as hundreds of inscriptions that show the integration of Cyprus into the Mediterranean Hellenistic *koine* (Vess-berg and Westholm 1956; Tatton-Brown 1985; Queyrel 1988; Connelly 1988; Mitford in general 1937-1980; Marcillet-Jaubert, Pouilloux *et al.* 1987; Yon 2004). One group however deserves particular attention, a collection of Cypriot epigraphical documents of the Hellenistic period that involve women either as recipients or dedi-cants of honorific dedications. It is common knowledge that Greek women were not strictly segregated to the private and domestic sphere and that they played a role in the religious and economic life of the Classical city; they were yet only rarely publicly celebrated through communication channels normally restricted to male citizens (Cohen 1996). These Cypriot documents not only show the impact of Ptolemaic rule on the social status of women in Cyprus but also the possible particularity of the island in the representation of female public image. The context of these inscriptions in both Cypriot historio-graphy and history needs some preliminary assessment. When looking at recent important contributions on Hellenistic women, which often incorporate the imperial period, such as the works by R. van Bremen (1996), A. Bielman (2002), or E. D. Carney (1991, 1993), mention of Cyprus is significantly missing. On the other hand, S. B. Pomeroy in *Women in Hellenistic Egypt* is at pains to find any evidence on Alexandrian women, and to present female members of the Ptolemaic court and priestesses of the royal cult, she is forced to look to Cyprus to sketch a realistic picture (Pomeroy 1984: 42-5). Apart from the passage in Polybius describing the horrid death of the courtier Agathocles and his family where there is mention of '*syntrophoi*' of Arsinoe III (Pol. 15.27 and 33; Rowlandson 1998: 33-4, no. 7), there is indeed hardly any evidence, except for the regnal dating of papyri referring to priestesses of the royal cult (Clarysse and Van der Veken 1983), for female members of the Alexandrian aristocracy, part of whom must have closely gravitated inside both the king's and the queen's entourage. The

[1] I would like to thank the organisers for their kind invitation and the stimulation of the conference. I am grateful to the British Academy for its many expressions of support during my Post-Doctoral Fellowship, as well as to King's College London for funding.

Cypriot inscriptions recording dedications to or by female members of Ptolemaic officials' families in Cyprus subsequently constitute a priceless contribution to our understanding of social networks in Ptolemaic politics.

This prominence of female dedications in Cyprus finds grounds in the combination of several contexts. The status of Cyprus within the Ptolemaic *pragmata* or empire, is certainly exceptional (Mitford 1953a; Bagnall 1976: 38-79). Ptolemy I had shown interest in Cyprus as early as 321 BC and ten years later his rule had been firmly ascertained. He punished those of the Cypriot kings who had sided with his rival Antigonus and abolished once and for all Cypriot kingship (*IG* XII:5 444 B 17; Diod. 20-1), a political act that none of the Ptolemies' predecessors, Assyrian, Egyptian or Persian, had ever attempted to do. Thanks to its strategic location facing the Seleucid kingdom, at the crossroad of maritime routes from and to the Aegean, and because of its natural resources in copper mines and timber essential to the Ptolemaic fleet, Cyprus was to stay in Ptolemaic hands until its annexation by the Romans in 58 BC (Mitford 1980); the island stood as the Jewel in the Crown, among possessions that stretched from the Black Sea to Phoenicia, even more so after the death of Ptolemy IV in 204 BC, and the loss of most of the dynasty's territories overseas (Hauben 1987; Hölbl 2001: 134-43; Marquaille 2001: 49-55). When Ptolemaic claims to the throne became an object for contention, as from the joint reigns of Ptolemy VI Philometor and his younger brother Ptolemy VIII Euergetes II in 170 BC, keeping hold of Cyprus for kings expelled from Alexandria, was a necessary way to keep access to the *basileia*, in other words to remain king (Hölbl 2001: 181-204). From the 2nd century onwards, the Cypriot population must have watched with incredulous eyes the shifts of power in Alexandria and its repercussions in Cyprus, especially since each king arrived in Cyprus with his own group of loyal friends and families, and possibly mercenaries.

Because of the importance of Cyprus to the survival of the Ptolemaic state, the administration of the island had always been closely supervised from Alexandria. Starting with the appointment of Menelaus, Ptolemy I's own brother, as *strategos*, and, probably thereafter, king in Cyprus (Diod. 20.47.3, 52.5; Paus. 1.6.6; Polyaen. 4.7.7; Bagnall 1976: 41, 188, 252-62), the government of Cyprus remained in the hands of the most eminent families of the Alexandrian court. From the end of the 3rd century the *strategos* became the king's full representative in Cyprus, supported by officials such as the ἐπὶ τῆς πόλεως, a Ptolemaic governor appointed to each of the Cypriot main cities, the *phrourarchos*, the commander of the garrison, and other Ptolemaic military and civic officials (Bagnall 1976: 45-73). They clearly developed in Cyprus a social and political structure of its own that acted as a royal reproduction of power structures in Alexandria, with the *strategos* now acting at the top of a political and social pyramid. These networks of power, already observed in the Persian empire (Briant 1996: 314-

66), reveal that the power of the Hellenistic monarch was not as absolute as it seemed, and the significant role of the king's entourage is in fact even more striking in the Hellenistic king's foreign policy and his representation outside Egypt (Mooren 1981, 1985). The Ptolemaic king, and sometimes his queen, could not ignore the family and friendship networks created by this political group. As the episode surrounding the rise and fall of Agathokles, as well as the various intrigues at the court of the young Ptolemy V may suggest (Pol. 15.3.25-36), the slow downfall of the Ptolemaic dynasty from the end of the reign of Ptolemy IV, rather than caused by the now obsolete idea of decadence within the Ptolemaic royal family, should be attributed to the divisions that arose within this political sphere.

In the 190s BC, the title of *archiereus*, high priest of local and royal cults on the island, was added to the functions of the *strategos* (*SEG* XXXI 1359; Mitford 1961a: 15-16 no. 40), soon to be followed in the 140s BC by the title of *nauarchos*, admiral, most probably of the whole Ptolemaic fleet (Mitford 1953b: 147, Bagnall 1976: 48-9). In addition to these functions, the strategos was συγγενής (kinsman) of the king, the highest rank in honorific aulic titles from the 2nd century onwards (Mooren 1975 on Ptolemaic court titulature). It was first attested in a dedication of a statue of Ptolemy VI Philometor by the strategos Ptolemaios, son of Ptolemaios, between 175 BC and 169 BC (*OGIS* 105, Mitford 1957: 183-84 no.3; Mitford 1961a: 20 no. 51). Before then, the office of *strategos* of Cyprus alone had conveyed the importance of the high official's status within the administration of the empire among the group of officials that Polybius (5.34.3-5) describes as the ἐπί τῶν ἔξω πραγμάτων διατεταγμένοι. The best example is Polykrates of Argos, son of Mnasiades. His father was the eponymous priest of the royal cult in Alexandria in 218/7 BC (Clarysse and Van der Veken 1983: 14 no. 73); Polykrates was *strategos* of Cyprus between 203 BC and 197/6 BC (Mitford 1961a: 15-16 no. 40, 17 no. 43; Bagnall 1976: 253-55); upon his return to Alexandria, he played a prominent role in the ceremony of *anakleteria* of the young Ptolemy V, which officially announced the young king's coming of age and accession to the throne, after which he became his first councillor (Pol. 5.64.4-6, 65.5, 82.3, 84.8; 18.54.1, 55.3-9; 22.17.3-7). We find a similar pattern in the earlier career of Pelops, son of Pelops, who was *strategos* of Cyprus between 217 BC and 209 BC (Bagnall 1976: 83-4), after serving in Cyrenaica (*SEG* XVIII 734); his father, Pelops, was one of the *philoi* of Ptolemy II and commanded Ptolemaic troops on Samos between 281 BC and 259 BC (*SEG* I 364); Pelops, the father, was also the eponymous priest in Alexandria in 264/3 BC (Clarysse and Van der Veken 1983: 6 no. 27; Mooren 1975: 60-1 no. 011). Following his Cypriot office, Pelops the son was still active at the court of Alexandria and a sufficient threat to Agathokles to be sent away as ambassador to Antiochos to invite him to remain friendly with Egypt (Pol. 15.25a.13). The primary role of the *strategos* and his subordinates was the projection and embodiment of

Ptolemaic power outside Egypt. This is particularly clear in Cyprus where the large group of honorific inscriptions dedicated to Ptolemaic officials carved on statue bases testifies to the intensive character of royal visibility throughout the island. They were ostensible marks of loyalty expressed by military, religious or political bodies, such as the 'koinon' of the Lycians, the members of the gymnasium, the priests of Aphrodite, the Guild of the Dionysiac artists, or the cities themselves.

To help in this diffusion of dynastic images and values, the Ptolemaic officials received the precious assistance of their family; not only their sons, who sometimes succeeded their fathers, but more particularly the female members of their family. The originality of this Cypriot phenomenon whereby actors of civic life in Cyprus felt the need to include wives or daughters in dedications to Ptolemaic agents lies, on the one hand, in the large number of dedications compared to other areas of the Hellenistic world, and, on the other, in the fact that they are attested as early as the 3rd century BC. These dedications offer a large panel of dedicants that are similar to those mentioned above in inscriptions related to Ptolemaic male officials, and present examples where women act as dedicants themselves. The longevity of these women's stay in Cyprus depended on that of their male relative's office, which considerably varied, from 1 to 16 years (Bagnall 1976: 45). Once the high official's term of service in Cyprus came to an end, these aristocratic families returned to Alexandria, but it is possible that some officials and soldiers were appointed to Cyprus on a permanent basis or retired with their family in Cyprus. Dual priesthoods, as will be shown, in both Cyprus and Alexandria suggest that the *strategos* and his family may have in fact divided their time between Cyprus and Alexandria, making it difficult on some occasions to assess whether these women were honoured for their actions or simply their status.

Inscriptions, however, record several reasons explaining why a woman should be honoured with a statue base. The first one is entirely related to the function of her husband or father. In such cases it is in fact possible that the inscription belonged to a larger family group of statues. For example Myrsine, the wife of the *strategos* Pelops, was honoured in Salamis (217-209 BC; Marcillet-Jaubert, Pouilloux *et al.* 1987: 38 no.74) and Palaipaphos (*OGIS* 84 = Mitford 1961a: 15 no.39) with terms similar in both dedications: Myrsine, wife of the *strategos*, is honoured for her husband's *arete* and *eunoia* towards the living sovereigns. The main target for these honours is not the accusative recipient but the genitive name, the male official, and he was the one, together with the honourand, to benefit from such publicity. Incidentally, it is worth adding, the attention of those who commented on similar inscriptions is, in the same manner, systematically drawn to the male figure and what there is to learn about his office. They surprisingly all keep silent about the yet remarkable staging of the female character. On a second level, the ultimate beneficiary of such inscriptions is

central power in Alexandria. In the statue of Myrsine set up by Ptolemaic military forces in Salamis, the troops, by marking their respect towards the *strategos'* wife, celebrate in parallel the *strategos* himself; the reason why Pelops' wife is honoured is her husband's loyalty to the king, loyalty which is consequently echoed by the troops in the present inscription. Women such as Myrsine came to be included in a kind of intermediate network of influence that a city or individuals could use to show their allegiance to the royal house. In other instances the careful listing of the officials' titles clearly indicates that what is at stake is the very reputation and status of the male relatives rather than the woman being honoured. For example by honouring his mother Eirene in Kition, Andromachos, himself an important man, bearing the court title of *diadochos* and acting as secretary of the troops, does not miss the opportunity to display the eminent position of his grandfather Ptolemaios, Eirene's father, as *strategos* and high-priest on the island (197?-181? BC, *SEG* XVI 787 = Yon 2004: 251-52 no.2022; Mitford 1957: 163-87, esp. 163-74; on Ptolemaios as the author of *Histories of Philopator*, which contained a list of royal courtesans: Ath. 425 e-f, Ogden 1999: 223). The Cretan Aristo combined codes of family values and Ptolemaic loyalty when she, together with her children whom she does not name, honoured her father-in-law Melankomas, the former ἐπὶ τῆς πόλεως in Kition and priest of the royal cult, proudly presenting herself as the wife of the current governor of the city (146-116 BC, *OGIS* 134, Yon 2004: 253-54 no.2024). Beyond the fact that such inscriptions confirm the extent to which women in the Greek world were integrated into their husband's family, it is interesting to see that as a woman Aristo was given the means to express the strength of her family ties.

Some inscriptions show the importance of matrimonial alliances between eminent families, in a fashion that is not dissimilar from the Ptolemaic alliance policy with heirs of Hellenistic dynasties (Hölbl 2001: 358-59), such as the betrothal of Eurydice and Soter's daughter Ptolemais to Demetrios Poliorcetes (Plut. *Dem.* 32.2), the union of Arsinoe (future Philadelphus) to Lysimachus in 299 (Paus. 1.10.3) or that of another daughter of Ptolemy I with Agathokles, son of Lysimachus (Paus. 1.9.6, 1.10.3). Women, as warrants of the integrity of the family's noble origins, naturally played a decisive role in a matrimonial system that functioned as a hermetic oligarchy, allowing marriages only between its members. Family connections were something to be given pride of place in dedications, so that when the wife of Leukos honours her father Philotimos, the name suggesting an aristocratic background, she describes herself as the wife of the secretary of the forces (180-150 BC, *OGIS* 154, Marcillet-Jaubert, Pouilloux *et al.* 1987: 44-45 no. 89). The emblematic union of Myrsine and Pelops was also an object of pride for these two representatives of the aristocratic milieu close to the royal house. The devotion of Pelops' family to the Ptolemaic kings has already been mentioned; Myrsine herself was the daughter of Hyperbassas, who was honoured by the Samian demos while in Ptolemaic service (*PP* VI 15772); Myrsine's sister, Iamneia, was committed to the Ptolemaic royal cult in Alexandria as *kanephoros* (basket-bearer) of Arsinoe Philadelphus (243/2 BC) and later as *athlophoros* (prize-bearer) of Berenike Euergetis (196/5 BC; Clarysse and Van der Veken 1983: nos. 48 and 96). But it is our *strategos* Polykrates who again provides a striking example. According to Polybius,

> '[Polykrates of Argos and Andromachus of Aspendus] were illustrious on the score of their private wealth, as well as on that of their respective countries; to which advantages Polycrates added those of an ancient family, and of the reputation obtained by his father Mnasiades as an athlete' (Pol. 5.64; bibliography on Polykrates in Walbank 1970: 589).

The 'Greek spirit' of Polykrates, as mentioned by Polybius in the same passage, was put at the service of Ptolemaic power when he competed in 198 BC, that is while he was still *strategos* in Cyprus, in the Panathenaic games, the most important games held in Athens every four years; in fact, during the same festival, his wife Zeuxo of Cyrene won a victory in a chariot race, while their daughters Hermione, Zeuxo and Eukrateia appeared on Panathenaic lists of victors for the year 202 BC (IG II² 2313 ll.8-10, 13-16, 60-61; IG II² 2314 ll.50, 92-94). Louis Robert remarked that the native city of Zeuxo was famous for its fine horses and chariots, as was Argos, the home city of Polykrates (Robert *BE* 1949: 202). It was a perfect match, a perfect family on the royal model, ostentatiously displayed thanks to a group of up to eight statues in the sanctuary of Aphrodite at Palaipaphos on Cyprus, representing Polykrates and Zeuxo surrounded by Polykrates' father, and the couple's sons and daughters (Mitford 1961a: 16-18 nos. 41-46). Recalling the Ptolemaic family and court's passion for horse races, these family statues perhaps celebrated the equestrian victories of the Polykrates clan and their Panhellenic fame, singing its value and *arete* as a family (Fantuzzi 2004; Thompson 2005; Van Bremen 2007). It seems clear that the presence of wives and daughters alongside Ptolemaic officials helped reinforce family values that had been always part of Ptolemaic propaganda and the idealised vision of the royal couple built, since the incestuous marriage of Ptolemy II with his sister Arsinoe II around 279 BC, on the divine model of Zeus and Hera (Theocr. *Id.* 17.131, Plut. *Moralia* 736e, Diod. 10.31.1).[2] It was therefore appropriate for the city of Kourion to honour its city commandant Demetrios of Thessaly jointly with his wife and children (200-193 BC), and Mitford's reconstitution shows that there was a separate statue of Demetrios' wife standing next to him (Mitford 1971: 91-4 no. 42). Women from the elite circle had fully integrated the sphere of political legitimation and took a fundamental share in power representation. This role is made plainly visible in the dedication made by the city of Chytroi in honour of Olympias (142-131 BC); she is described not by her patronymic but as daughter of Artemo, herself daughter of the former *strategos* Seleukos (*OGIS* 160). Artemo has become the necessary link, or 'bridge', between the city and royal power, and both mother and daughter were now conveying the eminence of the family's reputation.

Beyond the subsequent 'publicity' conveyed by these inscriptions, a specific motive is seldom mentioned. In the Greek East, evidence from the late Hellenistic period has shown that women increasingly appeared as benefactors; their sphere of action included buildings, games and festivals, public feasting and distribution of food, wine or money, receiving civic honours usually restricted to men (Van Bremen 1996). It is unlikely that they only held honorific offices, but what is important is that it became increasingly suitable to include them in public honours and manifestations. The religious role to which women's public position had previously been confined clearly appears in several instances. The majority of these inscriptions were found in sanctuaries and among them, pride of place was given to the sanctuary of Aphrodite at Palaipaphos, which cannot be solely attributed to the extensive works conducted at modern Kouklia (Maier 1967, 1985; Wilson 1974). All male Ptolemaic high officials held religious duties, primarily expressed through their commitment to the royal cult. We must bear in mind that the *strategos* was chief priest of all the cults, and that this title probably implied control over temple estates, the organisation of sacrifices and festivals, or the appointment of priests and priestesses. It is likely that there existed a link between the religious role of these officials and that of their female relatives, either as priestesses or religious benefactors. The only two examples where the function or title of the woman being honoured is specifically stated occur in a religious context. The first document is an inscribed pedestal of Boiskos dedicated by his mother Phanion, daughter of Boiskos, who is plainly described as 'priestess' (Mitford 1961a: 9-10 no. 19). The name Boiskos does not sound Cypriot and it is naturally tempting to recognise here the sister of Kallikrates of Samos, son of Boiskos and Ptolemy Philadelphus' admiral (Hauben 1970; Bing 2002/3). Kallikrates must have made regular visits to the island as chief commander of the Ptolemaic fleet, acknowledging the central position of Cyprus at the crossroad of Ptolemaic interests overseas. The reputation of his name in Cyprus is proved by the erection of his statue in the sanctuary of Aphrodite at Palaipaphos, the inscription being too damaged for us to recognise the identity of the dedicant(s) (Mitford 1961a: 9 no. 18). Kallikrates' family must have enjoyed long-term relationships with Cyprus as a statue of queen Berenice was erected by a certain Boiskos together with military officials; it has been recently dated by Hauben and Piejko to the middle of the 3rd century so it is likely that Boiskos here represents the son of Phanion, whose status was important enough to honour the Ptolemaic queen Berenice II (*OGIS* 20, SEG XXXI 1348, Hauben 1970: 71; Piejko 1981: 106-7).

---

[2] Diodorus mentions the famous incestuous marriages of Zeus and Hera alongside that of 'Ptolemy and Berenice' although he may have meant Ptolemy (II) and Arsinoe (II), the most famous of the incestuous Ptolemaic unions.

The title of 'priestess' in Boiskos and Phanion's inscription is intriguing because of its bareness. The location of the statue at Palaipaphos naturally points to a priesthood of Aphrodite. Despite the non-Cypriot origin of Phanion, Mitford has suggested that Phanion may have been the wife of a Kinyrad, from this local dynasty of priests who claimed descent from the Homeric hero, founder of Paphos and its sanctuary, or that she may have held the title *honoris causa*, repressing in both cases the idea that Phanion may have held a title specific to her function. Another explanation may stress the idea that Phanion, who came from an eminent family with interests in Cyprus, the nature of which may have been more extensive than commonly thought, was priestess of Aphrodite, transferring to the Ptolemaic elite an old Paphian tradition which associated members of the Paphian royal family with the cult of Aphrodite (Pindar *Pyth*. 2.15-16, Tacitus *Hist*. 2.3.1-2; *ICS* nos. 4, 6, 7, 16, 17; Baurain 1981; Maier 1989). The kings of Paphos traditionally held the charge of 'priests of the Wanassa' (Maier 1989: 376); this privileged status disappeared alongside Paphian monarchy around 310 BC according to Diodorus (Diod. 20.49.1). In the late 3rd century, the "*archos*" of the Kinyrads' is a certain Demokrates, son of Ptolemaios (Mitford 1961a: 13 no. 32; *BE* 1987: 724) and it should therefore be strongly suspected that by the 3rd century, the priesthood of the island's main cult was controlled by Ptolemaic agents, or by Cypriots durably linked to the royal house. The appointment of Phanion to the female priesthood of Aphrodite not only announced Ptolemaic supervision over the cults of the island, later illustrated by the title of *archiereus* given to the *strategos*, but also fitted the context of Kallikrates' role in Ptolemaic religious policy. Kallikrates played a decisive role in the implementation of two of the most important cults in Ptolemaic religious policy, the royal cult, of which he became the first eponymous priest in 269/8 BC (*P. Hibeh* II 199 line 12; Clarysse and Van der Veken 1983: 4-5 no.19), and the cult of the maritime goddess Aphrodite-Arsinoe, after Arsinoe II, whose temple was located near Alexandria, the foundation of which Poseidippos attributes to Kallikrates (Austin and Bastianini 2002 nos. 39, 116, and 119; Marquaille 2001: 193-234; Bing 2002/3; Criscuolo 2003: 324). The sanctuary of Aphrodite at Palaipaphos had become a showcase for royal power by the reign of Ptolemy II, reflecting Aphrodite's popularity at the court in Alexandria, where she was Euploia, the mirror of Ptolemaic maritime power and expansion. But she was also worshipped as goddess of marriage and as such protected the Ptolemaic incestuous royal couples (Robert 1966; Puelma 1982: 221-46 and 285-304; Gutzwiller 1992: 359-85). Aphrodite acted as a warrant of family love, and for men and women of the Ptolemaic hereditary elite in Cyprus, advertising their piety to such a caring goddess represented a political act coupled with religious devotion.

Our second example, also related to a priesthood tenure, concerns Artemo, daughter of the *strategos* Seleukos, in a dedication by a regiment based in Cyprus, where she is described, if the restoration is correct, as 'priestess of Queen and Goddess Kleopatra', that is the sister and wife of Ptolemy VIII, Kleopatra II (142-131 BC; *OGIS* 159, *SEG* XIII 587). Artemo was priestess of Arsinoe Philopator in Alexandria between the years 141 BC and 114 BC, therefore simultaneous with the time of the inscription (Clarysse and van der Veken 1983: 21-7 nos. 150-75). A Phoenician inscription found in Idalion dated to year 31 of Ptolemy son of Ptolemy, year 57 of the era of Kition and in the year when Amatosir, a Phoenician, was *kanephoros* of Arsinoe Philadelphus (255/4 BC; *CIS* I. 93; Mitford 1961a: 8) shows that Amatosir was a local priestess since another *kanephoros* is attested in Alexandria for the same year (Clarysse and Van der Veken 1983: 8-9 no. 36). It is not therefore unreasonable to assume the existence of a separate priesthood in Cyprus held by Artemo (contra Bagnall 1976: 68-9). The inscription specifically refers to Artemo's title; as a consequence, her connection with the royal cult, which was particularly popular with the Ptolemaic army, is likely to be related to the dedication itself. As it was common procedure in the Seleucid dynasty to appoint female members of the royal family and aristocracy as priestesses of the royal cult in the provinces (Ma 1999: 37; Bielman 2002: 43-9 no. 6; *CIG* 30), the close links that the *strategos* entertained with the royal family and his status as full representative of royal power in Cyprus must have given their wives and daughters a predominant role in the religious life of Cypriot cities.

No such documents as civic decrees showing women acting as benefactors to the city have been recovered from Cyprus, so that women's civic role, that is their contribution to the city, has to be re-constructed from inscriptions.[3] What was for example the motivation behind the honours attributed in Salamis to Olympias, the wife of Theodoros, by the Dionysiac artists in Cyprus (142-131 BC; Marcillet-Jaubert, Pouilloux *et al*. 1987: 40 no.79)? Is it possible, if the statue stood on its own, which cannot be proved, that she had sponsored their participation in a festival? We know from a letter addressed to the Boiotian city of Thespiae that Arsinoe III herself had donated a silver prize to victors at dramatic contests (dithyrambs, tragedy and comedy) during the festival of the Mouseia (Feyel 1942: 103-11 no. 5; Roesch 1989: 621-9, esp. 623-5). Aristocratic women from Alexandria may have followed this royal precedent in Cyprus. The inscription specifies that a statue of Olympias had been set up by the *grammateia* of the Dionysiac Technitai *in* Cyprus, who may therefore have been directly responsible to the island's gubernatorial couple for the promotion of the royal cult. The same Olympias' later contribution to the Lycian regiment in Cyprus is equally puzzling (123-118 BC; Mitford 1961a: 30 no. 80) and we may venture that she

---

[3] On the distinctions between 'civic', 'civil', 'official' and 'public' see Bielman 2002: 12-13.

perhaps improved their daily lives by the distribution of food or wine. Again, what was consisted in the involvement of Aristonike, the wife of Aristokrates, with the city of Paphos, for her to deserve a statue in the sanctuary of Aphrodite (114-107 BC; *OGIS* 163, Mitford 1961a: 35 no. 95)? It is naturally impossible to bring answers to these questions but it is safe to argue that the number of dedications involving women from the elite on Cyprus, and their diversity, entails that these women were acknowledged as public figures and active participants in the life of the Cypriot cities. They were publicly honoured perhaps not as much for what they actually did, but as women of influence close to the royal circle. Eirene, Artemo, and Olympias, Seleukos' daughter, were closely associated with the court in Alexandria, and must have been included in something resembling a queen's circle of 'Ladies-in-waiting'. They had all been eponymous priestesses of Arsinoe Philopator (Clarysse and Van der Veken 1983: 21-7 nos. 150-175; 33-5 nos. 150-75; 36-7 nos. 184b-186), Eirene for at least twenty-nine consecutive years. These non-institutional powers directly echo the role of the Ptolemaic *basilissa*, often conveyed in terms of political 'potential' (Carney 1991: 164; Savalli-Lestrade 2003: 66); the queen offered legitimacy as well as symbols of continuity and fertility to dynastic propa-ganda, although from the reign of Cleopatra II onwards, the Ptolemaic queen gained full political powers (Hölbl 2001: 194-204; Arsinoe II as pharaoh: Quaegebeur 1978: 258). This gradual development of the political stance of the *basilissa*, from Berenice I's association with Aphrodite, probably designed by the same agents who attached the name of Arsinoe Philadelphus to Ptolemaic thalassocracy, to the reign of Cleopatra VII acting as queen of an empire, progressively detached the powers of the Ptolemaic queen from its male counterpart. This resulted in a phenomenon pointed out by Ogden for the reign of Cleopatra VII:

'with Cleopatra, and before her Berenice IV and Cleopatra Selene, we reach the end-point of sister-marriage: birth from a Ptolemaic princess was now more important than birth from a Ptolemaic prince.' (Ogden 1999: 105).

Public representation of Ptolemaic aristocratic women linked to the royal house, as attested by Cypriot evidence, shows the fundamental role of royal mimetism; it also implies that the transmission of notions of *euergesia* and *eunoia* through women did not act only as a 'female pendant' to civic duties (Van Bremen 2003: 328).

This assumption is supported by the fact that we find the same social 'autonomy' or 'self-sufficiency' among aristocratic women in Cyprus. This is partly demonstrated by the dedication made to Paphian Aphrodite by Stratonike, daughter of Nikias, to Zeuxo, daughter of Ariston and wife of the *strategos* Polykrates (203-197 BC; Mitford 1961a: 16 no.41). Whereas Zeuxo's name and status are attached to both her husband and father, the

sole mention of Stratonike's patronymic indicates that she was either a maiden, or that her husband may have been dead. It could also well be, although more disputable, that what mattered here in the dedication and which would best convey the family's prestige was the mention of her father's name, Nikias. Stratonike's patronymic tied her to her family and must have been an object of pride. She describes herself as Alexandrian, and there is in fact something very masculine in this honorific exchange between two women, set up for reasons that unfortunately completely escape us. The only parallel for this period, despite its public and collective context, is the decree honouring Phaena and set up by the Koinon of the priestesses of Demeter at Mantinea (42/41 BC; *IG* V.2 266; Van Bremen 1996: 27-8). However the focus of our Cypriot inscription is rather the celebration by a member of the Alexandrian court of another member of this administrative elite that served the king's interests in his possessions. Zeuxo detains non-institutional powers thanks not only to her family ties but her husband's status, and the dedication allows these social and political elements to be reflected on Stratonike. That women were involved in a 'dialogue of power' (Ma 1999) at such an early date is certainly significant in the study of elites in the Hellenistic period. Since all these inscriptions convey power and family fame, revealing that women from the Greco-Macedonian elite had an integral share in legitimising Ptolemaic officials' authority in Cyprus, most of the time with the erection of a statue in conspicuous places, the Cypriot evidence is indicative of changing times and is characteristic of the Hellenistic period when the role of women was no longer limited to family realms. Instead, it projected family values in the public sphere. The influence of royal power and its agents – that is Ptolemaic officials, the court, the ruler cult and royal imagery – is here clear in the two-fold transfer of social power from male citizens to families in the Hellenistic period, and that of political power from the royal sphere to its elites. These inscriptions are also the reflection of royal trends among Hellenistic dynasties, and even more specifically mirror the growing status of the Ptolemaic queen. On a par with their fathers or husbands, these women equally made the link between Cyprus and royal power in Egypt, strengthening the status of Cyprus as a political and cultural extension of Alexandria in the Mediterranean.

Yet female dedications can also be found outside the Ptolemaic official sphere, where family values and ties are equally made public and reflect the multi-cultural aspect of Cypriot society. In the sanctuary at Palaipaphos, a statue of Onasion dedicated by both his mother and father, Andron and Stratonike (middle of the 2nd century; Mitford 1961a: 26 no. 66), may have stood not far away from a statue of the wife of Ptolemaios, most probably a Ptolemaic soldier or official, dedicated by him to Paphian Aphrodite (*SEG* XXXV 1468). Cypriots too boasted the ancestry of their family through the names of their female members, such as Echetime, daughter of Agapenor, honouring her children who both bear the equally very royal names of Agapenor and Evagoration (or Evagoratis) (*c*. 160 BC; Mitford 1961a: 24 no.61, *SEG* XX 201).[4] The statue of Pnytarion erected by the city and demos of Kition at the end of the 1st century BC is particularly emblematic of elite society in Hellenistic Cyprus (Yon 2004: 256-7, no.2030). According to the inscription, she was the daughter of Hipparchos, wife of Asclepiodoros, son of Asclepiodoros, himself son of Sillis, former gymnasiarchs and agoranomoi. Pnytarion's husband was the second founder of the sanctuary and high-priest of Asclepios and Hygiea. Surely an important woman, Pnytarion came from an old Cypriot family, who had married into a Semitic family, showing the creation of a new local elite combining different ethnic groups and its subsequent domination over military, economic and religious powers in the city. Again the specific role played by Pnytarion in relation to the city of Kition and the reason why she was honoured remain unfortunately unclear but it shows both the survival and permeation of social practices from Ptolemaic power elites to local aristocracies.

The Cypriot success of this public proliferation of parental links which gave prevalence to maternity and powerful women certainly owes to the eminence and reputation of the sanctuary of Aphrodite on Cyprus, suggesting that the Ptolemaic impact on female representation in Cyprus also corresponded to a typically Cypriot context. This conjunction of cultural and political conventions is perhaps what inspired the Alexandrian poet Posidippus in the 3rd century when he wrote the epitaph of this Cypriot grandmother named Onasagoratis (Austin and Bastianini 2002 no.47):

> This tomb holds Onasagoratis, who saw
> Her children and the successive generations of her children,
> four times twenty in all: so it was in the hands and hearts of eighty children
> that the very old woman was cherished.
> At the age of one hundred, the people of Paphos deposited here
> The blessed offspring of Onasa[s] in the [fire-devoured] dust.

Placed among other funerary epigrams celebrating women and themes commonly associated with such literary genre, such as death striking a woman in labour or before a maiden had a chance to marry, this poem describes the love and respect of a family for its female forebear. Onasagoratis herself had continued weaving the familial thread by echoing the name of her father, and also perhaps that of her *genos* – a king 'Unasagusu', or Onasagoras, is attested as king of Ledroi on a list of kingdoms paying tribute to the Assyrian king Esarhaddon

in 673/2 BC (Yon and Malbran-Labat 1995).[5] But Onasagoratis is here commemorated by the whole city; the poem in fact stresses how familial love finds resonance in civic honours. That Posidippus, a poet close to the court at Alexandria chose Paphos as an appropriate setting for the epigram, or whether he was commissioned to do so, reflects a reality in Ptolemaic Paphos that may have been familiar to Alexandrians.

To conclude, this short study of female representation in Cyprus, which primarily focused on inscriptions but will gain from a comprehensive analysis of other modes of representation such as statuary art, has several implications. As A. Bielman showed for the Aegean, Ptolemaic rule in Cyprus did have an impact on women's social status and redefined their integration into civic structures (Bielman 2004: 195-213). That it developed to such an extent, or rather that we have such a good illustration of it, also shows that the Ptolemies used existing ideological structures in Cyprus while reproducing power systems at work in Alexandria. Cypriot evidence also illustrates the role of women when defending the prestige of their family and the 'collective' nature of Hellenistic royal power, too often reduced to the figure of the king. The relative decline of the Ptolemies' charisma in the 2nd century in opposition to the longevity of the Ptolemaic dynasty is certainly there to prove the significance of power networks in Hellenistic politics. Finally, such inscriptions should have us question the functioning of parallel administrations, royal and civic, in Hellenistic empires, and their respective spheres of public representation. Were women of the Ptolemaic and local elites part of the same public sphere and what was their degree of permeability? When Cypriots took on royal functions as this became the case in the 2nd century, did Cypriot women enter the 'imperial' public sphere previously restricted to women from the Ptolemaic court circle and what consequences may this have had on the cultural life of the city? These questions remain unanswered for now but certainly do justice to the forgotten treasures of Cypriot history.

Appendix: Female Representation in Selected Honorific Inscriptions from Cyprus

These inscriptions involve women either as dedicants or recipients of honours addressed either to their family or directly to them. This list omits dedications strictly speaking with a religious content, unless they contain some political intent or indicate social transformations underlined in the paper. The bibliography points to the main reference only and is deliberately succinct. For a majority of documents the third column offers the original text of the inscription.

---

[4] Echetimos was one of the two 4th century kings of Paphos whose monumental tomb was uncovered at Palaipaphos: Maier and Karageorghis (1984) 217.

[5] Names in Onas- are typically Cypriot. In the famous Idalion Bronze Tablet (c. 478-470 BC), there is mention of the eponymous magistrate(?) Philokypros, son of Onasagoras, and the doctor Onasilos, son of Onasikypros, who is thanked by the king of Idalion: *SEG* XXXVIII 1499, Masson 1983: 233-44.

Paphos	3rd c. BC	The soldiers under the command of Nikanor honour Pra[och/ul]a daughter of Mnasimachos, from Epirus, the mother of Antiochos.	Mitford 1937 no.9
Old Paphos	Mid-3rd c.	Archetime daughter of Apelles is honoured by her children Samion and Onesilos	Mitford 1961a no.20
Cyprus (found in Charadros, Cilicia)	246/222	Statue base of Theodoros son of Demetrios from Arsinoe in Pamphylia, hegemon of Charadros, of Myraitha, his wife, daughter of Zenothemion, a Samian and their sons.	Mitford 1961b no.35
Old Paphos	246/222	His mother Phanion, daughter of Boiskos, priestess, honours Boiskos.	Mitford 1961a no.19
Old Paphos	225/200	Olympiodoros, son of Philokles, her husband, is honoured by Agemona daughter of Palaios and her children.	Mitford 1961a no.24
Old Paphos	217/209	The city of Paphos erected a statue of Myrsine, the strategos Pelops' wife, for Pelops' *eunoia* towards king Ptolemy and queen Cleopatra, Gods Philopatores, in the sanctuary of Old Paphos.	Mitford 1961a no.39
Salamis	217/209	The soldiers of the ? garrison dedicated a statue of Myrsine, daughter of Hyperbassas, the strategos Pelops' wife, for Pelops' *eunoia* towards king Ptolemy and queen Cleopatra, Gods Philopatores.	Salamine 74
Amathus	Late 3rd c.	Amathus honours Karpion, a Samian, son of Ammonios, his wife and children.	*BE* 1970 no.558
Old Paphos	203/197	Statues of Polykrates, *strategos* and archiereus, and his father, erected by the city of Paphos (no.43), standing next to a statue of his wife Zeuxo of Cyrene and son (no. 44). Polykrates' daughters Hermione, Zeuxo (and Eukrateia) also had their statues erected by the city of Paphos (no.45 possibly with that of another son of Polykrates.	Mitford 1961a nos.43-45.
Old Paphos	203/197	To Paphian Aphrodite, a statue of Zeuxo daughter of Ariston, Cyrenaean, wife of Polykrates, *strategos* and archiereus, was consecrated by Stratonike, daughter of Nikias, Alexandrian.	Mitford 1961a no.41
Kition area	3rd-2nd c.	Timokrates, son of Stasioikos is honoured by the thiasos of Artemis from Soanta together with Timagion, his wife, Timis, their daughter, as well as their sons including a son named Stasioikos, together with Aristion, Timis' daughter, Karion, Stasioikos' daughter, and her brother.	Kition 2019
Kourion	200/193	The city of Kourion honours Demetrios of Thessaly, governor of Kourion, his wife, and their children.	Kourion 42
Kition	197/181	A statue of Eirene, daughter of the strategos Ptolemaios, who was high priest of the cult of Artemis (d[espoina]?) of the gods, king Ptolemy and the other gods, was set up by her son Andromachos, diadochos and *grammateus* of the forces on Cyprus.	Kition 2022
Salamis	180/50 BC	The wife of Leukos, *grammateus* of forces stationed on Cyprus honours her father Philotimos son of Hecataion.	Salamine 89
Old Paphos	c. 160?	Demonike and ?, daughters of Leonnatos and Olympias, are honoured by the hegemon Chairias.	Mitford 1961a no.62
Old Paphos	Mid-2nd c. or 105/88	A statue of Xenophon [kinsman of the king, strategos], archiereus [over the island was dedicated by ?, daughter of ?], his wife and An[dromachos his son [...].	Mitford 1961a no.60
Kition	146/116	Statue base of Melankomas son of Philodamos, Aetolian, who was governor of the city, commandant and hipparch of the contingent, priest of the Theoi Euergetai, set up by Aristo, daughter of Dion, a Cretan, the wife of his son Melankomas, governor of the city, together with their children.	Kition 2024
Salamis	142/131	A statue of Olympias [daughter of ?], wife of Theodoros son of Seleukos, kinsman of the king, *strategos*, nauarchos and archiereus, was dedicated by the koinon of the island's *grammateia* of the artists of Dionysos.	Salamine 79
Old Paphos	142/131	Artemo?, daughter of Theodoros, son of Seleukos, kinsman of the king, strategos, nauarchos, archiereus of the island was honoured by the city of Paphos	Mitford 1961a no.72
Paphos	142/131	A statue of Artemo, the daughter of Seleukos, kinsman of the king, *strategos*, nauarchos, archiereus of the island, priestess of queen Cleopatra Goddess, was dedicated by the koinon? of the C[ilicians] stationed [on the island].	*SEG* XIII 587, Młynarczyk 1990: 158 Table B no.10

Chytroi	142-131	A statue of Olympias, the daughter of Artemo, daughter of Seleukos, one of the king's first friends, strategos, nauarch and archiereus, was dedicated by the city of [Chytroi?].	*SEG* XIII 557, *OGIS* 160
Old Paphos	127/124	A statue of a daughter of Lochos, [priest of the Muse Pieris and Hypereia, / son of Kallimedes, syngenes, hypermachos,] hypomnemato-graph, and strategos autokrator of Thebaid, was dedicated by the Koinon of the Lycian regiment in Cyprus.	OGIS 147; Mitford 1961a: 76 who offers an alternative reading; Młynarczyk 1990: 125 n.124
Old Paphos	123/118	A statue of [Polykrateia?], daughter of Theodoros, kinsman of the king, strategos, nauarchos and archiereus and his wife Olympias, was dedicated by ?.	Mitford 1961a no.82
Old Paphos	123/118	Olympias, Theodoros' wife, is honoured by the koinon of the Lycians on Cyprus	Mitford 1961a no.80
Old Paphos	116/107	The Priests of Paphian Aphrodite dedicated a statue of Helenos, kinsman of the king, strategos, archiereus, archikynegos of the island, ?, his wife, and Heliodora his daughter, for his benefaction towards them	*SEG* XVIII 583
Old Paphos	114/107	The city of Paphos dedicated a statue of Aristonike, daughter of Ammo-nios, wife of Aristokrates, kinsman, hypomnematograph and member of the Guild of the Dionysiac artists on Cyprus, for his *philagathia* towards it.	Młynarczyk 1990: 158 Table B no.15
Paphos	c. 88 BC	The city of Paphos dedicated a statue of ?, daughter of Onesandros, a Cypriot, kinsman of the king, priest for life of king Ptolemy Soter (in Alexandria) and of the Ptolemaion he had built, and *grammateus* of the city of Paphos.	Mitford 1939 no.18
Kition	1st c. BC	[Her]ois? daughter of Artemidoros son of Ariston, former gymnasiarch, had her statue erected by Strategis, daughter of Nauarchos, gymnasiarch and *hieromnemos* for life, ([Her]ois?) being her own daughter.	Kition 2027
Kition	1st c. BC	Pnytarion, wife of Asclepiodoros, daughter of Hipparchos is honoured by the city and demos of Kition.	Kition 2030

Bibliography

Special abbreviations
BE *Bulletin Epigraphique*
CIG *Corpus Inscriptionum Graecarum*
SEG *Supplementum Epigraphicum Graecum*

AUSTIN, C. and G BASTIANINI, eds, (2002) *Posidippi Pellaei quae supersunt omnia*. Milan, LED.

BAGNALL, R.S. (1976) *The Administration of the Ptolemaic possessions outside Egypt*. Leiden, Brill.

BAURAIN, C. (1980) Kinyras. La fin de l'âge du Bronze à Chypre et la tradition antique. *Bulletin de Correspondance Hellénique* 104, 277-308.

BIELMAN, A. (2002) *Femmes en public dans le monde hellénistique (IVe-Ier siècle av. J.-C.)*. Paris, Sedes.

BIELMAN, A. (2004) Egéries égéennes. Les femmes dans les inscriptions hellénistiques et impériales des Cyclades. IN: Follet, S. ed., *L'hellénisme d'époque romaine : nouveaux documents, nouvelles approches (Ier s. a.C – IIIe s.p.C), Actes du Colloque international à la mémoire de Louis Robert, Paris 7-8 juillet 2000*. Paris, De Boccard, 195-213.

BING, P. (2002-2003) Posidippus and the Admiral: Kallikrates of Samos. *Greek, Roman and Byzantine Studies* 43, 243-66.

BRIANT, P. (1996) *Histoire de l'Empire perse de Cyrus à Alexandre*. Paris, Fayard.

CARNEY, E.D. (1991) What's in a name. The emergence of a Title for Royal Women in the Hellenistic Period. IN: Pomeroy, S. ed., *Women's History and Ancient History*. London, University of Carolina Press, 154-72.

CARNEY, E.D. (1993) Foreign influence and the changing role of royal Macedonian women. *Ancient Macedonia* 5, 313-23.

CAYLA, J.-B. and HERMARY, A. (2003) Chypre à l'époque hellénistique. IN: Le Dinahet, M.-T. ed., *L'Orient méditerranéen de la mort d'Alexandre au Ier siècle avant notre ère*. Nantes, Editions du Temps, 232-56.

CÉBEILLAC-GERVASONI, M. and L. LAMOINE, eds (2003) *Les élites et leurs facettes. Les élites locales dans le monde hellénistique*. Rome, Ecole française de Rome – Clermont-Ferrand, Presses Universitaires Blaise-Pascal.

CLARYSSE, W. and G. van der VEKEN, (1983) *The Eponymous Priests of Ptolemaic Egypt*. Papyrologica Lugduno-Batava 24, Leiden, Brill.

COHEN, D. (1996) Seclusion, Separation, and the Status of Women in Classical Athens. IN: McAuslan, I. and P. Walcot, eds, *Women in Antiquity*. Oxford, Oxford University Press, 134-45.

CONNELLY, J.B. (1988) *Votive Sculpture in Hellenistic Cyprus*. Nicosia, Department of Antiquities of Cyprus.

CRISCUOLO, L. and G. GERACI, eds, (1989) *Egitto e Storia Antica dall'ellenismo all'età araba. Atti del Colloquio internazionale: Bologna, 31 agosto- 2 settembre 1987*. Bologna, CLUEB.

FANTUZZI M. (2004) The Structure of the *Hippika* in *P.Mil. Vogl. VIII 309*. IN: Acosta-Hughes, B, E. Kosmetatou *et al.* eds, *Labored in Papyrus Leaves. Perspectives on an Epigram collection attributed to Posidippus (P. Mil. Vogl. VIII 309)*. Washington DC, Harvard University Press, 212-24.

FEYEL, M. (1942) *Contribution à l'épigraphie béotienne*. Le Puy, Imprimerie de La Haute-Loire.

GUTZWILLER K. (1992) Callimachus' *Lock of Berenice*: Fantasy, Romance and Propaganda. *American Journal of Philology* 113, 359-85.

HAUBEN, H. (1970) *Callicrates of Samos. A contribution to the study of the Ptolemaic admiralty*. Studia Hellenistica 18, Leuven, Leuvense Universitaire Uitgaven.

HAUBEN, H. (1987) Cyprus and the Ptolemaic Navy. *Report of the Department of Antiquities Cyprus*, 213-26.

HÖLBL, G. (2001) *A History of the Ptolemaic Empire*. London, Routledge.

MA, J. (1999) *Antiochos III and the Cities of Western Asia Minor*. Oxford, Oxford University Press.

MAIER, F.G. (1967) Excavations at Kouklia (Palaepaphos) Site A. *Report of the Department of Antiquities Cyprus*, 29-49.

MAIER, F.G. (1985) *Alt-Paphos auf Cypern: Ausgrabungen zur Geschichte von Stadt und Heiligtum 1966-1984*. Mainz am Rhein, P. von Zabern.

MAIER, F.G. (1989) Priest Kings in Cyprus. IN: Peltenburg, E.G. ed., *Early Society in Cyprus*. Edinburgh, Edinburgh University Press, 376-91.

MAIER, F.G. and V. KARAGEORGHIS, (1984) *Paphos: history and archaeology*. Nicosia, A.G. Leventis Foundation.

MARCILLET-JAUBERT, J., J. POUILLOUX, *et al.* eds (1987) *Salamine de Chypre*. Vol. XIII: Testimonia Salaminia 2. Corpus épigraphique. Paris, De Boccard (= Salamine).

MARQUAILLE, C. (2001) *The External Image of Ptolemaic Egypt*. Unpublished Ph.D., London.

MEHL, A. (1996) Cyperns Städte im Hellenismus: Verfassung, Verwaltung und führende Gesellschaft. IN: Leschhorn, W., A.V.B. Miron, *et al.* eds, *Hellas und der Griechischen Osten*. Saarbrücken, SDV Saarbrücker Druckerei und Verlag GmbH, 127-52.

MASSON, O. (1983) *Les inscriptions chypriotes syllabiques: recueil critique et commenté*. Paris, De Boccard.

MITFORD, T.B. (1939), Contributions to the epigraphy of Cyprus. *Archiv für Papyrusforschung* 13, 13-38.

MITFORD, T.B. (1953a) The Character of Ptolemaic Rule in Cyprus. *Aegyptus* 33, 80-90.

MITFORD, T.B. (1953b) Seleucus and Theodorus. *Opuscula Atheniensia* 1, 130-71.

MITFORD, T.B. (1957) Ptolemy Macron. *Studi Calderini-Paribeni*. Vol. II. Milan, Ceschina, 163-87.

MITFORD, T.B. (1961a) The Hellenistic Inscriptions of Old Paphos. *Annual of the British School at Athens* 56, 1-39.

MITFORD, T.B. (1961b) Further Contributions to the Epigraphy of Cyprus. *American Journal of Archaeology* 65, 93-151.

MITFORD, T.B. (1971) *The Inscriptions of Kourion*. Philadelphia, American Philosophical Society (= Kourion).

MITFORD, T.B. (1980) Roman Cyprus. IN: Temporini, H. and W. Haase, eds, *Aufstieg und Niedergang der römischen Welt II.7.2*. Berlin, de Gruyter, 1285-384.

MŁYNARCZYK, J. (1990) *Nea Paphos. Vol. III: Nea Paphos in the Hellenistic period*, Warszawa, Editions géologiques.

MOOREN, L. (1975) *The Aulic Titulature in Ptolemaic Egypt. Introduction and Prosopography*. Verhandelingen van de Kononklijke Academie voor Wetenschappen, Letteren en Schoone Kunsten van België, Klasse der Letteren 78, Brussel, Paleis der Academiën.

MOOREN, L. (1981) Ptolemaic families. *Proceedings of the XVIth International Congress of Papyrologists, New York, 24-31 July 1980*. Chico, California: Scholars Press, 289-301.

MOOREN, L. (1985) The Ptolemaic court system. *Chronique d'Egypte* 60, 214-22.

MOOREN, L. (1998) Kings and Courtiers, Political Decision-Making in the Hellenistic States. IN: Schuller, W. ed., *Politische Theorie und Praxis im Altertum*. Darmstadt, Wissenschaftliche Buchgesellschaft, 122-33.

OGDEN, D. (1999) *Polygamy, Prostitutes and Death: the Hellenistic Dynasties*, London, Duckworth with the Classical Press of Wales.

OGIS: DITTENBERGER, W. (1903-5) *Orientis Graeci inscriptiones selectae*. Leipzig.

POMEROY, S. (1984) *Women in Hellenistic Egypt*. New York, Schocken Books.

PUELMA, M. (1982) Die Aitien des Kallimachos als Vorbild der römischen Amores-Elegie, I and II. *Museum Helveticum* 39, 221-46.

QUAEGEBEUR, J. (1978) Reines ptolémaïques et traditions égyptiennes. IN: Maehler, H. and V.M Strocka, eds, *Das ptolemaische Ägypten. Akten des Internationalen Symposions 27.-29. September 1976 in Berlin*. Mainz am Rhein, von Zabern, 245-62.

QUEYREL, A. (1988) *Les figurines hellénistiques de terre cuite. Amathonte IV*. Paris, De Boccard.

ROBERT L. (1966) Un décret d'Ilion et un papyrus concernant des cultes royaux. IN: Samuel, A. E. ed., *Essays in honor of C. Bradford Welles*. New Haven, American Society of Papyrologists, 175-211.

ROESCH, P. (1989) Les cultes égyptiens en Béotie. IN: Criscuolo, L. and G. Geraci, eds, *Egitto e Storia Antica dall'ellenismo all'età araba. Atti del Colloquio internazionale: Bologna, 31 agosto- 2 settembre 1987*. Bologna, CLUEB, 621-29.

ROWLANDSON, J. ed. (1998) *Women and Society in Greek and Roman Egypt*. Cambridge, Cambridge University Press.

SAVALLI-LESTRADE, I. (2001) Remarques sur les élites dans les *poleis* hellénistiques. IN: Molin, M. ed., *Images et représentations du pouvoir et de l'ordre social dans l'antiquité : actes du colloque, Angers, 28-29 mai 1999*. Paris, De Boccard, 51-64.

SAVALLI-LESTRADE, I. (2003) La place des reines à la cour et dans le royaume à l'époque hellénistique. IN: Frei-Stolba, R., A. Bielman, *et al*. eds, *Les femmes antiques entre sphère privée et sphère publique. Actes du Diplôme d'études avancées. Universités de Lausanne et Neuchâtel, 2000-2002*. Bern, Oxford, Peter Lang, 59-76.

TATTON-BROWN, V. (1985) Archaeology in Cyprus 1960-1985: Classical to Roman Periods. IN: Karageorghis, V. ed., *Archaeology in Cyprus 1960-1985*. Nicosia, A.G. Leventis Foundation, 60-72.

THOMPSON, D. (2005) Posidippus, Poet of the Ptolemies. IN: Gutzwiller, K.J. ed., *The New Posidipppus.*

A Hellenistic Poetry Book. Oxford, Oxford University Press.

Van BREMEN R. (1996) *The Limits of Participation. Women and Civic Life in the Greek East in the Hellenistic and Roman Periods*. Amsterdam, J. C. Gieben.

Van BREMEN, R. (2003) Family Structures. IN: Erskine, A. ed., *A Companion to the Hellenistic World*. Cambridge, Blackwell, 313-30.

Van BREMEN, R. (2007), 'The Entire house is full of Crowns': Hellenistic *agones* and the commemoration of victory, IN: Hornblower, S. and C. Morgan, eds, *Pindar's Poetry, Patrons and Festivals: from Archaic Greece to the Roman Empire*. Oxford, Oxford University Press, 346-75.

VESSBERG, O. and A. WESTHOLM (1956) *The Swedish Cyprus Expedition IV.3: the Hellenistic and Roman Periods in Cyprus*. Stockholm, The Swedish Cyprus Expedition.

WALBANK, F.W. (1957-1979) *A historical commentary on Polybius*. 3 vols. (1st volume republished in 1970), Oxford, Clarendon Press.

WILSON, V. (1974) The Kouklia Sanctuary. *Report of the Department of Antiquities Cyprus*, 139-46.

YON, M. ed. (2004) *Kition dans les textes. Kition-Bamboula V*. Paris, Editions Recherches sur les Civilisations (= Kition).

YON, M. and F. MALBRAN-LABAT (1995) La stèle de Sargon à Chypre. IN: Caubet, A. ed., *Khorsabad, le palais de Sargon II, roi d'Assyrie*. Paris, La documentation française, 159-79.

PART 3:

ART AND RELIGION

THE AEGEAN ORIGIN OF THE ANICONIC CULT OF APHRODITE IN PAPHOS
KATARZYNA ZEMAN

The Cyprus coast is the birth-place of Aphrodite*, the Greek goddess of love, who according to Hesiod (*Theogony* 188-95) was born from the sea foam and then arrived at the island where Graces clothed her and decorated her with golden ornaments. Scholars also mostly agree that the cult of Aphrodite had its beginnings on Cyprus (Hill 1944; Herter 1975; Karageorghis J. 1977, 2005), except those who, taking Herodotus' Aphrodite-Mylitta to be Astarte or Ishtar (*Histories* I.105 2-3), see her origins even farther East (Röscher 1883; Farnell 1896; Burkert 1985). The fact is the origins and beginnings of her cult were under strong influences both from East and West (Pirenne-Delforge 2001). In this paper I would like to underline one of the possible Aegean elements of her origins – Aphrodite's aniconic cult in Old Paphos.

The temple in Old Paphos in south-west Cyprus is considered to be the most important and oldest of Aphrodite's sanctuaries, dating from the Late Bronze Age and continuing in use until the 4th century AD and the official end of pagan cults. It had two phases of development: Sanctuary I was used from the LBA (*c.* 1200 BC, the transition between LCII and LCIII; Budin 2003: 171) to the Roman period; and Sanctuary II was built in the 2nd century AD. There was probably also a temple of Aphrodite dating to the Archaic period outside of the north-east city gate but it was destroyed by the Persians in 498 BC (Maier 1975: 79). In the 13th century AD a sugar refinery was erected here and local people used the former sanctuary as a source of building material (Maier 1975: 69). The remains of Sanctuary I, which is most interesting here, consists of two parts: a covered hall or a colonnade to the north and an open court to the south (Budin 2003: 171). The whole complex measures 67 x 70 m and it was accessible through at least one entrance in the Eastern wall of the court (Maier 1975: 75).

Aphrodite was always portrayed aniconically at her sanctuary at Paphos. That is to say, she was not repre-

sented by a cult statue, but by a baetyl (Tacitus *Historiae* II.3). A baetyl could be a symbol of a goddess; it could have her powers, or represent the goddess herself, just as the cult statue could. In the Kouklia Museum we can see the baetyl from the Paphian Sanctuary II (Fig. 1) which, unfortunately, was not found *in situ* (Karageorghis J. 2005: 30). Although there is no evidence, it is possible that the aniconic nature of Aphrodite's Paphian cult extends back into the Bronze Age (Maier 1975:79, Karageorghis V. 1992: 212). The baetyl from Aphrodite's sanctuary depicted on Roman coins (Fig. 2a) issued in the time between Augustus and Philip the Arab (Maier 1975: 70) may therefore have existed as early as the Bronze Age (Maier 1975: 79). The overall continuity at the sanctuary may support this hypothesis.

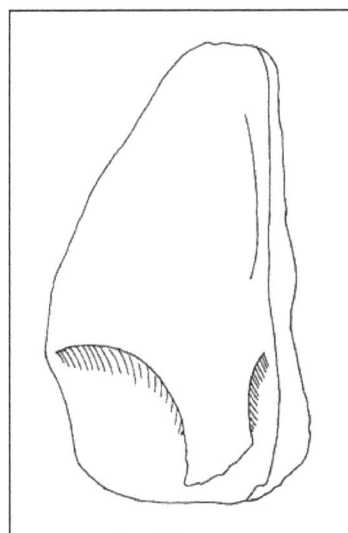

Fig. 1 – Baetyl from Aphrodite's Sanctuary in Old Paphos (drawing by author)

The most well known theory about the origins of aniconic cult in Paphos goes back to the Phoenicians. Evidence of

---

* I would like to thank Stephanie L. Budin for all her suggestions.

Fig. 2a – Detail from a Roman coin (drawing by author after Maier 1975, fig. 1)

Fig. 2b – Amygdaloid seal from East Crete (drawing by author after Evans 1928, fig. 66)

settlers from Phoenicia comes from the 9th century BC (Bisi 1986: 341), from sites like Kition or Amathus. The popularity of baetylic cult on the Levantine coast and the presence of such in Amathus where Aphrodite-Astarte was worshipped, make a good argument for Phoenician origins. Particularly significant could be the star of Astarte depicted with the Paphian baetyl on the Roman coins, which is, nevertheless, rather late evidence (Soyez 1972), based probably on the later trends towards syncretism between Aphrodite and Astarte (Budin 2004). But if we consider earlier, even Bronze Age beginnings of aniconic cult in Paphos, there could be an alternate possibility.

Aniconic cult was also a part of Bronze Age Aegean practice, most probably with Cretan origins. On Minoan seals we can see two types of baetylic representations; on both are depicted a naked or half-naked kneeling man or woman a) touching (Fig. 3a or b) holding arms around a big, rounded or oval stone (Fig. 3b). On such seals there can also be depicted a so-called sacred tree and/or a woman considered to be a goddess or a priestess, suggesting the scene was a part of a religious ritual, probably with ecstatic aspects and connected with fertility. Such representations are known from seals, rings and sealings from Ayia Triada, Kalyvia (Mesara), Sellopoulo (Knossos), Arkhanes, Zakros and Knossos; all have been well described, interpreted and analysed by Warren (1990: 195-201). Very interesting also is an amygdaloidal seal from East Crete with a stone (a baetyl?) inside a circular building with a conical roof, which could be a shrine (Evans 1928: 132) (Fig. 2b). There are also probable baetyls found on the Cretan sites of Vasiliki, Mallia, Gournia, Lasithi and Phylakopi, each having what appears to be one baetyl (Warren 1990: 202-5). We should also remember a trapezoidal altar where a baetyl was incorporated, from the sacred complex of Kephala Vasiliki, which was in use from LMIIIC until the Protogeometric period (La Rosa 2001: 222). Minoan baetyls probably also played a role in ceremonies for the dead (La Rosa 2001: 224-6). While the Paphian baetyl is conical in shape rather than oval or rounded as those represented in Cretan iconography, we should remember that those found in situ on Crete have different shapes themselves: rounded (Mallia), cuboid (Ayios Georghios, Lasithi) and plank-conical (Gournia).

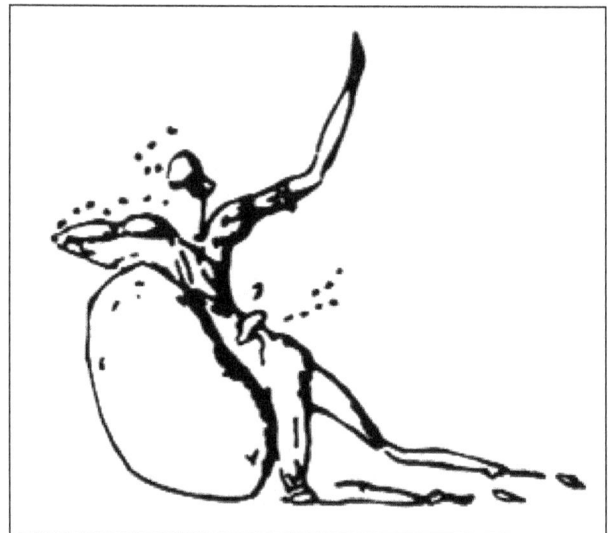

Fig. 3a – Man touching a baetyl, detail from a signet ring (Knossos, Sellopoulo tomb 3) (drawing by author after Popham 1974, fig. 14d)

The date of the erection of Aphrodite's sanctuary in Old Paphos is very close to the date of the arrival of Greek settlers there (Maier 1986: 312-14). There were also strong trade relations between this region and the Minoans and particularly the Mycenaeans even before the possible Aegean migrations (Karageorghis J. 2005: 17). The first trace of such contacts came from the LCI well in Paphos-Evreti from which came a LMIA cup. Then there

Fig. 3b – Man holding arms around baetyl, detail from a signet ring (Arkhanes, Tholos A) (drawing by author after Sakellarakis 1967, fig. 13)

are also 86 sherds in LHIIIA:2 style, several LMIIIB stirrup-jars and 343 examples of LHIIIB-style found throughout the remains of the Old Paphos (Maier and Karageorghis 1984: 55, 71). There are also examples of Aegean, especially Cretan, influences in the sanctuary of Aphrodite itself. First of all is a *larnax* found *in situ* in the south-western part of the colonnade (Maier and Karageorghis 1984: 96). Two Aegean style horns-of-consecration found, unfortunately not *in situ* (Maier and Karageorghis 1984: 99), also indicate strong Western influences. There was also one LCII pithos found in the Paphian Sanctuary that bears on one of its handles an impression of a cylinder seal with Aegeanising features (Maier and Karageorghis 1984: 96). The popularity of goddess with up-lifted arms figurines at the end of LBA and in CGI in Paphos is also significant (Karageorghis 2001: 325). They are well known from Mycenaean Greece, but even more so from Minoan Crete. The Cypriot examples are in type known from Crete, from sites like Gazi, Gournia, Karphi or Kephala Vasilikis (Budin 2003: 178).

The above examples show that an aniconic cult would not be an isolated example of Aegean influences in Aphrodite's cult in Paphos. They also show that there were several points in the history of the Paphian cult when such Aegean influence could have affected the goddess's iconography. Aniconism may have entered when Aegean influences were first being felt during early trade relationships; or when the earliest Aegean immigrants arrived at Old Paphos; or even later, when there was increased contact between Cyprus and the Aegean in the early Geometric period, concomitant with the popularity of the goddess with up-raised arms images.

That the Bronze Age residents of the Aegean may have spread aniconic aspects of cult is also supported by a separate case scenario, that of Arcadian Hermes. The god Hermes appears on the Linear B tablets from both Pylos (Gulizio 2000) and Knossos (Nosch 2000). The similarity of dialects between Arcadia and Cyprus (the Cypro-Arcadian dialect) suggests that this mountainous region of Greece was populated by a people closely related to those who migrated to Cyprus at the end of the Bronze Age. Here in Arcadia, Hermes was also worshipped with a strongly aniconic cult, where human worshippers put big stones near the crossroads, the terrain of the god of travel. They saw in those rocks Hermes himself, and these are the origins of herms, pillar-like statues of Hermes with just a head and genitals. In this instance it may be worth noting that Aphrodite's first sanctuary in the Aegean was also devoted to Hermes. This was Kato Symi in Crete, in use since MM times (Pirenne-Delforge 2001: 174). It was not their only common shrine: Aphrodite and Hermes were also worshipped together in Argos (Pausanias, 3, XV.10-11) and Samos. Their common origins in Crete may have led to a similar spread of aniconic imagery both east and north. In any case, the spread of aniconism in Hermes' cult shows that the Aegean origin of aniconism in Aphrodite's cult at Paphos would not have been unique.

In mythology we have two stories about the foundation of the Paphian Sanctuary. According to Homer the Cypriot king of Paphos, Kinyras, was the founder of the first temple of Aphrodite (Homer, *Iliad* XI.20). Tacitus claimed that it was Kinyras's father, king Aerias (Tacitus, *Historia* II.3). Kinyras is considered to be an Eteocypriot or a person of an Oriental origin (Karageorghis J. 2005: 15, 43). On the other hand, Pausanias states that it was the Greek Agapenor from Tegea, who, after the Trojan War settled on Cyprus, became the king of Paphos, and built the sanctuary for Aphrodite (Pausanias, 8, V.2). As in those myths, Aphrodite was a Cypriot goddess who took many aspects of her cult not only from the East, but also the West. In this case we should look to western, Aegean, even Cretan origins.

Bibliography

BISI, A.M. (1986) Le rôle de Chypre dans la civilisation Phénicienne d'Occident, IN: Karageorghis, V. ed., *Acts of the International Archaeological Symposium 'Cyprus between the Orient and the Occident'* Nicosia, Department of Antiquities, Cyprus, 341-50.

BUDIN, S.L. (2004) A Reconsideration of the Aphrodite-Ashtart syncretism, IN: *Numen, International review for the history of religions* 51:2, 95-145.

BUDIN, S.L. (2003) *The Origin of Aphrodite*. Maryland, CDL Press.

BURKERT, W. (1985) *Greek Religion*, Cambridge. Harvard University Press.

EVANS, A.J. (1928) *The Palace of Minos at Knossos*, vol. II. London, Macmillan & Co., Ltd.

FARNELL, L.R. (1896) *The cults of the Greek States.* Oxford, Clarendon Press.

GULIZIO, J. (2000) Hermes and e-ma-a2: The Continuity of his Cult from the Bronze Age to the Historical Period, IN: *Proceedings from the International Conference Antiquitas Viva*, Živa Antika 50, 105-16.

HERTER, H. (1975) Die Ursprünge des Aphroditekultes. IN: Vogt, E. ed., *Kleine Schriften*, Munich, Wilhelm Fink Verlag.

HILL, G. (1940) *A History of Cyprus.* Cambridge, Cambridge University Press.

KARAGEORGHIS, J. (2005) *Kypris: The Aphrodite of Cyprus, Ancient Sources and Archaeological Evidence.* Nicosia, The A.G. Leventis Foundation.

KARAGEORGHIS, J. (1977) *La Grande Déesse de Chypre et Son Culte à travers L'iconographie de L'époque Néolithique au Vième s. a.C.* Lyons, Maison de l'Orient Mediterranéen Ancien.

KARAGEORGHIS, V. (2001) The Great Goddess of Cyprus between the Aegeans and the 'Eteocypriots', IN: Laffineur, R. and R. Hägg eds, *Potnia: Deities and Religion in the Aegean Bronze Age*, Université de Liège, Liège, 323-7.

KARAGEORGHIS, V. (1992) On 'Baetyls' in Cyprus, *Levant* 24, 212.

LaROSA, V. (2001) Minoan Baetyls: Between Funerary Rituals and Epiphanies, IN: Laffineur, R. and R. Hägg eds, *Potnia: Deities and Religion in the Aegean Bronze Age*, Université de Liège, Liège, 221-7.

MAIER, F.G. (1986) Kinyras and Agapenor, IN: Karageorghis, V. ed., *Acts of the International Archaeological Symposium 'Cyprus between the Orient and the Occident'*, Nicosia, Department of Antiquities, Cyprus, 311-20.

MAIER, F.G. and V. KARAGEORGHIS (1984) *Paphos: History and Archaeology.* Nicosia, The A.G. Leventis Foundation.

MAIER, F.G. (1975) The Temple of Aphrodite at Old Paphos, *Report of the Department of Antiquities Cyprus*, 69-80.

NOSCH, M.-L.B. (2000) Schafherden unter dem Namenspatronat von Potnia und Hermes in Knossos, IN: Blakolmer, F. ed., *Österreichische Forschungen zur Ägäischen Bronzezeit 1998*, Phoibos Verlag, Wien, 211-15.

PIRENNE-DELFORGE, V. (2001) La Genèse de l'Aphrodite grecque: Le 'Dossier Crétoise', IN: Ribichini, S., M. Rocchi and P. Xella eds, *La Questione delle Influenze Vicino-Orientali sulla Religione Greca*, Consiglio nazionale delle ricerche, Roma, 169-87.

POPHAM M.R., E.A. CATLING, H.W. CATLING (1974) Sellopoulo Tombs 3 and 4. Two Late Minoan Graves near Knossos, *Annual of the British School at Athens* 69, 195-257.

ROSCHER, W.H. (1883) Lexicon der griechischen und romischen Mythologie, vol. I. Leipzig.

SAKELLARAKIS, J.A. (1967) Minoan Cemeteries at Arkhanes, *Archaeology* 20, 276-81.

SOYEZ, B. (1972) Le Betyle dans le Culte de l'Astarté Phenicienne, *Mélanges. Université Saint Joseph 47*, 149-69.

WARREN, P. (1990) Of Baetyls, *Opuscula Atheniensia* 18, 193-206.

THE WILD GOAT-AND-TREE ICON AND ITS SPECIAL SIGNIFICANCE FOR ANCIENT CYPRUS
LESLEY BUSHNELL

INTRODUCTION

One of the longest lived and most widespread images of the Ancient Near East and Eastern Mediterranean is a composition of two wild goats placed antithetically about a tree, usually referred to as a 'sacred tree'. Sometimes called 'The palm-and-ibex motif', it was the most ubiquitous of a group of motifs known as 'Animals at the Tree of Life' or 'Heraldic animal groups'. Whilst the image became popular throughout the region, particularly during the Late Bronze Age (LBA), most areas employed it for limited time periods. Ancient Cyprus was one exception. Once the goat-and-tree motif had arrived there during the Middle Bronze Age, it was adopted enthusiastically and persisted throughout the LBA and well into the Iron Age (IA). Its special significance for the island is the subject of this paper.

Hereafter, the goat-and-tree motif will be referred to as an *icon*, following Crowley's terminology for the discussion of Bronze Age art (Crowley 1992: 25). In order to avoid confusion over the myriad of terminologies used including image, motif, composition, theme etc. she defined the term *icon* as 'the memorable image, the means of organising subject matter'. In this case the *icon* typically consisted of wild goats in a variety of formal heraldic poses either side of a tree. The trees, usually stylised, represented deciduous trees, palms or conifers. The wild goats, often distinguished as *Capra ibex* or *Capra aegagrus* were most commonly depicted in the *rampant* (rearing up on their hind legs with forelegs in the air or against the tree), *statant* (standing with all four legs on the ground) or *couchant* (lying down) poses. Quite often they appeared to be eating the leaves of the tree. Whilst the basic composition of the icon endured over huge time spans and distances, local adaptations in style and content were frequent. For example, the original conifer on a stylised mountain, shown on icons from the Zagros region (Fig. 1), was replaced by a palm tree in

LBA Palestine (Fig. 2) and by a lotus in New Kingdom Egypt (Fig. 3). Birds were a frequent addition to the motif (Fig. 4), and the icon was often incorporated into a larger composition with human figures and/or mythological creatures (Fig. 5). Although it is extremely difficult to interpret the meanings of the icon, variations in use patterns indicate that they were almost certainly changed to meet the social needs of the receptive cultures.[1]

Fig. 1 – Drawing of impression from a marble seal from Iran from the Susa III-IV period (after Amiet 1980, illus. 537, pl. 34)

Numerous materials were used including luxuries like gold, silver, bronze, ivory and semi-precious stones as well as more everyday material such as ceramics. Whilst the range of goods was wide and included jewellery, vessels, furniture and personal items, the major medium for the icon was glyptic. Around 65% of the icons were found on seals, sealings, tablet impressions or signet rings. Vase decoration was another common medium

---

[1] This goat-and-tree icon was the subject of my MA dissertation (Bushnell 2005), for which I collected a total of 397 icons using mainly secondary sources such as catalogues, guides and reviews of various types of artefacts including seals, pottery, ivory, metal etc. The icons were analysed for patterns in their composition, materials and media, finds contexts, and regional and chronological distributions, and some interesting insights emerged.

Fig. 2 – Detail from jar from Megiddo LBIIA
(after Loud 1948, pl. 64:4)

Fig. 5 – Modern impression of an Elaborate Style cylinder seal from Cyprus of unknown provenance. (after Porada 1948, pl. IX, no. 17, after Frankfort 1939, pl. XLV, no. 1. Courtesy Archaeological Institute of America/American Journal of Archaeology)

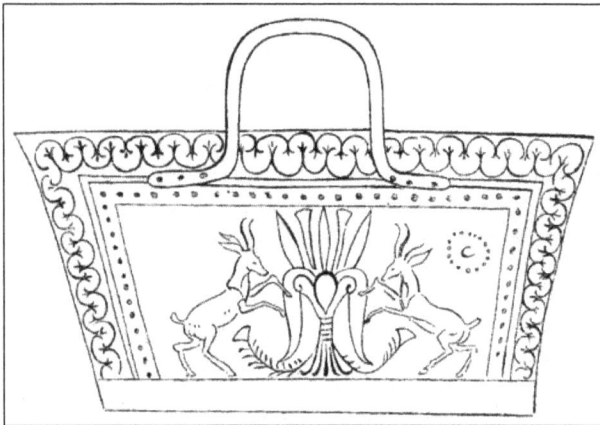

Fig. 3 – Drawing of a gold basket from the tomb of Rameses III (after Ohnefalsch-Richter 1893, fig. 107)

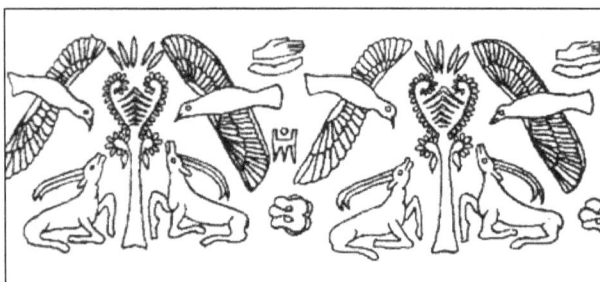

Fig. 4 – Drawing of an impression of a cylinder seal from Sinda (after Kenna 1967, illus. 27)

stand out as having a special affinity for the icon. They were Iran and Cyprus.

The high level of usage of the motif and its continuity in Iran is perhaps understandable. Contrary to many authorities who attribute the origin of the icon to Mesopotamia, my research indicates that it almost certainly originated in Iran, in the Susiana plain. Its special significance in Cyprus is more intriguing. The icon had no history there and was unknown before it was first imported in the late Middle Cypriot period. Yet by the LBA, it became even more popular in Cyprus than in Iran. Furthermore, at the end of the LBA, when the icon all but disappeared from the Eastern Mediterranean region, Cyprus retained a memory of the icon in elemental variations of it (Fig. 6), and was probably responsible for its re-introduction in the Early Iron Age (EIA), when there was a resurgence of the full iconic form. How is it possible to explain the long-lasting affinity Cyprus had for this motif?

Fig. 6 – Drawing of detail from a bowl from Kouklia Xerolimini, T9.7, c.1100-1050 B.C. (after Iacovou 1988, fig. 68)

THEORETICAL CONSIDERATIONS

Clarke (2005a: 81) pointed out that there are two key trajectories for cultural transmission and transformation.

accounting for 19% of the icons. There was also a complete range of contexts including funerary, cultic, administrative, palatial and settlement (Bushnell 2005).

The spatial and chronological occurrences of the icon are summarised in Table 1. The first appearance of the wild goat-and-tree icon was in the mid-4th millennium BC (Fig. 1), and it can be traced with few breaks to the IA and beyond. The zenith of its applications however, occurred in the LBA. In terms of spatial distribution, two regions

Table 1 – Spatial and Chronological Distribution of the Icon

Date	Greece	Crete	Anatolia	Cyprus	Palestine
Pre 4000 B.C	Neolithic	Neolithic		Neolithic	Chalcolithic 4500-3500 BC
4000 B.C.				Chalcolithic	(1)
3500 B.C.					Early Bronze I-III 3500-2200 BC (5)
3000 B.C.	Early Helladic	Early Minoan			
2500 B.C.				Philia c. 2500-2350	
		MMI LMIA (1)		Early Cypriot I-III c.2400-2000	MBIA/EBIV
2000 B.C.	Middle Helladic			Middle Cypriot 2000-1650 (3)	MBIIA-IIB 2000-1550 BC (3)
			Karum Kanesh II-Ib		
			Cappadoccian		
	LHI-LHIIIB2 1600-1200 BC (21)	LMIA-LMIIIB 1575-1200BC (4)	Old Kingdom	LCI-LCIIC 1650-1200 (39)	
1500 B.C.			Hittite 1500-1250 (6)		LBI-II 1550-1200 (26)
	LHIIIC 1200-1050 (1)	LMIIIC 1200-1050 (1)		LCIIIA-LCIIIB 1200-1050 (11)	Iron Age I (3)
1000 B.C.	Iron Age (3)	Iron Age (1)	Iron Age (3)	Iron Age CGI-III c.1050-750 (7)	Iron Age IIA-C (1)
500 B C. Key: (N) = No of icons				CAI-III c750-480 (10)	

Egypt	Syria	Diyala	N.Mesopotamia	S.Mesopotamia	Iran	Dilmun
	Prehistoric (1)		Ubaid	Ubaid	5th millennium (1)	Ubaid influence
Naqada I 4000-3500 (1)		4th millennium (6)	Tepe Gawra 4000-3500 BC (1)	Uruk I-II 4000-3500 BC	Susa I 4000-3000 BC (5)	Uruk influence
Naqada II	Protohistoric (1)		Uruk	Uruk III-IV Jemdet Nasr 3500-2900 BC (6)	Proto-Elamite 3400-2600 Susa II Silak III-IV Hissar I-II 3400-2600 BC (13)	
Naqada III						
Early Dynastic		Scarlet Ware EDI (1)	Ninevite 5	Early Dynastic 2900-2334 BC (6)		
	Early Dynastic (2)					
Old Kingdom 2681-2125 (2)	Early Syrian Akkadian (3)			Akkadian Ur III 2334-2000 BC (9)	Old Elamite 2600-1500 BC (9)	
FIP						
Middle Kingdom 2055-1650	Old Syrian (3)		Old Assyrian (2)	Isin-Larsa Old Babylonian 2000-1595 BC (2)		Early Dilmun 2000-1800 BC (22)
	Alalakh VI-V (1)					
SIP			Mittanian (1)			
New Kingdom 1550-1069 (21)	Ugarit R1-R2 Alalakh IV (29)	Mittanian (32)		Kassite 1590-1150 BC (12)	Middle Elamite 1500-1000 BC (22)	
			Middle Assyrian (19)			
TIP 21st-25th dynasties				Late Babylonian (2)		
			Neo-Assyrian (1)		Neo-Elamite 1000-550 (6)	
Late period			Achaemenid	Neo-Babylonian	Achaemenid (1)	

One is transmission through time, related to the phenomenon of continuity and long-term variation. Evolutionary theory and a system of cultural inheritance have been used to explain such modes of transmission (e.g. Boyd and Richardson 1985; Cavalli-Sforza and Feldman 1981). The continuity of the icon over several millennia in Iran can be explained within a framework of an inherited culture. Knowledge of its symbolism, embedded in religion, mythology and a mountainous environment, may have been transmitted from generation to generation, in a way that mimics biological inheritance (Shennan 1996: 286). Even after the knowledge became irrelevant to the society over time, memory and tradition could have maintained its symbolic value. This icon, along with other meaningful symbols, may have been transmitted as part of a mountain culture, sometimes called the Zagros Culture, which linked the peoples from Susa across the Diyala region and into Syria from at least the fourth through to end of the second millennium BC (Amiet 1986: 262-3; Stein 2001: 168).

The other trajectory is transmission and transformation of ideas through space by mechanisms that include trade and exchange, migration, invasion, enculturation, peer polity interaction etc. (Clarke 2005b: 137). The spatial transmission of the icon can best be illustrated by its distribution in the LBA when it reached the height of its popularity and its widest circulation. It was distributed throughout the Near East and the Eastern Mediterranean from Elam in the east through Babylonia, Assyria and to Palestine, Cyprus and Egypt and west to mainland Greece.

Of course, transmission of ideas can happen in both time and space but usually archaeological studies give precedence to only one of these trajectories. The goat-and-tree icon is an example *par excellence* of the transfer of iconography through both time and space. There was a general trend for early and continuous use of the icon in the east, a surge in all areas in the LBA with a shift to the west in the IA.

It is hard to believe that one intrinsic symbolic meaning of the icon was transmitted across such deep temporal and wide spatial divides. Since there were local changes of the composition of the icon to suit regional needs, it seems reasonable to suppose that meanings were adapted too. Questions of reception, choices and transformations made by the importing cultures also need a theoretical framework of consideration. If we accept that trade was a major route of transmission, then it is appropriate to apply economic theory to explain transformations of meaning. I have used Sherratt's model of the nature of Bronze Age exchange values which used the concepts of *prime value* and *added value* commodities (Sherratt and Sherratt 1991: 354-62) and was later refined to identify four dimensions of exchange value with prime value being divided into *convertible value* and *preciosity* while *added value* was assigned a subdivision of *cultural value* (Sherratt 1994: 62-3).

Convertible value goods such as precious and base metals can be used, stored, re-cycled and re-circulated. *Preciosity* refers to the value of goods that derives from their status as rare or exotic. Examples of these could be ivory or lapis lazuli. *Added* value is that conferred by craft or the manufacturing. It can be added to materials with prime value to enhance their worth e.g. a seal made of a semi-precious stone or repoussé gold work. Alternatively, workmanship can be used to enhance materials with little intrinsic value. Examples would be decorated ceramics or perfumed oil, used to create lifestyles or sets of values. *Cultural* value refers to the recognised social or ideological significance of a commodity such as a cult object. Iconography belongs to this type value. *Cultural* value can likewise be added to items which have *convertible, preciosity* or negligible value. It is the different combinations that distinguish the cultural reception of imported iconography.

During Bronze Age trade and exchange, it was in the economic interests of the elites to retain control over the all *prime* value goods. *Added* value commodities often carried the prestige of foreign and exotic lifestyles and meanings. Access to or understanding of the symbolic meanings of imported iconography similarly conferred or confirmed high status, so it was also preferable though more difficult, to restrict the flow of such *cultural* value goods, particularly if they were not attached to goods of high convertible or preciosity value. When access was not restricted or if it was subverted, the transmission of ideas filtered down to sub-elites via *added* and *cultural* value commodities.

THE ICON IN CYPRUS AND OTHER REGIONS OF THE EASTERN MEDITERRANEAN IN THE LBA

Widespread adoption of the icon in the LBA can easily be accounted for by the increase in trading networks and the improved efficiency of long-distance sea routes. This icon, like other images, had become part of an *international repertoire* of motifs (Crowley 1989: 245-66), and indeed the transmission rates to most regions were similar[2] (Table 2).

Cyprus was the highest consumer of this icon. Most of them appeared on luxury items, including imports, displaying fine artistry and workmanship. Where there was a provenance, they were frequently found in richly furnished tombs at major sites such as Enkomi. These were mainly *convertible* and *preciosity* value commodeties with high-level *added* value in terms of workmanship.

A gold signet ring from British Tomb 93 at Enkomi (LCIIA-LCIIC) has an engraved bezel depicting two

---

[2] The above average number of icons in the Diyala region is due to the discovery of Nuzi archive of sealings with a total of one thousand different glyptic designs (Stein 1993). This may have introduced an excavation bias to the results.

Table 2 – The Regional Frequency of the Icon in the LBA

Region	Number	Percentage
Anatolia	6	3%
Crete	6	2%
Cyprus	40	18%
Diyala	32	14%
Egypt	20	9%
Greece	21	9%
Iran	23	10%
North Mesopotamia	20	9%
South Mesopotamia	12	5%
Palestine	22	10%
Syria	28	12%

Fig. 8 – Gold mouthpiece from Klavdhia, 8a
with drawing of detail, 8b
(Courtesy of the British Museum, photo by author)

couchant goats, with attendant birds either side of a palm tree (Kenna 1971, no. 49, pl. XII). This icon is very similar to that punched on a gold foil 'mouthpiece' found in the same tomb (Fig. 7), except that the pose of the goats is *statant* rather than *couchant* (Goring 1983, no. 192). In contrast, the 'mouthpiece' from Klavdhia *Tremithos* (Malmgren 2003, 51, pl. 31) shows running goats, which atypically are heading in opposite directions (Fig. 8). The central 'tree' is Egyptianising in the form of a lotus. Two other examples of the lotus flower form can be seen in the icons represented on two blue faience vases from Kition *Bamboula* of unknown context. The iconography of one of these vases has been discussed by Caubet (1986); the other appears to be unpublished.

Fig. 7 – Gold mouthpiece from Enkomi Tomb 93
(Courtesy of the British Museum, photo by author)

A further notable example of a luxury item carrying this motif was a rectangular ivory gaming box from Enkomi. It is exquisitely carved on the two long sides with elaborate hunting scenes, but one of the short ends is decorated with two standing goats, either side of a rather scrubby little tree (Kepinski 1982, no. 808). Perhaps it has already been stripped of its leaves by the feeding animals.

Amongst the artefacts depicting the goat-and-tree icon, cylinder seals represented the highest proportion (61%). Many of these were finely cut cylinders of haematite, steatite, serpentine marble or other semi-precious stone. Cyprus did not have a seal-cutting tradition and workman-

ship and design of the cylinders can be traced to their Syrian origins (Porada 1948: 196). Nevertheless, by the early 14th century BC, Cypriot seal cutters had developed their own distinctive versions which have become known as the Elaborate Style (see example in Fig. 5). One exquisite cylinder from Sinda (Fig. 4) departs quite significantly from the canonical form. Instead of the rather crowded composition of the Elaborate Style, the slender, delicate forms of the goats and birds are rendered with symmetry and space.

It is instructive to compare the materials and media of the Cypriot icons from those of the neighbouring regions. In Egypt, the icons are again found on high status objects. Most of the items can be dated to the 18th dynasty. Two painted wooden caskets with triangular lids are interesting. Similar in construction and decoration, both were inscribed with the name of a Theban official, Perpuat (Killen 1994: 38-42, pls 29, 32, 39). On both caskets, the gable ends depict rearing animals seemingly nibbling at a stylised tree. One of the boxes has a variant of the icon which includes suckling young (Killen 1994: pl. 39). A silver jug from Bubastis has an impressed decoration on the neck and amongst the figured work is the wild goat-and-tree icon. But perhaps most spectacularly, a *rampant* three-dimensional goat forms a very substantial handle (Crowley 1989: 497). Other luxury materials include ivory inlays and faience.

The high status of the icon reached pharaonic level. A gold engraved basket was found in the tomb of Rameses III (Fig. 3). A stele fragment from the tomb of Amenhotep III is carved with *rampant* goats feeding at a lotus-style tree icon (Kepinski 1982, no. 936). This motif appears to have been a favourite with Tutankhamun since at least three luxury items with the icon were found in his tomb.

A chair made of ebony with ivory inlays has an icon which is split across the two gilded side panels. The outside panels have antithetical *couchant* ibexes, while the inside panels form the stylised tree (Carter 1922-33, I: 114 pl. LIX). A wooden bow inlaid gold also shows the wild goat icon (Carter 1922-33, I: 114). But perhaps the most remarkable is the icon found within the scene decorating a gold panel from his chariot. The icon appears as a tattoo on the arm of a Nubian prisoner as well as an embroidered pattern on his loin cloth (Kepinski 1982, nos. 941-3).

The vast majority of these Egyptian icons were thus on *convertible* or *preciosity* value goods with high *added value* from their workmanship. The *cultural* value of the icons had therefore been perceived as very high and access would appear to have been highly restricted to elite consumption. This concurs with the tight, state control of international trade and access to foreign exotica in 18th Dynasty Egypt.

Fig. 9 – Drawing of the impression of a Mitannian style faience cylinder seal with green glaze from Beth Shan (after Parker 1949, no. 52)

In complete contrast, in Palestine, there were few high value goods carrying the icon. Around half the icons were on Common Style glyptic (Parker 1949). The style was cursory and the designs all very similar. They featured two stylised horned animals whose heads and body parts were executed using a simple drilling technique. Sometimes the goats were not even antithetically placed around the tree, but faced in the same direction (Fig. 9). Likewise, the central tree consisted of a simple trunk with five or seven branches ending in globular foliage again produced by a simple drill. The quality of material was also low, usually glazed faience, or blue frit, made perhaps to resemble lapis lazuli. These items had no *prime* value and little *added* value in terms of workmanship. It would seem that the prestige of these items lay entirely in their *cultural* value, which had filtered down to a growing "sub-elite" population eager to break into the prestigious international club. Archaeological evidence indicates that

Mitannian Common style cylinder seals with this icon were mass-produced in Beth Shan workshops (Collon 1987: 62). They represented *import substitution* of more prestigious seals. Ownership of an imitation lapis lazuli seal seemed to have an important social meaning for sub-elite populations. The Beth Shan workshops started to export these seals to other 'sub-elite' markets including Megiddo, Lachish, Tell Far'ah and Tell Tanach and even back to Mitannian areas such as Alalakh, Tell al Rimah and Ugarit.

The palm-and-ibex icon was not limited to cylinder seals in Palestine. It was also a highly characteristic decoration on Bichrome ware from around Megiddo and Lachish in Late Bronze Age I-II. Like the cylinder seals, the ceramics did not have an inherent value. Instead, they seemed to possess a perceived *cultural* value related to their imported iconography. This is further suggested by the ceramic forms, mainly large drinking or pouring vessels such as kraters, jugs and goblets in Bichrome style (Amiran 1969, 161-5), recognised as social markers in the LBA. However, the figurative work of the painted pottery is individualistic and the forms are lively with real movement, as in Figure 2, in contrast to the more static, stylised glyptic.

With the two extremes of the transmission and transformation of the social meanings of the icons in the close neighbours of Cyprus, how is it possible to account for the exceptionally high popularity of the icon in Cyprus? Whereas Egypt had a long history of state-controlled international trade, Cyprus only became fully integrated into the maritime trade of the Eastern Mediterranean in the 14th and 13th centuries B.C., with the development of its copper export trade. Although Enkomi was an important centre for the copper industry, there is no evidence that trade was centrally controlled from there. Indeed, it seems probable that international trade was decentralised (Keswani 1996) with centres such as Maroni *Vournes* and Kalavassos *Ayios Dhimitrios* participating in trade. Luxury commodities became part of a cultural repertoire that created elite identities (Keswani 2004: 142-4) at these other centres. It was in the interests of newly emerging elites to restrict access to expensive and high prestige goods with exotic iconography. Hence, the wild goat-and-tree icon retained its high *cultural* value on a wide variety of *prime* value and *added value* goods.

I think that the decentralisation of trade may also have been key to the popularity of this foreign icon and the concept of eclecticism often levelled at LBA Cyprus. Despite this icon being part of an international repertoire, examination of the Cypriot icons reveals wide-ranging foreign influences. This may reflect the number of different coastal centres interacting with different foreign ports of trade.

Some Syrian influence was almost certain. This iconography has a long history in this area, and the Mitannian cylinders seem to have been a particular source of inspiration for Cypriot Elaborate Style seals, not that Cyprus was ever a mere passive recipient of ideas. The Cypriot cylinders were transformed to meet Cypriot needs and new features were introduced such as different tree styles (Fig. 5). One charming example illustrates Cypriot wit in adapting the icon with local themes. The all important copper ingots have been substituted for the goats and take pride of place either side of the 'sacred tree' (Fig. 10). Birds were a favourite addition in Cyprus (Fig. 4).

Fig. 10 – Impression of a cylinder seal from Cyprus (after Ohnefalsch-Richter 1893, pl. XXVII, no. 16)

Egypt, too, seems to have influenced the iconography, both in terms of imports and imitations. The two unprovenanced faience vases found in Kition were surely imported from Egypt. Not only was faience a typically Egyptian material, but the icons had lotus flowers and papyrus clumps as tree substitutes. The Klavdhia diadem (Figure 8), on the other hand, probably represents an influence rather than an import. Even though the lotus has been substituted for the tree, this type of gold work was very common on Cyprus (Goring 1983) and the diadem was clearly manufactured there.

Given the differences in consumption of the iconography and noting the disparity in styles, I would have to disagree with both Lubsen-Admiral (1998: 41) and Steel (1997: 40) that the iconographic transfer was from Palestine to Cyprus. To me, it is just not conceivable that the crudely carved cylinders were the inspiration for the fine artistry and high value of the Cypriot pieces. Neither is it probable that sub-elite *cultural* values of their near neighbours would have been adopted by the newly emerging elites of Cyprus.

Aegean involvement in the transmission of the icon is complex. The apparent rejection of the icon by LBA Crete could, I believe, be due to the fact that the wild goat already had a symbolic meaning in Minoan art, related to cultic activity and to hunting. Consequently, imported wild goat-and-tree imagery would have competed with, or subverted, entrenched meanings. The mainland attitude to the icon was different, and Mycenaean imagery incorporated this international icon. Whether Cyprus influenced Greece or *vice versa* is more difficult to disentangle.

Cyprus had imported quantities of Mycenaean pottery from the mainland (Wijngaarten 2002: 126), starting as early as LCI (*c.* 1550-1450 BC) and continuing throughout the LCII period (*c.* 1450-1200 BC). In the latter part of this time period, Cypriot potters were producing local imitations which have been labelled Pastoral Style or Rude Style. Pictorial kraters were particularly prestigious and frequently deposited in elite burials. Kraters depicting chariots were popular on Cyprus and appear to have been produced to meet a market niche amongst the Cypriot elite. The goat-and-tree icon, however, was not a common motif for this type of ware, so the unusual Mycenaean krater found in a Maroni tomb (Vermeule and Karageorghis 1982, pl. III.26) poses questions. Did this decoration (Fig. 11) represent a response to a Cypriot preference for the icon, as with other high *cultural* value icons, such as chariots? Or was it used for export because it was an international image? Did the Mycenaean use of the icon inspire the Cypriots to use it on local copies such as the Early Pastoral Style krater from Kazaphani (Fig. 12; Vermeule and Karageorghis 1982, pl. VI.6)?

Fig. 11 – Drawing of detail on Mycenaean krater found in a Maroni tomb (after Vermeule and Karageorghis 1982, pl. III.26)

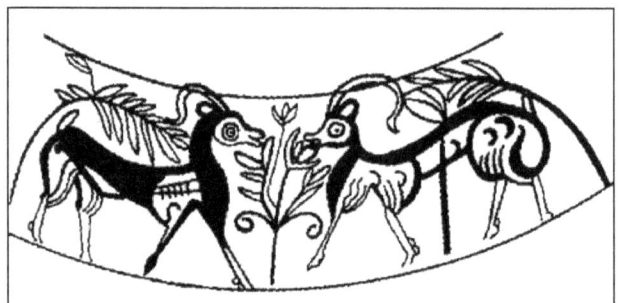

Fig. 12 – Drawing of detail on an Early Pastoral Style krater from Kazaphani (after Vermeule and Karageorghis 1982, pl. VI.9)

To conclude, I think that the seeming eclecticism in the attitudes of Cypriots to the icon reflected the major changes that occurred not only in long-distance trade of the LBA but also in urbanisation and social structure. The decentralisation of long-distance trade to a series of coastal urban centres was the type of trade that Keswani points out was responsible for the development of local hierarchy since it encouraged elites to 'secure their own exclusive supply of exotic prestige goods that were essential to maintenance of status and authority' (Keswani 2004: 154-5).

THE ICON IN THE IRON AGE

During the IA the icon was still a popular motif although only in a few regions. In Iran, it was northern areas such as Hasanlu, Ziwiye, Sialk and Luristan, that perpetuated its use during the Neo-Elamite period (c. 1000-640 B.C.) on some beautifully crafted luxury items such as a gold pectoral, a blue faience vessel and an ivory plaque as well as some of the famous 'Luristan bronzes' (Porada 1965, pls 33, 37, 72; Porada 1985, pl. 13). There were also some amazing three-dimensional icons in precious metals during the Achaemenid period (Porada 1965, pl. 50), although by this time the ibexes had often acquired wings. In other parts of the Near East, the icon was transformed, and whilst Neo-Assyrian and Neo-Babylonian seal iconography retained highly stylised sacred trees, the goats had often been replaced, either with richly dressed people or by mythological creatures such as genii or griffins (Collon 1987: 75-89). It is noteworthy that none of the Nimrud ivories, taken from Syrian areas, carries the icon, even though they were well represented by other symmetrical motifs.

In IA Cyprus, wild goat-and-tree icons were revitalised, appearing in new styles on ceramics. One fine example is a footed bowl of White Painted Ware from Palaepaphos *Xylinos* (Karageorghis 1997, pl. XX). The icon which almost fills one side of the bowl, depicts silhouetted animals, with exaggerated horns, feeding on a palm tree. Another is a lentoid flask in Bichrome I. The lively, running goats accompanied by birds are arranged around the circumference of the body (Karageorghis 2000, 78-9).

By the Cypro-Archaic era the icon has been rendered in a highly stylised form on Bichrome IV ceramics (Karageorghis 1974, pls XVII.19, XVII.21, XVII.34), such as the rosette-patterned, rather stout goats, nibbling at an elaborate lotus shown in Figure 13. The icon also reappeared on seals, this time as stamp seals (e.g. Reyes 2001, figs. 220, 228).

The survival of the motif in the IA Aegean is less evident. Certainly the number of prototypical icons found there is low. It may have been transformed into the 'Bird-and-palm' motif which became popular in the IA Aegean, particularly on Rhodes (Steel 1997: 45). They may, however, have retained the old goat-and-tree icon for manufacturing special export versions of the vases as on a very impressive Geometric krater, around 115 cm tall, exported to Cyprus in the 8th century BC from Euboia (Fig. 14). It is known that Cyprus forged strong links with Crete, Rhodes, Attica and Euboia from the 11th century onwards (Sherratt 1994: 24). The question is therefore whether these icons were survivals from the LBA dissemi-

Fig. 13 – Drawing of detail on Bichrome IV jug (after Ohnefalsch-Richter 1893, pl. XIX)

Fig. 14 – Drawing of Geometric krater, probably from Euboia, found on Cyprus (after Cesnola 1877, pl. XXIX)

nating from the Argolid to Euboia and the islands (including a previously resistant Crete), or whether they were IA re-introductions from Cyprus.

This leads to the vexed questions of what happened to the icon during the transitional phase between the LBA and EIA (c. 1200-1000 BC), when it almost disappeared from view. Only in Cyprus, did it seem to have survived the transition. The icons on two bronze tripods come from this era (Catling 1964, pl. 27e, pl. 29c-e). I believe that the icon also survived in the 11th century BC pictorial pottery where elements of the icon such as wild goats, trees and stylised hills can be traced in the newly developed silhouette style (Iacovou 1988, figs. 2, 36, 68, 72-3). An example is shown in Figure 6. This *pars pro toto* or elemental icon was perhaps an example of temporal transmission through memory and tradition. It seems possible that Cyprus kept the memory of this icon alive to burgeon again in the IA proper.

There is however some debate over evidence relating to pottery painting style which has implications for the icon during this transitional period. This debate relates to an assumption that Mycenaean LHIIIC or Sub-Minoan (LMIIIC) pottery influenced the Cypriot Silhouette Style of Proto White Painted Ware. If so, then by implication, an early Protogeometric bell krater (Fig. 15) or a LHIIIC Dodecanese vase (Fig. 16) which carried the wild goat-and-tree icon could have been the source for the re-introduction of the icon in the IA. However, according to Yon (1970: 311-17) and to Iacovou (1997: 66-8), the silhouette style introduced in LCIIIB (c 1125-1050 B.C.), was a Cypriot innovation that did not derive from the Mycenaean pictorial style. In accord with Yon, Iacovou (1997: 68) considered the suggestion of a Cretan/Minoan origin of the animal silhouette to be 'utterly unfounded'. They pointed to stylistic differences. For example, the Aegean depictions of animals have reserve eyes rather than solid silhouettes. Furthermore, it is strongly argued that the Cypriot examples of the silhouette style were earlier than the Aegean goat depictions on pottery (Iacovou 1988: 83-4). In short, a reverse influence could be argued (Iacovou 1988: 83).

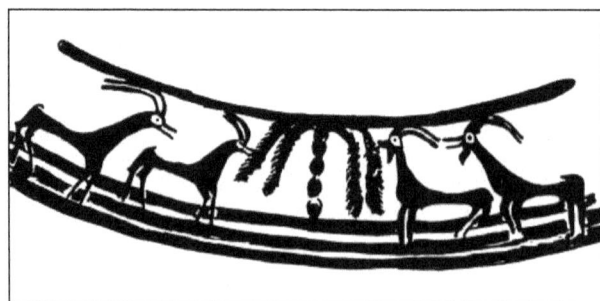

Fig. 16 – Drawing of detail from collared jar from Kalymnos c. 1100-1050 B.C. (after Vermeule and Karageorghis 1982, pl. XII.24)

the source of its re-introduction in the IA. In view of the relative rarity of the icon on the Greek mainland, together with the Euboean origin of the Cypriot vases, I would conjecture that the icon was revitalised on Cyprus in the IA, and re-introduced to the Aegean from there. However, it would have been used relatively little in its prototypical form except for specially commissioned export items, but it was probably transformed into the new bird-and-tree icon which became popular in the Aegean. There is also an intriguing speculation that the motif inspired the 'Wild goat style' or 'Rhodian style' that developed in the Aegean in 7-6th century BC but that must remain the subject for further study.

CONCLUSIONS

The original symbolism of the 'Wild goat-and-tree' imagery, rooted in Iran, may once have had religious or mythological meanings to the Zagros mountain culture of the third millennium BC.[3] By the time it had undergone long-term and widespread transmissions, the meaning of the icon must have been transformed. By the LBA, whatever the symbolic meaning that was ascribed to it by each receptive culture, its social meaning was clear. As one of an international repertoire of artistic motifs, this icon helped to declare the prestige of the owner. Whether this owner was one of really high status such as an Egyptian pharaoh or an aspiring 'sub-elite' varied with the region and the degree to which the icon had been restricted or subverted.

I suspect that its high popularity in LBA Cyprus coincided with a period of rapidly developing urbanisation and increased long-distance trade. It was a time when social hierarchies were being created and the acquisition of exotic foreign goods became an important part of this process. The resulting plethora of foreign influences mixed with local adaptations reflects a relatively new international player developing an iconographic ideology. By the end of the LBA and in the IA, Cyprus became a more confident international player with important roles

Fig. 15 – Drawing of an early Protogeometric bell krater c.1050-970 B.C. from the Fortetsa cemetery near Knossos (after Brock 1957, no. 45)

To the stylistic arguments of Iacovou, I would add some other evidence in favour of a survival and re-introduction of the icon stemming from Cyprus. Firstly, Cyprus utilised the icon more than the Aegean both in the LBA and in the IA. Secondly, even though Crete had three vases with the icon spanning LMIIIA2/LMIIIB to Protogeometric, it seems unlikely that a region which had largely rejected the icon throughout the LBA, would be

---

[3] See Bushnell 2005 for this argument, which space restraints here do not allow me to expand on.

in both metals export and commodity trading. The persistence of the popularity of the icon in the IA underscores Cypriot preferences. It also suggests possible involvement of Cyprus in its transmission west and its transformation to new icons.

Bibliography

Special Abbreviations
EIA Early Iron Age
IA Iron Age
LBA Late Bronze Age

AMIET, P. (1980) *La Glyptique Mésopotamienne Archaïque*. Paris, Éditions du Centre national de la recherché scientifique.

AMIET, P. (1986) Susa and the Dilmun Culture, IN: Al Khalifa, S.H.A., and M. Rice, eds, *Bahrain Through the Ages. The Archaeology*, London, Kegan Paul, 262-8.

AMIRAN, R. (1969) *Ancient Pottery of the Holy Land. From its Beginnings to the End of the Iron Age*. Jerusalem, Massada Press.

BOYD, R. and P.J. RICHERSON, (1985) *Culture and the Evolutionary Process*. Chicago, University of Chicago Press.

BROCK, J.K. (1957) *Fortetsa: Early Greek Tombs near Knossos*. Cambridge, Cambridge University Press.

BUSHNELL, L. (2005) *The Big Picture of a Little Icon. Tracing the Transference and Meaning of the Wild Goat-and-Tree Iconography in Near East and Aegean Art from the Prehistoric to the Iron Age*. Unpublished MA Dissertation, University College London.

CARTER, H. (1922) *The tomb of Tut-Ankh-Amen Discovered by the Late Earl of Carnarvon and Howard Carter. Volume 1*. London, Cassell.

CATLING, H. (1964) *Cypriot Bronzework in the Mycenaean World*. Oxford, Clarendon Press.

CAUBET, A. (1986) La Thème du Lion à Chypre au Bronze Récent: à Propos de Trouvailles de Kition – Bamboula, IN: Karageorghis, V. ed. *Acts of the International Archaeological Symposium 'Cyprus between the Occident and the Orient', Nicosia, 8-14 September 1985*. Nicosia, Department of Antiquities, 300-10.

CAVALLI-SFORZA, L.L. and M.W. FELDMAN, (1981) *Cultural Transmission and Evolution: A Quantitative Approach*. Princeton, Princeton University Press.

CESNOLA, L.P. (1877) *Cyprus: Its Ancient Cities, Tombs, and Temples: A Narrative of Researches and Excavations during Ten Years' Residence as American Consul in that Island*. London, John Murray.

CLARKE, J. (2005a) Transmissions and Transformations in Time and the Phenomenon of Continuity. IN: Clarke, J. ed. *Archaeological Perspectives on the Transmission and Transformation of Culture in the Eastern Mediterranean*. Levant Supplementary Series, Volume 2. Oxford, Oxbow Books, 81-3.

CLARKE, J. (2005b) Crossing Cultural Divides: Transmissions and Transformations in Space. IN: Clarke, J. ed. *Archaeological Perspectives on the Transmission and Transformation of Culture in the Eastern Mediterranean*. Levant Supplementary Series, Volume 2. Oxford, Oxbow Books, 137-9.

COLLON, D. (1987) *First Impressions. Cylinder Seals in the Ancient Near East*. Chicago, University of Chicago Press.

CROWLEY, J. (1989) *The Aegean and the East. An Investigation into the Transference of Artistic Motifs between the Aegean, Egypt, and the Near East in the Bronze Age*. Jonsered, Paul Åströms Förlag.

FRANKFORT, H. (1939) *Cylinder Seals*. London, Macmillan.

GORING, E. (1983) *Late Cypriot Goldwork*. Unpublished PhD thesis, Bedford College, London.

IACOVOU, M. (1988) *The Pictorial Pottery of Eleventh Century B.C. Cyprus*. Studies in Mediterranean Archaeology LXXVIII. Göteborg, Paul Åströms Förlag.

IACOVOU, M. (1997) Images in Silhouette: The Missing Link of the Figurative Representations on the Eleventh Century B.C. Cypriote pottery, IN: Karageorghis, V., R. Laffineur, and F. Vandenabeele, eds, *Four Thousand Years of Images on Cypriote Pottery, Proceedings of the Third International Conference of Cypriote Studies, Nicosia, 3-4 May, 1996*. Brussels, Liège, Nicosia, The A.G. Leventis Foundation, 61-71.

KARAGEORGHIS, V. and J. des GAGNIERS (1974) La Céramique Cypriote de Style Figuré. *Age du Fer (1050-500 av J.C.)*. Rome, Edizioni dell'Ateneo.

KARAGEORGHIS, V. (2000) *Ancient Art from Cyprus. The Cesnola Collection in the Metropolitan Museum*. New York, Metropolitan Museum of Art.

KARAGEORGHIS, V., LAFFINEUR, R. and VANDENABEELE, F. eds (1997) *Four Thousand Years of Images on Cypriote Pottery, Proceedings of the Third International Conference of Cypriote Studies, Nicosia, 3-4 May, 1996*. Nicosia, The Leventis.

KENNA, V.E.G. (1967) The Seal Use of Cyprus in the Bronze Age, II, *Bulletin de Correspondance Hellénique* 91, 552-77.

KENNA, V.E.G. (1971) *Catalogue of the Cypriote seals of the Bronze Age in the British Museum*. Studies in Mediterranaean Archaeology XX:3. Göteborg, Paul Åströms Förlag.

KEPINSKI, C. (1982) *L'Arbre Stylisé en Asia Occidentale 2ᵉ Millénaire avant J.-C*. Paris, Recherche sur les civilizations.

KESWANI, P. (1996) Hierarchies, Heterarchies, and Urbanization Processes: the View from Bronze Age

Cyprus. *Journal of Mediterranean Archaeology* 9, 211-49.

KESWANI, P. (2004) *Mortuary Ritual and Society in Bronze Age Cyprus*. London, Equinox.

KILLEN, G. (1994) *Ancient Egyptian furniture II. Boxes, Chests and Footstools*. Warminster, Aris and Phillips.

LOUD, G. (1948) *Megiddo 2, Seasons of 1935-39 by the Megiddo Expedition*. Chicago, University of Chicago Press.

LUBSEN-ADMIRAL, S.M. (2001) A Proto White Slip Ware jug with ibex heads. IN: Karageorghis, V., E. Czerny and I.A Todd eds, *The White Slip Ware of Late Bronze Age Cyprus: Proceedings of an International Conference in Honour of Malcolm Wiener*. Nicosia, The A.G Leventis Foundation, 43-52.

MALMGREN, K. (2003) *Klavdhia-Tremithos. A Middle and Late Cypriote Bronze Age Site*. Jonsered, Paul Åströms Förlag.

OHNEFALSCH-RICHTER, M. (1893) *Kypros. The Bible and Homer*. London, Asher.

PARKER, B. (1949) Cylinder Seals from Palestine. *Iraq* 11, 1-43.

PORADA, E. (1948) The Cylinder Seals of the Late Cypriote Bronze Age, *American Journal of Archaeology* 52, 178-98.

PORADA, E. (1965) *The art of Ancient Iran. Pre-Islamic cultures*. New York, Crown Publishers.

REYES, A.T. (2001) *The Stamp-Seals of Ancient Cyprus*. Oxford, University of Oxford School of Archaeology.

SHENNAN, S. (1996) Cultural Transmission and Cultural Change. IN: Preucel, R.W. and I. Hodder, eds, *Contemporary Archaeology in Theory*. Malden MA, Blackwell, 282-96.

SHERRATT, A. and SHERRATT, S. (1991) From Luxuries to Commodities: The Nature of the Mediterranean Bronze Age Trading Systems. IN: Gale, N. ed. *Bronze Age Trade in the Mediterranean*, Studies in Mediterranean Archaeology, 90. Göteborg, Paul Åströms Förlag, 351-84.

SHERRATT, S. (1994) Commerce, Iron and Ideology: Metallurgical Innovation in 12th-11th century Cyprus. IN: Karageorghis, V. ed. *Proceedings of the International Symposium. Cyprus in the 11ᵗʰ Century B.C.* Nicosia, The A.G. Leventis Foundation, 59-106.

STEEL, L. (1997) Pictorial White Slip – the Discovery of a New Ceramic Style in Cyprus. IN: Karageorghis, V., R. Laffineur and F. Vandenabeele, eds, *Four Thousand Years of Images on Cypriote Pottery, Proceedings of the Third International Conference of Cypriote Studies, Nicosia, 3-4 May, 1996*. Brussels, Liège, Nicosia, The A.G. Leventis Foundation, 37-47.

STEIN, D. (1993) *Das Archiv des Šilwa-Teššup. Heft 9. The Seal Impressions (Catalogue)*. Wiesbaden, Harrassowitz Verlag.

STEIN, D. (2001) Nuzi Glyptic: the Eastern Connection. IN: Hallo, W.W. and I. J Winter eds, *Seals and Seal Impressions, Proceedings of the XLVᵉ Rencontre Assyriologique Internationale*. Bethesda, CDL Press, 149-83.

van WIJNGAARDEN, G.J. (2002) *Use and Appreciation of Mycenaean Pottery in the Levant, Cyprus and Italy (1600-1200 BC)*. Amsterdam, Amsterdam University Press.

VERMEULE, E. and V. KARAGEORGHIS. (1982) *Mycenaean Pictorial Vase Painting*. Cambridge MA, Harvard University Press.

YON, M. (1970) Sur une Répresentation Figure Chypriote. *Bulletin de Correspondance Hellénique*, 94, 311-17.

REPRESENTATION OF MUSIC IN MEDIEVAL CYPRIOT ICONOGRAPHY: EVIDENCE FROM NATIVITY SCENES*
SAVVAS NEOCLEOUS

Music is a theme of Christian iconography of Medieval Cyprus relatively neglected by scholars. The bulk of the iconographic material survives mainly as church frescoes dating from the early twelfth to the sixteenth century and provides us with a treasury of information about medieval Cypriot musicians and musical instruments. This paper attempts to explore the representation of musical images in surviving iconographic sources of Medieval Cyprus using, as examples, wall paintings of the Nativity of Christ. The selection of the Nativity scenes is justified by the emphasis on musical instruments given there. These instruments are being played by the shepherds of the Nativity.

According to Luke the Evangelist, an angel of the Lord appeared to the shepherds who were near the Nativity Cave keeping guard over their flock and delivered them the good tidings: 'Today, your Saviour is born in the city of David' (Luke 2:11). Generally in Byzantine art, the episode of the annunciation to the shepherds is placed in the upper right half of the Nativity scene (Acheimastou-Potamianou 2001; Vokotopoulos 2001; Leventes 2000). Here, an angel is represented turning to the shepherds to announce to them the glad tidings of Christ's birth. Sometimes only one shepherd is depicted, either with or without an instrument, regularly a *floyéra* (flute) (Anoyanakis 1979: 147-9, 161-3; Liavas 2000: 42-3), an end-blown open-ended tube with six or seven fingerholes. Also quite frequent is the case where two shepherds are

represented, normally none of them holding an instrument. However, the group of the shepherds more usually consists of three men, of whom the attitudes and ages vary. Most often, we see an old man, a middle-aged man and a beardless young man. The latter is generally represented seated with crossed legs and playing an instrument, usually a *floyéra*.

The representation of a shepherd holding a musical instrument – always aerophone – in Byzantine art might be due to a misinterpretation of the word 'αγραυλούντες' which describes the shepherds in St Luke's Gospel (Luke 2:8) and is translated as 'abiding in the field'. The Byzantine painters had mistaken the 'αγραυλούντες' as a synonym of 'αυλούντες', that is translated as playing the classical Greek instrument *aulos* (*avlós*) or an aerophone in general (Argyrou 2001: 218).

THE EVIDENCE

As has been said, the frescoes under examination date from the early twelfth to the sixteenth century. During this period of five centuries within which the paintings were executed, Cyprus had been part of the Byzantine Empire (until 1191), had formed a kingdom under the French Lusignan dynasty (1192-1489), and finally came under the rule of the Most Serene Republic of Venice (1489-1571). Our evidence is arranged in chronological order so as to observe whether there is any alteration over time in the representation of the shepherd-musicians.

The Church of the Panayia at Trikomo (Stylianou and Stylianou 1985: 486-91) retains part of the oldest extant representation of the Nativity in Cyprus, dating from the early twelfth century. Here, the three shepherds of differentiated ages are represented (Fig. 1). The youngest one is fairly richly attired and, seated on a rock, is shown playing his *playíavlos*, an instrument played in the same

* I would like to thank the Holy Archbishopric of Cyprus and the Holy Bishopric of Morphou for the kind permission to publish the photographic material that I use in this paper. I would also like to express my gratitude to the Bank of Cyprus Cultural Foundation for the kind permission to use photographic material from the calendar for 2000 of the Bank of Cyprus Group entitled '*The Birth of Christ*' *The Nativity as depicted in the Byzantine Art of Cyprus* (Figs 1-7 and 10-14). Moreover, my thanks are due to Mr Christos Argyrou for the concession of the photograph of the Nativity of Christ at the Church of *Ayios Herakleidios* at the Monastery of *Ayios Ioannes Lampadistes* in Kalopanayiotes village (Figs 8-9).

Fig. 1 – Detail from the Nativity of the Church of Panayia at Trikomo (Courtesy of the Bank of Cyprus)

manner as the modern transverse flute and which, as it is usually assumed, migrated from India into Byzantium in the tenth century (Anoyanakis 1979: 162; Montagu *et al.*, 2001: 31-5). The second representation of the same instrument in medieval Cypriot mural iconography is found in the Nativity scene at the Church of the Holy Apostles at Perachorio (Stylianou and Stylianou 1985: 422-4). This Nativity, dating between the years 1160 and 1180, is poorly preserved. As Stylianou and Stylianou argue, 'compared with the rest of the paintings, it is rather crude in workmanship and rustic in style, qualities which we often meet in this popular scene in Cyprus, even when the rest of the paintings are of a polished character.' (1985: 422). As in the Nativity at Panayia at Trikomo, in the Nativity at the Holy Apostles the three shepherds of different ages are portrayed. The youngest one is shown seated and playing his *playíavlos*.

It is possible that both the painters of the churches of Panayia at Trikomo and of the Holy Apostles at Perachorio were Constantinopolitan masters (Stylianou and Stylianou 1985: 423, 488) and reproduced a current Byzantine iconographic type. As Stylianou and Stylianou state, 'Cyprus was in direct contact with the artistic developments in Constantinople in the twelfth century, whence masters of outstanding merit were often summoned to decorate its churches.' (1985: 423). However, it is not beyond the bounds of possibility that the *playíavlos* was used in a medieval Cypriot context: it would have made perfect sense to include, in a biblical scene – especially in the 'popular scene' of the Nativity, an instrument which in local terms appeared realistic.

The Church of Panayia tou Arakos at Lagoudera in Pitsilia (Stylianou and Stylianou 1985: 157-85; Winfield and Winfield 2003) is decorated with excellent wall paintings dating from 1192, a year after Cyprus passed from Byzantine into Western hands. As Stylianou and Stylianou argue, the frescoes in the Church of Panayia tou Arakos 'represent the metropolitan, classicising school in its full bloom in style, iconography and technique, and

they stand on the border-line as the climax of Byzantine art of the Comnenian period.' (1985: 158). On the right of the Nativity scene, the shepherds are represented receiving the glad tidings from the angel (Fig. 2): *Μή φοβείσθε, ιδού γαρ ευαγγελίζομαι υμίν χαράν μεγάλην ήτις έσται παντί τω λαώ* ('Do not be afraid! For, behold, I bring you tidings of great joy, which shall be to all the people' (Luke 2:10)). In this case, as in the churches of Panayia at Trikomo and Holy Apostles at Perachorio, all three shepherds are depicted. The youngest one is handsomely garbed and is shown at some distance from the other two. He is isolated at the top right-hand corner having just stopped playing his musical instrument, a *floyéra*, and having turned his face to the angel (Fig. 3).

Fig. 2 – Detail from the Nativity of the Church of Panayia tou Arakos (Courtesy of the Bank of Cyprus)

The Church of Ayios Nikolaos tes Steges (Stylianou and Stylianou 1985: 53-75), situated in close proximity to Kakopetria village, has preserved wall paintings that date from various periods, from the eleventh to the seventeenth centuries. The depiction of the Nativity dates from the mid-fourteenth century (Fig. 4). The Virgin is represented seated, with a suckling newborn Christ, whom she holds in her arms. This iconographical detail is indeed very rare in Byzantine art and its prototypes lie in the East (Stylianou and Stylianou 1985: 68-71). The example of this position in the Church of Ayios Nikolaos tes Steges is the only one known in the medieval iconography of Cyprus. However, the uniqueness of the depiction of the Nativity in Ayios Nikolaos tes Steges is due not only to the posture of the Virgin: this fresco, painted around one and a half centuries after Cyprus ceased to form part of

Fig. 3 – Detail from the Nativity of the Church of Panayia tou Arakos (Courtesy of the Bank of Cyprus)

happening around them. Moreover, they appear to wear fourteenth-century-style hats, with turned up brims coming to a point in the front (Norris 1999: fig. 377), although in mainstream Byzantine art the Nativity shepherds are usually depicted bareheaded (Vokotopoulos 2001: 15). Therefore, it may be suggested that they could be seen not as Nativity shepherds but rather as two Cypriot musicians of the mid-fourteenth century who create in the scene of the Nativity an atmosphere redolent of the musical sounds of medieval Cyprus.

The first of the musicians (Fig. 5), seated on rocks, plays his instrument, perhaps a *floyéra* or a *zournás* (shawm) (Baines and Kirnbauer 2001; Anoyanakis 1979: 163-8; Liavas 2000: 50-1). The *zournás* is an oboe-type instrument, i.e. with a double reed, and has seven fingerholes and one thumbhole. It reached Byzantium from the Islamic East during the eleventh and twelfth centuries, and its earliest representation, occurring in a Nativity scene in Sakli Kilise in Cappadocia, dates from the mid-eleventh century (Argyrou 2001: 219 n. 15; Maguire 1981: fig. 63). The high-pitched and penetrating sound of the *zournás* made it suitable for use outdoors.

Fig. 4 – The Nativity of the Church of Ayios Nikolaos tes Steges (Courtesy of the Bank of Cyprus)

Fig. 5 – Detail from the Nativity of the Church of Ayios Nikolaos tes Steges (Courtesy of the Bank of Cyprus)

the Byzantine Empire, does not conform iconographically to any of the 'classic' Byzantine treatments of the shepherds.

The two young musicians portrayed in the Nativity at Ayios Nikolaos tes Steges can hardly be seen as the Nativity shepherds. None of them seem to participate in the Nativity episode. No angel addresses either of the two. Both give all their attention to the playing of their instruments and do not seem to be distracted by what is

The second shepherd-musician (Fig. 6), seated next to a cistern, plays his *tsamboúna*, a type of bagpipe (*áskavlos*) (Anoyanakis 1979: 168, 177, 179-84, 200-1; Liavas 2000: 46-9; Cocks *et al.*, 2001). The representation of a shepherd playing a bagpipe in the Nativity scene is very rare in Byzantine iconography (Stylianou and Stylianou 1985: 71; Argyrou and Myriantheus 2004: 24). As Argyrou points out, the bagpipe of the Nativity at Ayios Nikolaos tes Steges constitutes the earliest known example in the monumental painting of the Byzantine world (Argyrou 2001: 221; Argyrou and Myriantheus 2004: 24). The bagpipe, an instrument which traces its origins back to the most ancient civilizations, reached Greece from Asia, approximately during the first or second century A.D. The *tsamboúna* consists of the bag (*aski*), made from the skin of a goat or kid, the mouthpiece, made from cane, wood or bone, and the part that produces the sound, made from a grooved wooden base to which two wooden cane pipes are attached with wax.

Fig. 6 – Detail from the Nativity of the Church of Ayios Nikolaos tes Steges (Courtesy of Bank of Cyprus)

As regards the representation of bagpipers in medieval Cypriot Nativity scenes, Argyrou asserts that it is an element introduced from the Western iconography (Argyrou 2001: 221-2, 228; Argyrou and Myriantheus 2004: 24). In Western art a shepherd-bagpiper frequently appears amongst the shepherds in the scene of the Annunciation to the Shepherds – not in the Nativity scene, as Argyrou argues – since the thirteenth century (Argyrou 2001: 221; Wieck 1988: 61, 64). It is worth mentioning here that, unlike Byzantine iconography, Western iconography treats the Nativity and the Annunciation to the Shepherds as two separate iconographic subjects (Wieck 1988: 60-1, pls 3-4, pls 20-1, figs 36-7; Harthan 1977: 28, 54, 87, 95, 130). However, there is a strong possibility that the bagpipe was used in a medieval Cypriot context instead of being merely an alien instrument reproduced from the Western iconography. Additionally, as has been already suggested, the bagpiper at Ayios Nikolaos tes Steges, not appearing to participate in any way in the Nativity episode, challenges us to see him independently from the whole scene, perceiving him as a musician of the surrounding Cypriot environment.

The Church of Panayia tes Asinou (Stylianou and Stylianou 1985: 114-40), situated close to Niketari village, is decorated with wall paintings dating from various periods. The Nativity scene at the church dates

from the third quarter of the fourteenth century. The shepherd (Fig. 7) is represented playing his musical instrument, maybe a *zournás* or a *floyéra*. He is dressed in clothing of the fourteenth-century. His body garment is a tunic having full, tight sleeves finishing in a band at the wrist. The tunic, reaching to about the knees, is gathered at the waist by a belt or cord (Norris 1999: 260-2). The shepherd's hat, with the brim turned up at the back and coming to a point in the front, is characteristic of the contemporary fashion (Norris 1999: fig. 377; Gies and Gies 2005: 127), while the rolled ends of the shepherd's hair is a fashion worn during the period (Norris 1999: 267, fig. 298f). Next to the shepherd, propped up against the rocks, is his crook on which his hand-woven bag is hung. The garment, the hat, and the style of hair of the shepherd-musician suggest that the model behind him may well have been again an amateur or a professional musician of the medieval Cypriot surroundings.

Fig. 7 – Detail from the Nativity of the Church of Panayia tes Asinou (Courtesy of Bank of Cyprus)

The Church of Ayios Herakleidios (Stylianou and Stylianou 1985: 292-305) at the Monastery of Ayios Ioannes Lampadistes in Kalopanayiotes village dates from the eleventh century. The church has preserved two series of wall paintings. According to Stylianou and Stylianou, the latest of the two series dates to *c*. 1400 and 'constitutes an interesting ensemble of late Byzantine paintings of an individual character in some respects, with no parallel in the island' (1985: 298). The same scholars state that they 'have not been able to trace a parallel in monumental painting outside the island either' (Stylianou and Stylianou 1985: 298). This series of paintings includes the representation of the Nativity (Fig. 8). The Nativity shepherd (Fig. 9), being isolated at the bottom right-hand corner, does not seem to partake at all in the Nativity episode. As in the case of the two shepherd-musicians at the Church of Ayios Nikolaos tes Steges, no angel announces the birth of the Saviour to him. Seated cross-legged and surrounded by his sheep, he carries on playing his musical instrument, a *zournás*, ignoring what is happening around him. The shepherd-musician is shown in a contemporary hose with foot part combined, and a tunic reaching to about the knees and having short-armed sleeves that made it suitable for the sunny climate of Cyprus. He also wears a hat with a wide brim that protects his head from the sun (Norris 1999: 261, 426). In his isolation, the young man of this Cypriot Nativity scene 'of an individual character' invites us to view him individually as the full-length portrait of a musician of late-fourteenth/early-fifteenth century Cyprus, rather than a Nativity shepherd.

Fig. 9 – Detail from the Nativity of the Church of Ayios Herakleidios at the Monastery of Ayios Ioannes Lampadistes (Courtesy of Mr Christos Argyrou)

Fig. 8 – The Nativity of the Church of Ayios Herakleidios at the Monastery of Ayios Ioannes Lampadistes (Courtesy of Mr Christos Argyrou)

Fig. 10 – Detail from the Nativity of the Church of the Archangel Michael at Pedoulas (Courtesy of the Bank of Cyprus)

The Church of the Archangel Michael at Pedoulas (Stylianou and Stylianou 1985: 331-43) is decorated with wall paintings by the local artist Minas, dating from 1474. The Nativity, 'the most rustic of all the New Testament cycles' in the same church according to Stylianou and Stylianou (1985: 334), does not follow iconographically the standard Byzantine treatments of the Nativity shepherds. Here, as in the Church of Ayios Nikolaos tes Steges, two young shepherds are represented (Fig. 10). Each of them holds an instrument, intended to be either a *floyéra* or most probably a *pithkiávli* (Anoyanakis 1979: 149-52; Liavas 2000: 44-5), a Cypriot member of the class of ducted flutes, i.e. flutes with a whistle mouthpiece. The *pithkiávli* has six frontal fingerholes, or six frontal fingerholes and one rear thumbhole, and is usually made from cane. It is still played in Cyprus, though ever more rarely.

The first shepherd of the Nativity at the Archangel Michael at Pedoulas has just stopped playing his musical instrument and is receiving the good tidings from the angel sent by God. He holds his musical instrument with his right hand and with his left a crook, almost identical to that which occurs in the Nativity at the Church of Panayia tes Asinou. At some distance, the second shepherd holds his instrument with his left hand while he feeds a black goat with his right; totally absorbed in his daily tasks, he appears to ignore the celestial message. One could assume, based on the unconventional manner of representing the two shepherds, that the painter was inspired by contemporary Cypriot reality. Dressed in contemporary tunics with tight sleeves, hoses with foot parts combined (Norris 1999: 261, 425-6, fig. 377), and wearing hats, presumably of the contemporary fashion (I have not been able to trace identical or similar hats in other paintings in or outside Cyprus), the two young men portrayed in the Nativity at the Archangel Michael at Pedoulas could be understood as a reference to the amateur musicians of fifteenth-century Cyprus.

The Church of the Holy Cross of Ayiasmate (Stylianou and Stylianou 1985: 186-218) is situated close to Platanistasa village in the Pitsilia area, and is decorated with wall paintings by the fifteenth-century artist Philip Goul. Inscriptions over the south and the north doors record that the church was erected and its walls painted in 1494. The Nativity scene (Fig. 11) is considered one of the rare examples representing the Magi twice: once as they ascend the rugged landscape by horseback and once as they offer their gifts to the newborn Christ. The scene, however, seems to be unique for another reason: the representation of the shepherds. Four shepherds are represented in a way that boldly breaks with the Byzantine tradition. The three of them in their working clothes obviously do not participate in the episode of the Nativity: one is represented high up on the rocks ready to catch an unruly sheep with his crook. The other two are shown at the bottom right-hand corner milking their sheep. The classical Byzantine representation of the Nativity shepherds seems to have been adapted to the local environment. The artist, inspired by contemporary Cypriot living habits, enhanced the Nativity depiction with two bucolic scenes which, in local terms, appeared realistic.

The fourth shepherd (Fig. 12), an old man seated cross-legged, has stopped playing his *tsamboúna*, and turns his head to listen to the angel announcing the birth of Christ. Despite the fact that he is iconographically closer than the other three shepherds to Byzantine tradition, his musical instrument is not the conventional *floyéra*. It is a *tsamboúna*, an instrument that has already been seen in the Nativity scene of the Church of Ayios Nikolaos tes Steges. According to Argyrou, the *tsamboúna* represented

Fig. 11 – The Nativity of the Church of the Holy Cross of Ayiasmate (Courtesy of the Bank of Cyprus)

Fig. 12 – Detail from the Nativity of the Church of the Holy Cross of Ayiasmate (Courtesy of the Bank of Cyprus)

in the Nativity scene of the Holy Cross of Ayiasmate constitutes the second earliest known example in monumental art of the Byzantine world (Argyrou 2001: 221; Argyrou and Myriantheus 2004: 24). As has been mentioned, the earliest one is that in Ayios Nikolaos tes Steges. Although Argyrou asserts that the depiction of bagpipers in Cypriot Nativity scenes is a Western influence, we have argued that the possibility that the bagpipe was used in a medieval Cypriot context should not be ruled out. As regards specifically the Church of the Holy Cross of Ayiasmate, since the painter Philip Goul – inspired by the contemporary reality – enhanced the popular Nativity scene with two bucolic scenes, it would have been only too logical to also insert an instrument which in local terms seemed realistic.

82

The Church of the Transfiguration of the Saviour at Palaichori (Stylianou and Stylianou 1985: 256-86) is an early sixteenth-century chapel that has preserved one of the most complete series of wall-paintings of the period. As Stylianou and Stylianou suggest, the frescoes of the church date from the second decade of the sixteenth century. The shepherd of the Nativity (Fig. 14), seated cross-legged, has stopped playing his musical instrument, a *floyéra*, a *pithkiávli* or a *zournás*, and turns his head to the angel announcing the glad tidings. The shepherd's light-coloured, short-sleeved tunic, the contemporary hat that he wears with a wide brim to shade the face from the midday sun (Norris 1999: 262, 426; Wieck 1988: pl. 4, pl. 15a), and the fact that he is represented barefoot, indicate that this young man constitutes a reference to a Cypriot amateur musician playing his instrument while watching over his grazing flock in a warm summer day in early sixteenth-century Cyprus.

fashion worn during the period (Norris 1999: 433, fig. 607c). It is also worth noting that in the Nativity at the Church of the Archangel Michael, in contrast to all the others we have examined, the shepherd-musician is portrayed playing his instrument seated not on the ground, but on a bizarre chair with a hollow seat and a conical base: this unquestionably represents an actual practice of the time. The young man's attire and hairstyle, and the fact that he is depicted playing his *zournás* seated on a stool, suggest an overlap of the shepherd of the Nativity and a contemporary Cypriot musician.

Fig. 14 – Detail from the Nativity of the Church of the Archangel Michael at Vyzakia (Courtesy of the Bank of Cyprus)

Fig. 13 – Detail from the Nativity of the Church of the Transfiguration of the Saviour at Palaichori (Courtesy of the Bank of Cyprus)

The Church of the Archangel Michael at Vyzakia (Stylianou and Stylianou 1985: 110-13) retains one of the most interesting sets of wall paintings of the sixteenth century, presenting a folkloric character, infused with Venetian iconographic elements. The Nativity shepherd (Fig. 14) is depicted ignoring the angel announcing the birth of Christ and keeping on playing his musical instrument, a *zournás*. He is dressed in contemporary clothing. He wears a tunic with loose sleeves (Norris 1999: 426, figs 593-4), and a tall hat shaped like a pointed bag. His long hair touching his shoulders at the back is a

CONCLUSION

In this paper, using as evidence monumental representations of the Nativity of Christ, I have attempted to explore what we can learn about medieval Cypriot music. Public images such as the frescoes were to a great extent intended to explain the word of God to an illiterate or marginally literate audience. The catechetical function of the depictions of the Nativity was to make clear the deeper meaning of the Incarnation of the Saviour and to allow reception by a wider audience. In medieval Cyprus they did so by adapting, to a certain extent, local cultural environment, as the iconographic material we have examined attests. Without precisely following the 'standards' of Byzantine iconography as found elsewhere, especially after Cyprus ceased to form part of the Byzantine Empire, the medieval Cypriot Nativity representations display details which reflect more closely the habits of the contemporary local society by and for whom the frescoes were painted.

Although the other protagonists of the Nativity such as Christ, the Virgin, Joseph, the angels and the Magi are more or less standardised in medieval Cypriot art in conformity with the Byzantine tradition, the shepherds are developed in Cypriot iconography, especially from the thirteenth century henceforth, in a more innovative and imaginative way which suggests that they are a local adaptation to this iconography. Each of the depicted shepherd-musicians of the Nativity may well represent a musician of medieval Cyprus.

It must be kept in mind, however, that the musical instruments are generally depicted as one component of the religious scene. The purpose of the frescoes was not to convey precise depictions of musical instruments but to preach the Christian message. Therefore, many of the instruments are either shown in insufficient detail which prevents their positive categorisation, or are so unreliable that on many occasions it is far from clear whether a *floyéra*, a *pithkiávli*, or a *zournás*, was intended. Nevertheless, what seems almost indisputable is that music played a prominent part in medieval Cypriot society.

Bibliography

ARGYROU, C. (2001) Παραστάσεις Μουσικών Οργάνων στις Εκκλησίες της Κύπρου (12ος – 16ος αιώνας). Η Βυζαντινή Παράδοση και Δυτικές Επιδράσεις. *Επετηρίδα Κέντρου Μελετών Ιεράς Μονής Κύκκου* 5, 215-28.

ARGYROU, C. and MYRIANTHEUS, D. (2004) *Ο Ναός του Τιμίου Σταυρού του Αγιασμάτι*, Lefkosia, Bank of Cyprus Cultural Foundation, Holy Bishopric of Morphou.

ACHEIMASTOU-POTAMIANOU, M. (23 December 2001) Η Γέννηση του Χριστού στη Βυζαντινή Μνημειακή Ζωγραφική. *Η Καθημερινή Επτά Ημέρες: Η Γέννηση του Χριστού στο Βυζάντιο*, 14-20.

ANOYANAKIS, F. (1979) *Greek Popular Musical Instruments*, Athens, National Bank of Greece.

BAINES, A.C. and KIRNBAUER, M. (2001) Shawm. IN: Sadie, S. and Tyrrell, J. eds., *The New Grove Dictionary of Music and Musicians*, 2nd ed., 6, London, Grove's Dictionaries, 228-37.

CHATZECHRISTODOULOU, C. and MYRIANTHEUS, D. (2002) *Ο Ναός της Παναγίας της Ασίνου*, Lefkosia, Bank of Cyprus Cultural Foundation, Holy Bishopric of Morphou.

COCKS, W.A., BAINES, A.C. and CANNON, R.D. (2001) Bagpipe. IN: Sadie, S. and Tyrrell, J. eds., *The New Grove Dictionary of Music and Musicians*, 2nd ed., 6, London, Grove's Dictionaries, 471-84.

GIES, F. and GIES, J. (2005) *Daily Life in Medieval Times: a Vivid, Detailed Account of Birth, Marriage and Death; Food, Clothing and Housing; Love and Labor in the Middle Ages*, Hoo, Kent, Grange.

HARTHAN, J. (1977) *Books of Hours and their Owners*, London, Thames and Hudson.

LEVENTES, A.C. (January 2000) Η Γέννηση του Χριστού στη Βυζαντινή Τέχνη. *Corpus* 12, 80-5.

LIAVAS, L. (2000) *Ελληνικά Λαϊκά Μουσικά Όργανα, Greek Folk Musical Instruments*, Athens, Ministry of Culture, Directorate of Folk Culture.

MAGUIRE, H. (1981) *Art and Eloquence in Byzantium*, Princeton N.J., Princeton University Press.

MONTAGU, J. (2001) Duct flute. IN: Sadie, S. and Tyrrell, J. eds., *The New Grove Dictionary of Music and Musicians*, 2nd ed., 7, London, Grove's Dictionaries, 643.

MONTAGU, J., BROWN, H.M., FRANK, J. and POWELL, A. (2001) Flute. IN: Sadie, S. and Tyrrell, J. eds., *The New Grove Dictionary of Music and Musicians*, 2nd ed., 6, London, Grove's Dictionaries, 26-48.

NORRIS, H. (1999) *Medieval Costume and Fashion*, New York, Dover.

STYLIANOU, A. and STYLIANOU, J.A. (1985) *The Painted Churches of Cyprus: Treasures of Byzantine Art*, London, Trigraph for the A.G. Leventis Foundation.

VOKOTOPOULOS, P.L. (27 December 2001) Μέση και Ύστερη Βυζαντινή Περίοδος. *Ιστορικά: Η Γέννηση του Χριστού στην Τέχνη* 115, 12-19.

WIECK, R.S. (1988) *The Book of Hours in Medieval Art and Life*, London, Sotheby's.

WINFIELD, D. and WINFIELD, J. (2003) *The Church of the Panaghia tou Arakos at Lagoudhera, Cyprus: the Paintings and their Painterly Significance*, Washington, D.C., Dumbarton Oaks Research Library and Collection.

PART 4:

LANDSCAPE STUDIES AND HERITAGE

MANAGEMENT

AGIOS GEORGIOS, PEGEIA – CAPE DREPANON: INTEGRATING AN EXCAVATION SITE INTO AN ARCHAEOLOGICAL LANDSCAPE
KONSTANTINOS TH. RAPTIS AND OLGA-MARIA BAKIRTZIS

INTRODUCTION

Agios Georgios at Pegeia is a well-known place of pilgrimage in the Paphos district that was founded on Cape Drepanon, the westernmost point on Cyprus, a counterpart to the shrine of St Andrew at the east end of the island. Between 1952 and 1955, under the direction of A.H.S. Megaw, the Cypriot Department of Antiquities excavated three three-aisled Justinianic and post-Justinianic basilicas and a bath (Megaw 1960: 345-51, 1974: 59-88). The excavations have been continued in the past decade by the Aristotle University of Thessaloniki (1992-8) and the Hellenic Ministry of Culture's Archaeological Expedition in Cyprus (from 1999 onwards) under the direction of Charalambos Bakirtzis, uncovering structures adjacent to the basilicas, establishing the connection between the monuments, and showing that an extensive unwalled settlement occupied the site in the Roman and Early Christian period (Bakirtzis 1995: 247-53, 1996: 153-61, 1997: 327-32, 1998: 46-7, 1999: 35-48, 2001: 155-70)

THE EARLY CHRISTIAN SETTLEMENT (Fig. 1)

The centre of the settlement, on the neck of the cape, is occupied by the complex belonging to Basilica A (Fig. 2), with adjacent structures on the north side and an open quadriporticus and a peristylar baptistery on the west side. To the north side of the latter is annexed a smaller three-aisled basilica with a transept (Fig. 3) (Megaw 1974: 71-2; Papageorghiou 1985: 314-15; Michaelides 1992: 101, 2001: 43;), and to the west side a two-storey bishop's residence in the style of a Graeco-Roman house (Bakirtzis 2001: 158). To the north of the complex around Basilica A the excavations have uncovered a bath in a large courtyard, in which a subterranean tomb of the Roman period, accessed by a staircase, was used to collect the effluent from the bath (Bakirtzis 2001: 158). To the north-east, at the side of the road leading inland, are the remains of the complex belonging to the three-aisled basilica Γ (Fig. 4) (Megaw 1974: 72) with adjacent structures along the north side (Bakirtzis 2001: 158-9).

The residential area of the settlement faces the sea at the foot of the southern slope of the cape, where parts of houses, underground cisterns, and the three-aisled basilica B (Fig. 5) have been excavated (Megaw 1974: 72; Bakirtzis 2001: 158-9).

The settlement's necropolis, with two types of monumental tomb, arcosolia and loculi, hewn out of the rock (Bakirtzis 1999: 35-48; Anastasiadou 2000: 333-47), occupies the brow of the steep cliff rising from the west and north-west shore of the cape.

The Early Christian settlement on Cape Drepanon faces the sea, though, owing to erosion of the rocky coastline, there is no trace of an ancient harbour. However, a marine archaeological survey has shown that there were anchorages just off the southern tip of Cape Drepanon, one of them in the sheltered bay of Maniki, visible from the administrative centre of the Early Christian settlement (Giangrande, Richards, *et al.* 1987: 185-97; Hadjisavvas 1995: 95).

The settlement is not mentioned in contemporary sources. However, the morphological similarity of the ecclesiastical buildings to monuments of the Aegean and other areas influenced by Constantinople, the basilicas' architectural members of Proconnesian marble imported into Cyprus (Raptis and Vasiliadou 2005: 199-224), and other marble objects, like sigmoid altars, and luxurious marble plates, the marble ambo with the inscription 'For the blessing of sailors' (ΥΠΕΡ ΕΥΧΗΣ ΝΑΥΤΩΝ) (Michaelides 2001: 43-56), the plethora of amphoras, the pottery imported from Egypt, and the fact that the settlement faced the sea, where Early Christian anchorages have been located, bear witness to its connections with the sea, the Aegean, Constantinople, and Egypt.

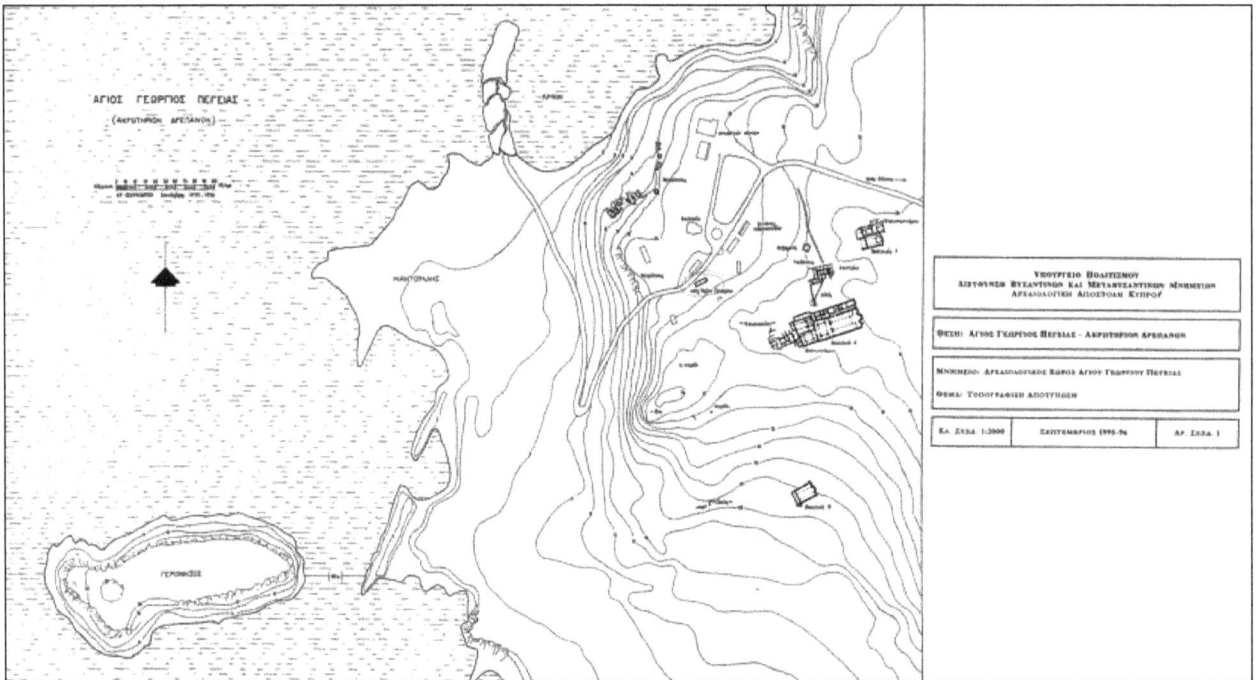

Fig. 1 – Cape Drepanon. Archaeological site of Agios Georgios at Pegeia. Topographic documentation
(Courtesy of the Hellenic Archaeological Expedition in Cyprus)

Fig. 2 – Basilica A (Courtesy of Hellenic
Archaeological Expedition in Cyprus)

Fig. 4 – Basilica Γ (Courtesy of Hellenic
Archaeological Expedition in Cyprus)

Fig. 3 – Three-aisled basilica with transept (Courtesy of
Hellenic Archaeological Expedition in Cyprus)

Fig. 5 – Basilica B (Courtesy of Hellenic
Archaeological Expedition in Cyprus)

Fig. 6 – Map of Eastern Mediterranean (Courtesy of Hellenic Archaeological Expedition in Cyprus)

In the Early Christian period Constantinople was supplied with grain from Alexandria. The annual grain fleet followed a route via Cyprus, Rhodes, Chios, and Tenedos. Its geographical position (Fig. 6), coupled with a study of its architectural remains, shows that the unwalled Late Roman settlement on Cape Drepanon, cut off from the interior of the island by the Akamas Mountains, facing the sea, and situated at the westernmost extremity of Cyprus and in the middle of the sea route between Alexandria and Rhodes, became a port of call for the grain fleet in the Early Christian period, probably when Constantine the Great was sole augustus. It developed especially in the reign of Justinian (AD 527-65), when the institution of the *annona civica* was reorganised, and under his successors, which was a period when, archaeological data shows, the settlement was flourishing, with new basilicas and public buildings being constructed (Bakirtzis 1995: 247-51, 1997: 330, 2001: 157).

As a port of call for the grain fleet, the settlement became inactive after the Persians captured Alexandria in AD 618, and was abandoned in the mid-seventh century, probably after the Arab conquest of Egypt in AD 642 and

the consequent cessation of the grain deliveries to the Byzantine capital. This data is supported by the numismatic evidence, because the latest coin found during the excavation so far is a *follis* of Constantine II of the year AD 641-2. After the mid-seventh century and when the Arabs settled in Paphos, the settlement on Cape Drepanon was an anchorage of purely local significance (Bakirtzis 2001: 159).

THE MEDIAEVAL SHRINE (Fig. 1)

Cape Drepanon was known by the Cypriots for the local shrine of St George a long time before the discovery of the Early Christian basilicas and the excavation of part of the Early Christian settlement. The shrine had developed very early around the aisle-less chapel of St George (Fig. 7), which according to excavation data was founded in the late thirteenth or early fourteenth century.

The origins of the shrine that grew up on the natural plateau north-west of the neck of the cape, between the basilicas and the necropolis, are unknown, though they do

Fig. 7 – Medieval chapel of St. George. Interior (Courtesy of Hellenic Archaeological Expedition in Cyprus)

Fig. 8 – Removal of undesirable self-propagating grassy vegetation

Fig. 9 – Path

testify to the continuation of Christian worship on the site of the Early Christian basilicas, the ruins of which were visible in the mediaeval period. It seems that from the start the shrine was limited to the little chapel of St George, outside which, until a few years ago, there was a tree on which pilgrims used to hang their votive offerings.[1]

Stone structures were gradually built around the church to serve the pilgrims' needs. The shrine was surrounded by a stone enclosure and was self-sufficient, having its own water cistern for garden produce and probably an oil press. The only road from Pegeia led to a gate in this enclosure. The shrine was supplied with water from the Avakas gorge by a communal cistern and fountain (which no longer survive) at the side of the road outside the enclosure. In the modern period a stone-built, domed Church of St George was constructed, which now dominates the area.

THE ARCHAEOLOGICAL SITE

The site of the Early Christian settlement on the neck of the cape, the tranquillity of the natural environment, and the religious atmosphere of the shrine together create a monumental landscape that is imbued with historical memory and spirituality. This applies especially to the site of basilica A and its associated complex, which occupies the highest point in the area, commanding not only the southern slope of the cape, the rocky south-west coast, and Yeronissos island, but also the natural plateau to the north-west with the shrine of St George.

Inside the fenced archaeological site the monuments are surrounded by drystone walls, which act as retaining walls for the various levels, and mastic trees (*Pistachia lentiscus*) (Fig. 9), which in places have formed an impe-

netrable natural barrier that visually separates the monuments. The microenvironment of the site is seaso-nally supplemented by diverse low-growing vegetation (Fig. 8): spring sees the appearance of, among others, poppies (*Papaver rhoeas*), yellow chrysanthemums (*Chrysanthemum coronarium*), and asphodels (*Asphodelus aestivus*), while summer produces wild oat (*Avena sterilis*), fleabane (*Inula/Dittrichia-viscosa*), caper (*Capparis spinosa*), and various types of thorn.

The elevation on which the archaeological site is located,[2] the gentle contours of which are emphasised by dry-stone walls marking the boundaries of old properties, is covered with self-propagating brush-like vegetation consisting mainly of native evergreen species, such as mastic (*Pistachia lentiscus*), carob (*Ceratonia siliqua*), and wild olive (*Olea europaea*), and certain naturalised species, such as prickly pear (*Opuntia ficus-indica*). Before the excavation of the Early Christian basilicas began, early in

---

[1] Similar cult is mentioned at the Church of St Solomone, Kato Paphos, and elsewhere on Cyprus, where the practice is widespread (Panaretos 1969).

[2] The area under discussion, like most of the district of Paphos, is in the geotectonic zone of Mamonia, which consists of allochthonous, eruptive (serpentine, pillow lava), sedimentary (psammite, illuvium, pelite), and to a lesser extent metamorphosed rocks (crystallised limestone and schist), the age of which varies between 210 and 95 million years (Tsintidis, Hadjikyriakou, *et al.* 2002).

the 1950s, most of the cape was covered with agricultural land, growing mainly cereal crops, while the built environment was limited to the few buildings connected with the shrine. Today, however, the overall picture has been supplemented by banana plantations and ornamental plantings of mainly exotic species around the roads and the newly built tourist facilities. It is a natural conesquence of the area's tourist and economic development, which, in the space of a decade, has brought about major changes in both the built and the natural surroundings of the archaeological site.

INTEGRATING AN EXCAVATION SITE INTO AN ARCHAEOLOGICAL LANDSCAPE

Owing to the dramatic changes that have taken place in the natural and built landscape of Cape Drepanon in the last decade and as a natural consequence of the progress made by the archaeological investigations on the site, the Hellenic Ministry of Culture's Archaeological Expedition in Cyprus, in association with the Cypriot Department of Antiquities, which is responsible for protecting the monuments and the archaeological site, has undertaken to draw up and gradually implement a study for the maintenance and development of the site. Since the site was op ened to the public, development has become necessary because, owing to the gradual excavation of the monuments since the early 1950s, the site is now fragmented by fences and paths. These served various excavation needs, but are a barrier to modern visitors' communication with the site. Apart from having visual contact with the antiquities, visitors want to know what purpose they served and to understand the nature of the settlement and its place in the historical, social, and political context that gave birth to it, and also to appreciate the peace and tranquillity of the archaeological landscape.

The aims associated with the development of the extensive archaeological site of Agios Georgios at Pegeia are: to maintain the ruins by restoring the damage to the architectural remains and the colourful mosaic floors of the monuments of the Early Christian settlement; to highlight their historical and archaeological importance by developing and unifying the archaeological site; and at the same time integrating it into a wider cultural landscape that will be in keeping with the natural environment, the history, and the religious character of the area.

As a result of the excavations and the protective measures that have been put in place at various times, the site is independent, self-contained, and self-sufficient. In view of this, the interventions will be governed by the following general principles:[3]

i. It is proposed that the consolidation works consist of non-invasive procedures that will prolong the duration of the materiality of the ruins without creating foreseeable problems and will preserve the authenticcity of the monuments and the archaeological site.

ii. There will be no major interventions, nor will any new structural features be added. Building ruins within ruins simply creates a stage set and destroys the self-sufficiency and self-existence of the archaeological site.

iii. Non-invasive plantings are proposed, which will make the site more friendly to visitors and help to integrate the excavation site into the wider cultural landscape, while requiring minimal care and attention.

The work on the architectural remains of the monuments of the Early Christian settlement is limited to small-scale interventions of a consolidatory nature and is intended to maintain, protect, and highlight the authenticity of the antiquities and the monumental landscape. Any consolidation work is carried out with mortar that is compatible with the already existing mortar, as well as with traditional materials used in Cypriot architecture. Wide use of concrete is avoided as it has been proved to be inefficient in past consolidation work, since it has caused new structural problems.

Special attention has been paid to positioning and partially restoring the numerous marble architectural members unearthed during the excavation of the site. As part of the development of the archaeological site the two marble columns that were restored in the 1950s have been conserved and their capitals have been returned to them, one Corinthian capital in Basilica A (Fig. 10) and one Ionic impost capital in Basilica B. Intact marble capitals have been moved and placed along the stylobates of the two basilicas (Raptis and Vasiliadou 2005: 211).

The mosaic floors (Michaelides 1992: 101; Mastora 2003: 266-7) that have been lifted, conserved, and replaced in the past will be conserved *in situ*: the mosaic surface will be consolidated where necessary, cracks will be sealed, the surrounding mortar replaced, isolated detached *tesserae* consolidated, and the surfaces mechanically cleaned.

---

[3] Bearing in mind the international conventions enshrining the principles of the preservation and conservation of cultural heritage, especially the Venice Charter of 1964: Article 1: 'The concept of an historic monument embraces not only the single architectural work but also the urban or rural setting in which is found the evidence of a particular

civilization, a significant development or an historic event. This applies not only to great works of art but also to more modest works of the past which have acquired cultural significance with the passing of time.' Article 5: 'The conservation of monuments is always facilitated by making use of them for some socially useful purpose. Such use is therefore desirable but it must not change the layout or decoration of the building. It is within these limits only that modifications demanded by a change of function should be envisaged and may be permitted.' Article 13: 'Additions cannot be allowed except in so far as they do not detract from the interesting parts of the building, its traditional setting, the balance of its composition and its relation with its surroundings.' Article 15, paragraph 3: 'All reconstruction work should be ruled out a priori. Only anastylosis, that is to say the reassembling of existing but dismembered parts, can be permitted. The material used for integration should always be recognizable and its use should be at least that which will ensure the conservation of a monument and the reinstatement of its form.'

Fig. 10 – Basilica A. Restoration of column and capital (Courtesy of Hellenic Archaeological Expedition in Cyprus)

But apart from carrying out localised, mainly consolidation procedures on the material remains of the buildings of the Early Christian settlement, it will be possible to bring out the distinctive geographical and historical identity of the site only by integrating the monuments into a wider archaeological landscape that will extend not only over the fenced area, but over the entire cape.

Inside the excavation site, it is considered especially important to unify it with a single encircling fence, to restore the visual connection between the monuments, to lay paths that will allow visitors to circulate around the monuments without violating their materiality, to integrate the ruins into the natural landscape with the help of plantings of native vegetation (Figs 11-12), and to link the archaeological site with the mediaeval shrine and the devotional character of the area in such a way that the former will partake of the spirituality of the latter, while the latter will acquire tangible historical depth.

More specifically regarding the development of the immediate environs of the monuments, the undesirable self-propagating grassy vegetation will be removed by hand at least twice a year (Fig. 8); repairs will be made to

Fig. 11 – Cape Drepanon. Archaeological site of Agios Georgios at Pegeia. Present state
(Courtesy of Hellenic Archaeological Expedition in Cyprus)

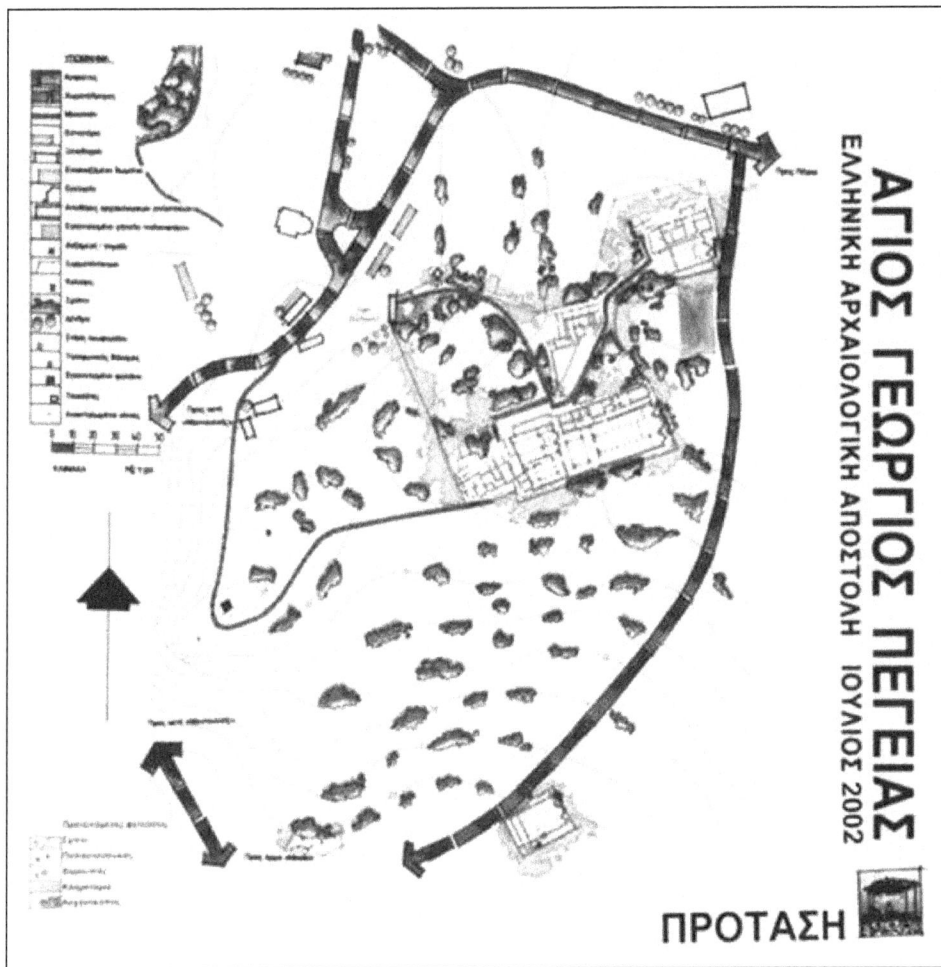

Fig. 12 – Cape Drepanon. Archaeological site of Agios Georgios at Pegeia. Proposal
(Courtesy of Hellenic Archaeological Expedition in Cyprus)

the dry-stone walls, which both supplement the fencing around the monuments and help to retain the walls of excavated earth around the monuments; new paths will be laid between the monuments, and the existing ones will be repaired and bordered with new dry-stone walls or plantings in such a way that visitors will be led to the entrances to the monuments along the pathways of the Early Christian urban tissue and will be helped towards a better understanding of the space. The empty space between and around the monuments will be filled with plantings of the self-propagating flora of the cape in order to enhance the relationship between the archaeological and monumental landscape and the natural environment. At the same time the fencing will be supplemented to visually isolate the archaeological site from the modern developments around. In order to display the monuments and for the benefit of visitors, seating will be provided in shady areas, from where visitors will have a comprehensive view of the excavated complexes of the Early Christian settlement and gain an understanding of how its urban tissue developed and its relationship with the sea.

In order to link the archaeological site with the wider environs of the monuments and the shrine of St George, a number of measures will be taken to give the entrance to the site the form and character of a traditional Cypriot farmhouse, and also of the shrine itself with its air of self-sufficiency. This will be enhanced by the rustic architecture of the site warden's office, which is the consolidated and restored stone stable in which pilgrims used to keep their pack animals. Trees will be planted around the office and beside the stone seats, mainly carobs (*Ceratonia siliqua*) and olives (*Olea europaea*); and a 'traditional' vegetable garden has been created in the courtyard behind the office with such ground-covering edible species as vegetable marrow (*Cucurbita pepo*), cucumber (*Cucumis sativus*), and water melon (*Citrullis vulgaris*), which are also cultivated in the wider agricultural area of Pegeia. The public could use the flat area to the north of the site warden's office as a resting place as they enter and leave the site. This notion will be reinforced by the construction of a wooden pergola with a grapevine (*Vitis vinifera*) growing over it, which will offer shade during the very hot summer months. Fruit trees will also be planted, together with certain ornamental bushy species that are found on most Cypriot farms and which go well with the character of the site warden's office. These include the fruit-bearing citrus (*Citrus lemon, Citrus sinensis*), pomegranate (*Punica granatum*), mulberry (*Morus alba*), which is the tree most commonly used for shade in Cypriot courtyards, and the ornamental West Indian jasmine (*Plumeria alba*), lantana (*Lantana camara*), Spanish jasmine (*Jasminum grandiflorum*), myrtle (*Myrtus communis*), and oleander (*Nerium oleander*). The shrine's existing water cistern will be consolidated, waterproofed, and restored to supply water for the archaeological garden, the new plantings, and the vegetable garden.

CONCLUSION

The archaeological site occupies a large area on the neck of Cape Drepanon and is visible from all sides of the hill: the complex of basilica Γ can be seen from the area to the north of the site and that of basilica A from the south and the west. The restored column of the latter, topped by a Corinthian capital, rises above the site.

After the space around the monuments has undergone non-invasive development and the empty spaces have been filled with plantings of self-propagating native species, the archaeological site's relationship with the pre-existing natural landscape will have been fully restored. From inside the site visitors' visual connection with the built environment of the surrounding area, which is now characterised chiefly by tourist infrastructure, will be considerably reduced.

The microenvironment inside the developed archaeological site not only screens the monuments from the modern developments in the wider environs, but also connects the archaeological landscape of the settlement with the natural landscape of the cape and the sea in the distance.

Among the few more modern features that will still be visible from within the newly developed archaeological site is the stone Church of St George, which towers on the plateau to the northwest of the site, emphasising Cape Drepanon's status as a place of pilgrimage and the continuity of the devotional tradition.

Bibliography

ANASTASIADOU, T. (2000) The Rock-Cut Tombs at Agios Georgios tis Pegeias, Paphos District, Cyprus. *Report of the Department of Antiquities Cyprus*, 333-47.

BAKIRTZIS, Ch. (1995) The Role of Cyprus in the Grain Supply of Constantinople in the Early Christian Period. IN: Karageorghis V. and D. Michaelides eds, *Proceedings of the International Symposium 'Cyprus and the Sea', Nicosia 25-26 September 1993*, Nicosia, 247-53.

BAKIRTZIS, Ch. (1996) Description and Metrology of Some Clay Vessels from Agios Georgios, Pegeia. IN: Karageorghis V. and D. Michaelides eds, *The Development of the Cypriot Economy from the Prehistoric Period to the Present Day*, Nicosia, 153-61.

BAKIRTZIS, Ch. (1997) Η θαλάσσια διαδρομή Κύπρου–Αιγαίου στα Παλαιοχριστιανικά χρόνια. *Acts of the International Symposium 'Cyprus and the Aegean in Antiquity. From the Prehistoric Period to the 7th century A.D.', Nicosia (8-10 December 1995)*, Nicosia, 327-32.

BAKIRTZIS, Ch. (1998) Les Basiliques de Ayios Yeoryios. *Le Monde de la Bible* 112, 46-7.

BAKIRTZIS, Ch. (1999) Early Christian Rock-Cut Tombs at Hagios Georgios, Peyia. IN: Patterson Ševčenko N. and C. Moss eds, *Medieval Cyprus: Papers in Art, Architecture and History in Memory of Doula Mouriki*, Princeton University Press, 35-48.

BAKIRTZIS, Ch. (2001) Αποτελέσματα ανασκαφών στον Άγιο Γεώργιο Πέγειας (Ακρωτήριον Δρέπανον), 1991-1995. *Πρακτικά του Γ΄ Διεθνούς Κυπρολογικού Συνεδρίου (Λευκωσία, 16-20 Απριλίου 1996)*, Nicosia, 155-70.

GIANGRANDE, C., G. RICHARDS, D. KENNET and J. ADAMS (1987) Cyprus Underwater Survey, 1983-1984: A Preliminary Report. *Report of the Department of Antiquities Cyprus*, 185-97.

HADJISAVVAS, S. (1995), Cyprus and the Sea: The Archaic and Classical Periods. IN: Karageorghis, V. and D. Michaelides eds, *Proceedings of the International Symposium 'Cyprus and the Sea'*, Nicosia 25-26 September 1993, Nicosia, 95.

MASTORA, P. (2003), Διερεύνηση της διατήρησης και αποκατάσταση του ψηφιδωτού δαπέδου του κεντρικού κλίτους της βασιλικής Α στον Άγιο Γεώργιο Πέγειας. *Ε΄ Συνάντηση Βυζαντινολόγων Ελλάδος και Κύπρου*, Κέρκυρα 3-5 Οκτωβρίου 2003, Τόμος περιλήψεων, Κέρκυρα, 266-7.

MEGAW, A.H.S. (1960) Early Christian Monuments in Cyprus in the Light of Recent Discoveries. *Akten des XI. Internationalen Byzantinisten-Kongresses. München 1958*, Munich, 345-51.

MEGAW, A.H.S. (1974) Byzantine Architecture and Decoration in Cyprus: Metropolitan or Provincial?, *Dumbarton Oaks Papers* 28, 59-88.

MICHAELIDES, D. (1992) *Cypriot Mosaics*, Nicosia.

MICHAELIDES, D. (2001) The Ambo of Basilica A at Cape Drepanon. IN: Herrin, J., M. Mullett, and G. Otten-Froux eds, *Mosaic, Festschrift for A..H.S. Megaw*, British School at Athens Studies 8, London, 43.

PANARETOS, A. (1969) *Δενδρολατρεία*, Nicosia.

PAPAGEORGHIOU, A. (1985) L'Architecture Paléo-chrétienne de Chypre. *Corsi di Cultura sull'Arte Ravennate e Bizantina* 32, 314-15.

RAPTIS, K. and S. VASILIADOU (2006) Διαχρονική χρήση, διαδοχικές θέσεις και απόπειρα επανένταξης των μαρμάρινων αρχιτεκτονικών μελών των βασιλικών Α, Β, Γ Αγίου Γεωργίου Πέγειας (Πάφος): από την παραγωγή στα παλαιοχριστιανικά λατομεία της πρωτεύουσας στη διαμόρφωση του αρχαιολογικού χώρου. *Report of the Department of Antiquities Cyprus* 2005, 199-227.

TSINTIDIS, T.Ch., G.N. HADJIKYRIAKOU and Ch.S. CHRISTODOULOU (2002) *Δένδρα και Θάμνοι στην Κύπρο*, Nicosia.

TSINTIDIS T.Ch. (1995) *Τα Ενδημικά Φυτά της Κύπρου*, Nicosia.

A COMPARATIVE STUDY OF HERITAGE MANAGEMENT
IN ISRAEL AND CYPRUS
DEIRDRE STRITCH

This paper presents a very brief overview of some of the key factors which have influenced archaeological heritage management in Israel and the Republic of Cyprus, and the respective responses of heritage managers to the similar historical and contemporary factors at play in both countries. The archaeological infrastructure of both Israel and the Republic of Cyprus is indebted to the local Ottoman and, particularly, British colonial past; the result being highly-centralised heritage management systems, centred on government, antiquities' departments or authorities. Since independence, the archaeological profession and academia in these two countries have been both driven and constrained by similar factors, ranging from questions of ethnogenesis to the problems caused by rapid development and urbanisation. Both countries faced enormous external and internal pressure on their territorial and ethnic integrity from the time of their formation. This resulted in an intense need or desire to confirm the Jewish or Greek character of each country. Professional archaeologists played a significant role, either consciously or unconsciously, in this quest. Furthermore, in both countries tourism forms a crucial element of the local economy and the archaeological heritage of each country has been commandeered as an essential component in this industry (Silberman 1997).

Despite these many similarities in the history, structure and problems faced by archaeology in Israel and Cyprus, differences also exist in the ways that both countries have addressed these issues and challenges. This paper gives a brief overview of the approaches taken to archaeological practice and heritage management in each country. In addition some of the common problems confronted by both countries are analysed. Finally, these case studies are used as a basis from which to make suggestions for possible approaches towards creating a more sustainable and multi-vocal, cultural heritage practice.

THE SYSTEM IN CYPRUS

Protection of the archaeological heritage of Cyprus operates within a highly centralised system centred on the Department of Antiquities. The Department was founded in 1935 by the British Colonial Authority and is a direct branch of government, falling, along with a number of other departments, within the Ministry of Communications and Works. The drawbacks of functioning as a member of the civil service have been felt in recent years, and the benefits of reorganising the Department of Antiquities or its transfer to the Ministry of Education and Culture are being considered in an effort to enable the Department to modernise and make itself more effective, though no decision has yet been reached (mcw.gov.cy).

A PYRAMIDAL STRUCTURE

The Department is headed by a Director, supported by two senior officials who head the two major branches of the Department; the Curator of Museums (and Surveys) and the Curator of Monuments and Sites.[1] All rescue excavations within Cyprus are carried out by the Department of Antiquities, which is also responsible for the granting of licences for research excavations. According to Greene,

> '... there are only limited formal intra-governmental mechanisms for coordinating development planning and cultural resource preservation, and the work of the Cyprus Survey, the primary means in the past by which the Department gathered information on antiquities outside the major known sites, has been curtailed since the 1970s.' (Greene 1999: 50).

---

[1] 'Surveys' is not usually quoted nowadays as proper surveys are no longer carried out by the Department, only rescue surveys etc.

Within the centralised system extant in Cyprus, much authority over, and responsibility for, antiquities policy lies with the Director of the Department, and much rests, therefore, on the personal character and aims of this individual. This fact impacted on, and shaped, the Department's response to questions of cultural-resource management (Greene 1999: 47). The rescue of the Late Bronze Age site at Agios Dhimitrios, threatened in 1979 by the construction of a multi-lane divided highway between Nicosia and Limassol is a case in point. The discovery came too late to realign the road, so the Department could only rescue as much of this part of the site as possible before it was destroyed. The Department, however, did not respond by initiating its own excavations; instead at the personal request of the Director of the Department, Vassos Karageorghis, the *Vasilikos Valley Project* (an independent group researching the prehistory of the area) were called upon and accepted the challenge of rescuing the site. This case is symptomatic of the ambivalent response to the problem of rescue and salvage work in Cyprus that existed up until the 1990s, when a more systematic approach to rescue excavation was adopted. In the case of the site at Agios Dhimitrios, it is fair to say that were it not for the presence and willingness of the *Vasilikos Valley Project* team to take onboard the rescue excavation, the road construction would undoubtedly have resulted in the loss of much important archaeological information.

In this case, I suggest that the personal interest of Professor Karageorghis in this particular site and period ensured the site's rescue and preservation. As Director of the Department of Antiquities from 1963 until 1989, it was inevitable that the personality of Professor Karageorghis would have an overwhelming influence on the nature of archaeological conduct in Cyprus. Cypriot archaeology is undoubtedly indebted to this individual's vigour and enthusiasm in promoting Cypriot archaeology at home and abroad and in striving to achieve best practice in the field, particularly in the areas of prompt publication and site preservation. Unfortunately, such a pyramidal structure within the Department meant that inevitably a void was created on Professor Karageorghis' retirement that has proved difficult to fill, and poses the question of whether or not it is beneficial for one person to wield such influence over the profession both academically and in the field.

CHRONOLOGICAL SUBJECTIVITY

The Cypriot Department of Antiquities is responsible for the protection of remains from all periods of Cyprus' past, however, later periods have traditionally received far less attention. Also, in contrast to the concentration on certain periods of prehistory is the lack of attention paid to monuments and artefacts from periods conceived of as negative or painful in the national consciousness, in particular the Ottoman period. The Department of Antiquities of Cyprus, for example, has an impressive

collection of artefacts from the Neolithic period through to the Crusader period, but the collection becomes meagre thereafter. The roles and narratives attributed to archaeological monuments in the landscape is another feature of this historical and cultural selectivity. Many Venetian and Ottoman period buildings have been reused as museums, as at Kouklia and Limassol, but the history of the buildings themselves and their role in their local community have been ignored.[2] In this way, the physical, historical environment is manipulated and transformed to provide concrete evidence and reminders of a particular authoritative text, whilst eclipsing unwanted pollutants to that text.

MEETING THE NEEDS OF TOURISM

Another major factor which influenced site management and conservation decisions in Cyprus is the tourist industry. After independence, the Director of the Department of Antiquities was directly involved with government in the development and promotion of so-called cultural tourism, through the investment in large-scale excavations at monumental sites. Many of the buildings and mosaics uncovered, however, were in urgent need of conservation and consolidation, but the Department lacked the services of specialised architects and conservators (Hadjisavvas 1995: 2). Furthermore, the Turkish invasion in 1974 put additional pressure on the southern half of the island; in 1973, 70% of tourists to the island were attracted to the Famagusta and Kyrenia districts (Hadjisavvas 1995: 2). With the Turkish invasion of the island in 1974, and subsequent occupation of the northern half of the island, the tourist trade, previously absorbed by Famagusta and Kyrenia, and the problems it engendered now emerged at Limassol, Paphos and Agia Napa.[3] This meant that in the post-invasion years the Department had to deal with hurried development as well as the burden of normal conservation and funding issues.

The Department of Antiquities had limited financial resources and even more meagre specialised service expertise with which to deal with the demands of the accelerated threat to, and exposure of, archaeological remains. Finances would have to be generated and the reconstruction of theatres, such as at Salamis, Kourion and Soloi, perceived to have the greatest earning potential, became a management priority. Within the framework of the promotion of cultural tourism, theatres are a natural choice for the direction of conservation funds. They have the same potential for use in the present as they did in antiquity, thus there is reason for reconstructing them even when a similar amount of surviving material would not warrant reconstruction in another type of building (Wright 1994: 2). The reconstruction of archaeological remains is, however, a

---

[2] A notable exception is the Medieval sugar mill at Kouklia-Stavros.

[3] For a discussion of the effects on the Cypriot economy and environment, and of the dependency of the economy on the tourist industry see Vasilliou 1994.

contested issue. The Charter of Venice, adopted by the International Council of Monuments and Sites in 1965 only allows *anastylosis* and not reconstruction on excavation sites (icomos 1996; Schmidt 1997: 46). An important example of *anastylosis* in Cyprus is the Sanctuary of Apollo Hylates near Kourion (Fig. 1) where work was carried out by the American Expedition. In addition to *anastylosis,* however, many monuments in Cyprus underwent quite considerable reconstruction for which large amounts of new material were sometimes required, most obviously in the case of the theatres already mentioned. Furthermore, the reconstructtion of these monuments ensured their prominence both in the physical landscape and in the topos of public imagination, thus promoting and giving permanence to the narrative of illustrious Hellenism associated with them. In more recent years, archaeologists at the Neolithic site of Choirokoitia and, most notably, at the Chalcolithic site of Lemba, have utilised experimental techniques by reconstructing typical buildings from these sites outside of, but nearby, the site itself in order to facilitate and aid site interpretation, illuminate the construction methods used and relieve the pressure of large visitor numbers on the sites themselves. It is noteworthy, however, that in the case of Lemba, these steps have been the initiative of the excavators themselves, as part of an experimental research project, and not of the Department of Antiquities (though it was carried out with the Department's co-operation).

the cultural resources of that part of the island. The Department of Antiquities was actively engaged in the development of this area through an investment in certain types of sites for tourist consumption. Archaeological activity was focused on the monumental sites of Paphos, Kourion, and Amathus (Hadjisavvas 1995: 3). Despite claims that the Department became more organised in its approach to conservation in the 1980s and 1990s, large scale development of archaeological sites, often carried out at the expense of conservation issues, continues in Cyprus, most controversially at the Graeco-Roman sites at Kourion (Fig. 2) and Nea Paphos. This focus on development, as opposed to conservation, is harmful because high visitor numbers is one of the main factors leading to site destruction through wear and tear and deliberate damage. A balance is required between creating archaeological parks with unmanageable and unsustainable numbers of visitors and not attracting any visitors at all, so that a monument and all that it may have to offer, educationally, aesthetically etc, is not lost to the public. This is a balance, which is not often struck as a result of the current planning and management environment in either Cyprus, or indeed Israel, as will now be outlined.

Fig. 2 – View across Kourion (photo by author)

Fig. 1 – Example of anastylosis in Cyprus: Sanctuary of Apollo Hylates (photo by author)

The 1974 invasion of Cyprus by Turkey further drove development in the south, which in turn put pressure on

THE SYSTEM IN ISRAEL

In theory, Israel, like Cyprus, supports a state-controlled, highly-centralised system for the management of archaeological heritage. In reality, however, a number of organisations and groups in Israel (all either directly or indirectly linked to government) have decision-making responsibility and control over archaeological sites. It is the Israel Antiquities Authority, however, an independent government authority (Baruch and Vashdi 2005), that has primary responsibility for archaeology in Israel.

The Israel Antiquities Authority (henceforth the IAA) was founded 15 years ago in the spring of 1990. It was restructured out of the former Department of Antiquities, which was a direct branch of the Ministry of Education and Culture. The IAA is still affiliated with the Ministry but is now a more autonomous body in its actions and decision-making, as was the aim. The restructuring of the Department allowed the new IAA to expand its apparatus, both administratively and professionally and to retain independently earned revenues (Silberman 1997: 74). According to Rabinovich, between 1990 and 1994, the Authority quadrupled its number of full-time staff, and its annual operating budget increased from $2 million to $22 million (1994: 44). The reorganisation of the Department of Antiquities was in part inspired by two things; a realisation on the part of government of the potential of archaeology to attract tourists and the personal character of its new director, General Amir Drori.

A PYRAMIDAL STRUCTURE

Up until the appointment of Drori to the position of Director of the Department of Antiquities in 1988, the post had always been held by a professional archaeologist and Drori's appointment caused some concern at the time. The General, however, brought his military skills to bear on the re-structuring of the old Department of Antiquities into the new IAA, turning it into a highly organised administrative body. The internal structure of the IAA, rather like in Cyprus, is pyramidal, with much power vested in the hands of the Director. The Director is not required to have any archaeological training or experience, and to date this has been the case. The Director is appointed by the Minister of Education and Culture and the two individuals who have held this post, Drori, and Shuka Dorfman have come from the upper echelons of the army. Within the department, the Director is all powerful. He is responsible for policy formation and retains the ability to change the law, to the extent that he can have entire areas rezoned as either archaeological or non-archaeological, should he choose.

Directors are appointed for a period of five years, but this period can be extended. During the first two years he takes courses in archaeology and management etc, and throughout the tenure he is supervised by the Authority Council. This council, comprising sixteen members, is directly appointed by the Ministry of Education and Culture and includes the Director-General of that Ministry. Members of this council can be loosely divided into two groups of eight, the first comprising government officials, many from economic posts, and the second, academics and representatives of other interested groups, in particular religious groups. The

Director of the IAA meets with this council every two months, but is not obliged to implement any of its suggestions, indicating the lack of power actually exercised by the Council.[4] As is also clear from the composition of the Council and its remit, various government branches, particularly Religion and Finance have (when allowed) an inordinate say in how the I.A.A. is run, which, when combined with the fact that the Director-General of the I.A.A. itself is not required to have archaeological expertise, is worrying. The ramifications of this fact can be seen in the increased say of the religious right in archaeological matters, such as the excavation and reburial of human remains and in the intense excavation of certain sites such as Beth Sean for the explicit purpose of providing local employment and the generation of tourist revenue.

AN EFFECTIVE RESPONSE TO RESCUE ARCHAEOLOGY

The IAA is responsible for the overseeing of rescue or salvage excavation in Israel. For the purposes of archaeology, Israel is gridded into $10km^2$ units and each unit is served by a group from the IAA. The process for the detection, monitoring and excavation or further protection of endangered sites is highly efficient because it requires the tight co-ordination of all three divisions (archaeology, logistics and finance) of the IAA. Constructors have the option of choosing any qualified company, including the IAA, to carry out the actual excavation of sites identified by the IAA. There are a small number of private rescue archaeology companies in Israel, mostly connected to university archaeology departments. This institutional link arose out of the need for publication facilities, as without prompt publication no license to excavate in Israel will be granted.

On the completion of excavation, the site is once again examined by the IAA to determine that no further work is required. The project cannot end until the IAA sign it off. Private companies are allowed to retain artefacts from such excavations for a period of ten years to allow for analysis and publication but they must be returned to the IAA at the end of that period. The IAA retains a vast, but exceptionally well-catalogued and organised centre for the storage and study of artefacts at Har Hotzvim in Jerusalem.

---

[4] Ephraim Stern was named chairman of the Archaeological Council in December 2000, following the resignation of the former chairman, Moshe Kochavi, in protest at the appointment of Shuka Dorfman, a military man with no archaeological training, as Director of the I.A.A. On the appointment of Dorfman, Stern said that a non-archaeologist in the role was a problem, though not an insurmountable one for him. According to Feldman, Stern claimed that the Archaeological Council will have more influence on Dorfman than it had on Drori 'because Dorfman will need to look to others for their expertise in archaeology' (Feldman 2001). Feldman was also of the opinion that Stern would make the Archaeological Council more active than it had been; in the brief period he had held the post he had already convened two meetings of the Council in two months whereas in recent years the Council had met only occasionally (Feldman 2001).

CHRONOLOGICAL SUBJECTIVITY

The IAA's salvage policy and work, has created a significant counter-weight to the traditional Biblical-oriented approach to research archaeology in Israel, which had created an important, but extremely subjective body of archaeological information (Braun 1992: 29), colouring our understanding of the entire archaeological record. The Law of Antiquities in Israel [A.L. 1978] generates a further chronological bias in archaeological activity, as it only provides for the protection of remains dating earlier than 1700, or those later than that date which the Minister of Education and Culture has declared to be antiquities (antiquities.org.il 2005a). Conservation laws enacted in 1978 provide for the protection of buildings dating from later periods, but in general it is only the façade of such buildings that is retained while entire interiors have, and continue to be, gutted in modernisation processes. Accompanied by a widespread disinterest in preserving or promoting the remains from later periods, the result, as in Cyprus, is a dearth of physical testimony to the country's more recent, and in particular, Ottoman past. However, the salvage work conducted by the IAA draws no distinction between biblical and non-biblical remains in its decision-making with regard to excavation, salvage and rescue, thus greatly expanding the body of information available from other periods in Israel's past.

Due to the fact that the Director has prerogative over the final fate of a site, regardless of advice provided by archaeologists, architects and planners, the all-pervasive power of the Director-General within the IAA has the potential to make this rescue and salvage system less fair and unbiased than is currently the case (antiquities.org.il 2005b). Given that there is no requirement for the Director-General to be an archaeologist or have undergone archaeological training, it is clear that the placing of so much decision-making power over questions of archaeological practice in his hands may on occasion prove problematic.

Many concerns also rest on the financial orientation of the IAA, which has acted as contractor to non-academic groups wishing to excavate for various ideological reasons, and on the increasing rift between the IAA and the academy in Israel. It could therefore be argued that the IAA in gaining efficiency and increased autonomy through being restructured, did so at the cost of close ties with the greater academic community and entered into a precarious economic relationship with private groups with their own vested interests. These are all thoughts to be borne in mind by those responsible for the structuring or restructuring of archaeological heritage management organisations both in Israel and elsewhere, such as in Cyprus, where a restructuring of the current Department of Antiquities is being considered. That a restructuring might prove beneficial is not in question but these benefits should be sought without compromising the integrity of the Department.

SHARED MANAGEMENT OF SITES

Nationalistic and economic agendas further enter the archaeological picture in Israel as a result of the fact that, in many cases, the IAA shares guardianship of a number of the roughly 20,000 archaeological sites in Israel with other authorities, all of which have some connection to the government. Sites located with national parks or those deemed to be of particular value to the state can be scheduled as Israel Nature and National Parks Protection Authority sites, and are then administered and maintained by the INNPPA. Other interested parties may also put in proposals for the running of archaeological sites. Most of these groups are semi-governmental or have been formed by government, and are involved in the development of specific urban areas, such as East Jerusalem or the old city of Jaffa in Tel Aviv. While the approval of the IAA Director-General is required for any change to be made to a protected site, problems of various kinds, from interpretation to matters of physical conservation, still arise. For example, the East Jerusalem Development Company Ltd. which manages the Ophel Archaeological Garden, Jerusalem Archaeological Park and Davidson Exhibition and Virtual Reconstruction Center, have presented these interconnecting, and multi-period sites in such a way as to place all conservation and interpretation focus on the remains associated with the Jewish Second Temple, to the exclusion of the other Roman to Mameluke period remains. The Davidson Centre, itself, is located in rooms that were originally part of the basement of the seventh to eighth century Umayyad Palace (about which information is not provided, mirroring the situation previously described in Cyprus). Along with this lack of information, the placement of the Centre erases the significance of the palace as an historic monument, and in a deliberate way eclipses its original importance.

It could be argued that the intervention of organisations other than the IAA in the management of archaeological sites provides a financial resource pool otherwise unavailable to maintain as many sites as possible. The reality, however, is that only a select number of sites pertaining to the interests, economic or ideological, of the groups in question actually receive such management interest. Meanwhile, the overall result of the participation of such groups in the management of archaeological sites in Israel is that there are great variations in the quality and quantity of conservation measures carried out from site to site, and perhaps more importantly, that there are vastly greater opportunities for more extreme versions of official nationalist narratives to enter the mainstream under the guise of objective scientific fact. For example, the Israel Nature and National Parks Protection Authority is the largest group outside of the IAA responsible for the preservation, maintenance and promotion of archaeological sites as well as the presentation of archaeological knowledge. The major aims of the INNPPA are to generate income and inculcate a sense of unity and attachment to the land among a disparate community (Killebrew 1999: 19). In the 1990s, the INNPPA, with the assistance of the Government Tourist Organisation, was involved in the major development of a select number of archaeological sites with the aim of increasing Israel's prominence in the international tourist market. Excavations were carried out and huge sums of money invested in the infrastructure of certain sites, the biggest being Masada, but also in the monumental sites at Caesarea and Beth Shean.[5] The carrying out of excavations with the explicit aim of promoting tourism rather than expanding our knowledge of the past is highly questionable given that excavation is by its nature destructive and archaeology is a non-renewable resource. Furthermore, while reconstruction work as defined earlier, was limited, it was carried out nonetheless on theatres, while toilets and other public facilities were built into the remains of 'lesser' monuments at Masada and Caesarea, indicating yet again the problems associated with accommodating high visitor numbers (Figs 3-4).

Fig. 4 – Caesarea: craft shops built into/underneath archaeological remains (photo by author)

Fig. 3 – Public toilets built into the remains (photo by author)

The nature of tourism in Israel also affects the choice of sites for promotion and the manner in which they are promoted. Most tourists coming to Israel do so as part of pre-organised groups, with set itineraries centred on well-known sites. The result is that a small number of archaeological sites with international religious, historical or visual appeal and which regularly appear on touring itineraries become the focus of conservation and promotion, while prehistoric and/or smaller less impressive sites remain neglected. To a lesser extent this same process of site selection can be seen at play in Cyprus as evidenced at the sites of Kalavassos and Choirokoitia (Figs 5-8). The Neolithic site of Kalavassos *Tenta*, despite having originally received quite substantial investment in order to make it ready for public presentation, has lower than expected visitor numbers. This fact stems in part from the correlation between civil service working hours and site opening times, resulting in the limiting of access to the site both to tourists and more importantly to native Cypriots. Choirokoitia, on the other hand, receives high visitor numbers, and thus generates a high income, and so its opening hours have been extended. This extension of visiting hours is a response to increased visitor numbers but in turn generates higher numbers, as tour operators and private individuals are allowed greater flexibility in their itinerary, and the site becomes a 'must-see' on account of its popularity. Over time this can only lead to the deterioration of both sites.

Fig. 5 – Kalavassos Tenta (photo by author)

---

[5] At Caesarea, a seaside walkway was built against the cautioning of archaeologists, who warned that it would be washed out to sea during the first winter. The walkway was built and was, indeed, washed out to sea the next winter.

Fig. 6 – Kalavassos Tenta: view from inside
the protective structure (photo by author)

Fig. 7 – Choirokoitia (photo by author)

Fig. 8 – Choirokoitia: reconstructions to side
of archaeological site (photo by author)

De la Torre and MacLean blame such situations on a lack
of communication between the cultural and tourism
sectors of government, but in the case of Cyprus it can
happen that both agencies are actually working together in
the promotion of certain sites to the potential exclusion of
others (de la Torre and MacLean 1997: 11). This highlights the need for professional conservators, archaeologists and indeed local communities to be involved at all
stages of the decision making process in order to ensure
that the best interests of the sites (and therefore all parties
with vested interests in them) are preserved. At present
this does not happen in either Israel or Cyprus.

CONCLUSION

The managers of the archaeological heritage in Israel and
Cyprus are confronted by the major question posited for
cultural resource managers everywhere in the world; that
is how to decide whose past to preserve for whose future
and how. In the models discussed today, we have seen
how both direct and indirect government authority over
the archaeological heritage has resulted in a situation
whereby ideological and financial concerns have
frequently been prioritised and perhaps more importantly
have silenced the nuances and complexities of actual
historical processes in time and space. Economic agendas
place value for money above preservation or other
knowledge-based concerns whilst at the same time they
are used to bolster ideologically derived narratives.
Tourism can indeed be of benefit not just to society but to
archaeology, but forceful marketing which becomes
economical with the truth, and excessive visiting numbers
that damage sites are pitfalls that need to be avoided
(Fowler 1992, 128). The creation of independent regula-
tory bodies comprised of representatives of all interested
parties including government, would be one way of en-
suring that a more multi-vocal and responsible archaeology takes place. It is only with the existence of such
bodies that the profession of archaeology can hope to
flourish and move beyond the current, all-pervasive
constraints of the nation-state.

This is a general principle that needs to be endorsed
internationally, not just in Cyprus and Israel, and is
essential if all the values of a site – aesthetic, scientific,
historic, financial and educational – are to be identified
and preserved. The involvement of all interested parties
from local communities, archaeologists through to
tourist agencies is therefore necessary to ensure that
conflicts of interests and competing or conflicting
values (such as may exist between scientific and
financial interest in a site) are heard and negotiated
without loss to the cultural heritage or to the values
themselves (Sullivan 1997: 16). The existence of such
inclusive, decision-making bodies is thus vital for the
development and implementation of long-term, feasible
management plans for archaeological sites and monuments. Ultimately, in this way more multi-vocal
readings of the past may materialise and the layerings
and nuances of history and cultural identity may be
allowed to emerge.

Bibliography

Antiquities.org.il(a) (2005) *Interpretation: Definition.* Internet. Available from: <http://www.antiquities. org.il/article_Item_eng.asp?sec_id=42&subj_id=228& autotitle=true&Module_id=6> [Accessed 6 September 2005]

Antiquities.org.il(b) (2005) *Archaeological Excavations in Israel.* Internet. Available from: <http://www. antiquities.org.il/article_Item_eng.asp?sec_id=41&sub j_id=227&id=202&module_id=#as> [Accessed 6 September 2005]

BARUCH, Y. and R.K. VASHDI (2005) *From the Israel Department of Antiquities to the Founding of the Israel Antiquities Authority.* Internet. Available from: <http://www.antiquities.org.il/article_Item_eng.asp?se c_id=38&subj_id=154#MMMas> [Accessed 6 June 2005]

BRAUN, E. (1992) Objectivity and Salvage Excavation Policy in Mandate Palestine and the State of Israel: An Appraisal of its Effects on Understanding the Archaeological Record. IN: Shay, T. and J. Clottes eds, *The Limitations of Archaeological Knowledge.* Etudes et Recherches Archéologiques de l'Université de Liège 49, 29-38.

De la TORRE, M. and M. MACLEAN (1997) The Archaeological Heritage in the Mediterranean Region, IN: de la Torre, M. ed. *The Conservation of Archaeological Sites in the Mediterranean Region. An International Conference Organised by the Getty Conservation Institute and the J.P. Getty Museum, 6-12 May 1995.* Los Angeles, The Getty Conservation Institute, 5-14.

FELDMAN, S. (2001) First Person: Changes at the Top, Ephraim Stern Named Chairman of Archaeological Council. *Biblical Archaeological Review* 27:3. Internet. Available from: <http://www.basarchive.org/ bswbBrowse.asp?PubID=BSBA&Volume=27&Issue= 3&ArticleID=6&UserID=2297&> [Accessed 21 June 2005]

FOWLER, P. (1992) *The Past in Contemporary Society: Then, Now.* London & New York, Routledge.

GREENE, J.A. (1999) Preserving Which Past for Whose Future? The Dilemma of Cultural Resource Management in Case Studies from Tunisia, Cyprus and Jordan. *Conservation and Management of Archaeological Sites* 3, 43-60.

HADJISAVVAS, S. (1995) Cyprus Department of Antiquities, 60 Years After. The Monuments Branch. *Report of the Department of Antiquities Cyprus.* Cyprus, Department of Antiquities, 1-9.

ICOMOS (1996) *The Venice Charter: International Charter for the Conservation and Restoration of Monuments and Sites.* Internet. Available from: <http: //www.icomos.org/venice_charter.html> [Accessed 18th April 2006]

KILLEBREW, A. (1999) From Canaanites to Crusaders, the Presentation of Archaeological Sites in Israel. *Conservation and Management of Archaeological Sites* 3, 17-32.

mcw.gov.cy, *Department of Antiquities,* Internet, Available from: <http://www.mcw.gov.cy/mcw/mcw.nsf/ Main?OpenFrameSet> [Accessed 5 May 2004]

RABINOVICH, A. (1994) Inside the Israel Antiquities Authority. *Biblical Archaeological Review* 20:2. Internet. Available from: <http://www.basarchive.org/ bswbBrowse.asp?PubID=BSBA&Volume=20&Issue= 2&ArticleID=2&UserID=2297> [Accessed 21 June 2005]

SCHMIDT, H. (1997) Reconstruction of Ancient Buildings, IN: de la Torre, M. ed. *The Conservation of Archaeological Sites in the Mediterranean Region, An International Conference Organised by the Getty Conservation Institute and the J. Paul Getty Museum, 6-12 May 1995.* Los Angeles, The Getty Conservation Institute, 41-50.

SILBERMAN, N.A. (1997) Structuring the Past: Israelis, Palestinians, and the Symbolic Authority of Archaeological Monuments. IN: Silberman, N.A. and D.B. Small eds, *The Archaeology of Israel: Constructing the Past, Interpreting the Present.* Sheffield, Sheffield Academic Press, JSOT Series 237, 62-81.

SULLIVAN, S. (1997) A Planning Model for the Management of Archaeological Sites, IN: de la Torre, M. ed. *The Conservation of Archaeological Sites in the Mediterranean Region, An International Conference Organised by the Getty Conservation Institute and the J. Paul Getty Museum, 6-12 May 1995.* Los Angeles, The Getty Conservation Institute, 15-26.

VASSILIOU, G. (1994) *Tourism and Sustainable Development.* Transcript of Paper Presented at Global Conference on the Sustainable Development of Small Island Developing States: Case Study No. 2 14th April 1994, 1-38.

WRIGHT, G.R.H. (1994) Care of Monuments in Cyprus. *Archaeologia Cypria* III, 1-3.

www.ingramcontent.com/pod-product-compliance
Lightning Source LLC
Chambersburg PA
CBHW061008030426

42334CB00033B/3405